This book is dedicated to the memory of
The Reverend Ch'eng Ching-yi, D.D., L.L.D.
and
The Reverend A. Raymond Kepler, D.D.
whose devoted labors did so much to make
the dream of a Church of Christ in China a reality.

Contents

Foreword, 9

1 A New Century, 13

2 Movements Toward Unity, 21

3 The Rise of Chinese Leadership, 39

4 A Church United, 53

5 The Synods—Their Areas and Characteristics, 68

6 The Church of Christ in China—The Early Years (1927-37), 83

7 The Years of the War with Japan (1937-45), 110

8 Ventures in Mission, 132

9 Rehabilitation and Renewal (1945-49), 153

10 The New Day in China, 172

11 The Church of Christ in China—Goals and Achievements, 195

Appendices, 214

Bibliography, 226

Index, 229

Foreword

The Church of Christ in China was one of the earliest efforts in the twentieth century to bring together a wide range of churches with varying origins and traditions in the spirit of Christian unity. The first church union in China to go beyond confessional lines, it was conceived and developed in a period of grave political crisis, civil war, and foreign invasion, when normal communications were disrupted and the nation was politically divided. The Church of Christ in China's most trying hours came only two decades after its founding, with the coming to power in China of a Communist regime basically hostile to all religious activity. In spite of tremendous difficulties, however, the union grew and developed significantly. At present, when almost no organized church life is visible in China, it seems opportune to record something of this Church's life and to seek to evaluate its significance, especially as those who had knowledge and experience within its framework are fast passing from the scene.

Dr. A. Raymond Kepler, the first General Secretary of the Church of Christ in China, had planned to write a history of the Church. After Dr. Kepler's death in 1942, Dr. A. J. Fisher, who had been active in the life of the CCC since its earliest days, was asked by the General Assembly office of the Church to prepare such a history. Mrs. Fisher reported in a letter to me that Dr. Fisher made "a study and outline of the Church history . . . while under 'house arrest' in 1941-42" (in Shanghai). "This was to be the basis of a history to be written later in Chinese." This study, after editing, was left with Church officials in Shanghai but disappeared during the war with Japan.

After the war, Dr. Fisher, who although he had already reached the age of retirement was back in Shanghai for a year at the request

9

of the Church of Christ in China, rewrote his history. Two copies of his typewritten manuscript were found among his papers at his death in 1967. One copy went to the Hong Kong Council of the Church of Christ in China, the other to the University of Oregon Library with other papers. Entitled "Building a Christian Church in China," it consisted of more than two hundred pages of typescript, describing in some detail the historical beginnings of the church bodies which became part of the Church of Christ in China and the early development of the Church. In 1971, the China Program of the East Asia Working Group, National Council of Churches of Christ in the USA, asked me to undertake a history of the Church of Christ in China. Including all the North American mission boards which cooperated with the Church, the China Program generously provided for the expenses involved in research and preparation of the manuscript.

Fisher's manuscript is dated 1947 and therefore did not cover the later years of the life of the Church of Christ in China. Nevertheless, it has been a valuable source of information to the author. Additional information has come from a wide range of material, including the modest publications of the Church itself, the correspondence of mission boards and individuals, and references in *The Chinese Christian Year Book* and *The Chinese Recorder,* as well as the digests of minutes of General Assemblies and of General Council meetings. The most important sources are listed in the bibliography.

I corresponded with a number of those who worked in the CCC framework, and many have shared information and documentary material which I want to acknowledge gratefully. Special mention should be made of the help given by E. Bruce Copland and by W. H. Clark. The latter shared much documentary material on the Yunnan Mission of the CCC and was most generous in editorial comment. I also acknowledge with gratitude the invaluable advice and assistance of M. Searle Bates.

What I have attempted is a brief, popular history—not highly documented—which I hope will be informative and accurate. While some mention is made of the missionary beginnings leading to the development of the churches that became part of the Church of Christ in China, this is a history of that Church and not of the missions, though I do not mean to slight their important role. As one who was fortunate enough to know almost all the early leaders of the Church of Christ in China and who deeply sympathized with the strong desire of that leadership for a truly Chinese Church that would transcend the denominationalism of the West and respond to Christ's call to mission in their own land, I feel strongly that this adventure in unity was of considerable significance and a worthy chapter in the history of the Christian church.

A major source of information was found in the extensive material in the Missionary Research Library in New York. Appreciation should also be expressed to the Board of World Mission of the United Church of Canada and the Library of Victoria College, the University of Toronto; to the United Presbyterian Commission on Ecumenical Mission and the Presbyterian Historical Society in Philadelphia; and to the Sage Library of the New Brunswick Theological Seminary of the Reformed Church in America for access to archival materials and for assistance rendered by staff in each instance.

Finally, a word of tribute should be voiced for all those servants of the Church, Chinese and missionary, who had a share in the movement for unity which culminated in the Church of Christ in China, and the many who quietly and devotedly participated, often under great difficulty, in danger and deprivation, in the work and witness of that Church. Many of them are already gone from our midst; most of their names have already disappeared from man's notice. But they are known to God, and their labors have surely borne good fruit.

W. C. M.

Chapter One: A New Century

Protestant mission work in China dates back to the arrival of Robert Morrison in Canton in 1907, though Protestants had been at work in adjacent areas for some time and were already working on translation of the Bible into Chinese. Roman Catholic missions had begun as early as the thirteenth century. Although there were several breaks in their witness, there had been a continuing mission since the able Jesuit Matteo Ricci had introduced Western science as a means of promoting the Christian cause at the close of the sixteenth century.

By 1870 the Roman Catholic Church numbered approximately 400,000 believers and there were two hundred and fifty European missionaries at work. By 1897 the number of Catholics had increased to 532,448, while there were seven hundred and fifty-nine European missionaries and four hundred and nine Chinese priests. Believers were required to go through a period of probation and instruction before receiving baptism. Orphanages and schools (mostly at the primary level) had been established in many areas, many of the missionaries dispensed simple medication, and some clinics and modest Christian hospitals had begun to operate. Distribution of alms was common, frequently on condition that recipients become catechumens. Conversion was commonly influenced by the rights guaranteed Christians by the treaties with Western powers and especially the protectorate over Roman Catholic missions and converts assumed by the French. Increasing use was made of Chinese workers as catechists, and a program of theological training for the priesthood was established.

The Russian Orthodox Church had a mission in Peking from the early seventeenth century, but its chief ministry was to the descendants of Russian prisoners taken in 1685 and to the diplomatic community. It proved useful in the training of scholars and translators, but its influence in the Chinese community was negligible. In the latter half of the nineteenth century, efforts began to reach Chinese, though only very modest results had been attained by the close of the century.

Protestant work in the nineteenth century had hardly touched the fringe of the great mass of the Chinese people. On the other hand, in many ways it was already exercising considerable and growing influence. From the first convert won by Morrison after long years of lonely labor, there had grown a church of some 100,000 communicants by 1900 and a Christian community of perhaps double that size, largely concentrated in a few coastal provinces. While in that number were many whose lives showed no great change from those of unbelieving neighbors, there were also many Christians whose character, dependability, sacrificial devotion, and freedom from vice deeply impressed the Chinese. Protestant emphasis on education (especially of women) and medicine; its opposition to foot-binding, illiteracy, and opium; and its use of the vernacular language were important factors in the awakening of Chinese nationalism and the increasing demand for change in a static society. Christianity also helped to give thoughtful Chinese a glimpse of the moral idealism and humanitarian aspects of Western culture, in contrast to the commercialism and militarism so evident in the tensions between the Western powers and Chinese officials. It was already true that many of China's younger leaders, especially in education and medicine and in the ranks of those who sought change, were Protestant Christians or had been educated and influenced by Protestant institutions.

Among the earliest activities of Protestant missionaries in China were literature and education. Schools and printing presses were tools for acquainting the Chinese with the Gospel message. The first Protestant school was established in Canton soon after the arrival of Elijah C. Bridgeman in 1830, and by 1832 he was publishing *The Chinese Repository* in English to educate Westerners about China.

Almost everywhere Protestant missionaries went, schools were established, mostly at the primary level; not only for boys, but for girls as well, an innovation for China. Traditional Chinese subjects were included, but there was a strong emphasis on modern Western learning which was to have important consequences for the development of new educational approaches by the Chinese in the twentieth century. By 1900 there were more than 2,000 Protestant Christian schools in China, including forty or fifty middle schools and six colleges, with a total enrollment of approximately 40,000 students.

The number of Protestant missionaries and societies in China rapidly increased, especially in the latter part of the nineteenth century, until by the beginning of the new century they were at work in almost every province and there were almost five hundred mission stations. Kenneth Scott Latourette (*A History of Christian Missions in China*) gives the breakdown in 1874 as 48% Americans, 44% British and 4% Europeans. Important elements in the constitution of the missionary body were the large number of women (more than half of them unmarried) and a relatively high proportion of laymen, particularly educators and medical workers. The historian Searle Bates estimates that of about 2800 Protestant missionaries in China in 1900, 60% were women and nearly half the men were laymen. Chinese salaried workers (5-6,000) were double the number of missionaries and also included many women. A substantial number of mission boards and societies were represented, chiefly related to the traditional denominations, with the major exception of the nondenominational China Inland Mission.

Literature continued to play an important part in the missionary enterprise. The Bible and portions of it were published in large quantities, usually in a modified form of the classical language but increasingly in the various dialects. There grew to be an impressive list of Chinese Christian publications, mostly religious and Biblical in nature but including biographies, histories, and other general works. Especially important was the preparation of textbooks in every field of modern knowledge for the Christian schools. Periodicals played an important part in the literary expression of Protestant Christians, at first chiefly in English, but later in Chinese, including the vernacular. By 1900 eleven mission presses were in service. Most of the literature in the early years was prepared by missionaries; efforts to encourage Chinese authors were not very successful, even in later years. A Society for the Diffusion of Christian and General Knowledge Among the Chinese was founded and by 1906 became the Christian Literature Society for China, a major publisher of Christian books.

Medical work was part of the Protestant effort in China from the very beginning. By 1900 there were two hundred and forty Protestant medical missionaries in China, one-third of them women. The numerous medical institutions scattered around the country included China's first asylum for the insane, established by Dr. J. G. Kerr in Canton; a number of leprosaria; and refuges for opium addicts. There was a strong emphasis on the training of Chinese nurses, medical assistants, and doctors. Such beginnings led to the later development of some of the most influential medical schools and made a great contribution to the growth of a modern medical profession in China. A number of Chinese, particularly women, were able to go abroad for excellent medical training and returned to establish or head Chinese hospitals. Missionary doctors also produced the first modern medical literature in Chinese through translation or original works and developed a Chinese medical terminology. The China Medical Missionary Association, organized in 1887, "was the first to bring to bear on all China Western medical science and was probably the first group . . . to begin to plan for the health of the entire Empire" (Latourette, p. 460).

Missionaries soon became keenly aware of the desperate needs of the handicapped, and a number of schools for the blind were early established. These not only provided a home for blind children, most of whom would traditionally have become beggars, but taught them handicraft skills and reading and writing by a modified system of Braille. Notable among them was the school at Palichuang, outside Peking, established by the Scottish missionary William Hill Murray. Work for the deaf was also begun in several places in the nineteenth century. Protestant missionaries were among the first to oppose the cruel practice of footbinding for girls and were a strong influence against the opium trade, concubinage, and gambling. In times of famine and flood they threw their considerable strength and resources into the efforts to bring relief to the victims of disaster.

China at the Turn of the Century

The early years of the new century in China were full of turmoil and uncertainty. China, a proud and ancient nation once serene in its highly developed civilization and confident in its central place in the world of men, once so powerful that envoys from European nations had to approach its rulers with obeisance, was fast approaching the end of an era. Content in its own ways, ruled by the Manchus, one dynasty in a long list of vigorous and hardy barbarians who had conquered the Chinese but had in turn been conquered and corrupted by power and luxury, the great empire had come to a standstill in a rapidly changing world. The Manchus, who had given China some of the ablest rulers in all history, were increasingly isolated by their ambitious and self-seeking servants the eunuchs. Wounded and hurt by internal weakness and external aggression, China, as one recent writer has put it, staggered into the twentieth century.

The tide of Western expansionism grew increasingly strong as treaty ports were forced open and Western trade found its way into the tottering empire. Japan, too, was eager not to miss the opportunities enjoyed by the Western powers. It was strong with the sense of power and nationalism awakened by its newly reorganized and Westernized state and by its growing military might. A decisive defeat had been administered to the Chinese in 1894-5 and Formosa and the Pescadore Islands taken, while China virtually relinquished its claims to Korea and the Liaotung Peninsula in Manchuria. The Western powers, however, forced the revocation of the cession of Liaotung to the Japanese and pressed for new concessions for themselves. Most of the Liaotung Peninsula was subsequently leased to Russia, while expanded treaty rights, spheres of influence, and new openings for trade and development were granted the colonial powers.

By the late nineteenth century, many thoughtful Chinese recognized the weakness of the failing empire, which in traditional fashion had lost its vigor and greatness and was increasingly weakened by incompetent leadership, palace intrigue, and corruption. Reformers such as Sun Yat-sen, Kang Yu-wei, and Chang Chih-tung spoke out for change and won the hearing of many, including the young Emperor, Kwang Hsu. Western-style schools were authorized, including Peking University (a powerful influence in later years), a modern national army was proposed, and major reforms in the classical pattern of government were ordered. It seemed that much-needed changes in Chinese society were on the way.

However, the forces of traditionalism and resistance to change were strong and were abetted by the strong aversion of many to the ways of the hated foreigners. Officeholders and the establishment of the day did not easily give way and the reformers were young and inexperienced, as was the Emperor who supported their cause. In September 1898 the powerful and conservative Empress Dowager (Tzu Hsi), suspicious of change and distrustful of Western ways, again seized power and put the Emperor under restraint. A number of reform leaders were executed, others went into hiding, and the changes that had been promulgated were annulled.

The missionary enterprise in China was deeply involved in these critical developments, both as an instrument of change and an object of resentment. More and more venturing into the interior of China, where they were generally unwelcome, the missionaries were irritants in the body politic. Rumors of unorthodox and offensive practices (using the eyes of the dead to make silver, cutting off limbs, and eating babies were among the charges) were given wide credence. Resentment against demands for protection by foreign governments, against interference in lawsuits (much more common in Roman Catholic practice than Protestant), and against foreign encroachments were all factors in opposition to the missionary, led by the gentry, who violently opposed change.

> Wherever a missionary travelled and spoke, wherever he distributed a book, organized a school, or opened a hospital, he introduced conceptions which, if put into effect, would disrupt many old institutions. The Protestant missionary's attitude toward bound feet, toward the education of women, toward the content and method of all education, toward honors to ancestors, concubinage, religious festivals and the use of the vernacular for literary purposes—to mention only a few of his most prominent innovations—could not but prove revolutionary. Everyone influenced by him was a threat to the older fabric of Chinese life. (Latourette, p. 476)

Throughout the history of Christian missions in China, there had been difficulties and strong opposition, with many incidents of violence. In the troubled atmosphere of the close of the nineteenth century and the beginning of the twentieth, such incidents increased markedly. Resentment against the foreigner and the changes for which he was in part responsible flared into widespread violence with the Boxer uprising in 1900. Directed against all foreign influence and led by the secret society whose Chinese name (the Society of Righteous Fists) was roughly translated as "the Boxers," it was secretly encouraged by the Empress and many of her advisors, though opposed by others, some of whom were able to mitigate its excesses. When an expedition of Allied troops (European, American, and Japanese) tried to reach Peking, they were defeated, though they did manage to seize the Taku coastal forts near Tientsin. The German ambassador in Peking was murdered. The Empress ordered all foreigners killed. Westerners and Japanese in Peking, with a number of Chinese Christians and the protection of a few hundred troops, gathered in the Legation Quarter and a Catholic cathedral in the north city, where they came under heavy attack by Boxers and Imperial troops until relieved by an Allied expedition from Tientsin in late August.

The brunt of the violence fell upon the missionaries and Chinese Christians, chiefly in Chihli (later called Hopei) and Shansi provinces. Property destruction and loss in lives were frightful. Almost fifty Roman Catholic missionaries were killed; close to two hundred Protestants (of whom almost a third were children). About 2,000 Chinese Protestants lost their lives, and an estimated 30,000 Catholics. The toll would have been much higher if a number of Chinese viceroys in Shantung, central, and south China had not ignored orders from Peking and maintained order in their own areas.

In its attempt to eliminate foreign influence, including the Christian movement, the uprising failed. It was clear to many Chinese that change had to come. In the revulsion against the faults and failures of their ruler and the bloodshed and fanaticism of the Boxers, a wave of enthusiasm for reform swept over the nation.

For the Christian movement, the losses had been heavy. But the courage and constancy of the Christian martyrs deeply impressed many. While some defected, most Christians stood firm in their faith. The brutality of the Allied troops as they engaged in executions and looting was an adverse factor, but missionary interpreters were able in a number of instances to restrain violence and save lives. The dramatic events of the siege in Peking and the killing of so many Christians had focused attention on China and there was no lack of missionary replacements for those whose lives had been taken.

The attitudes of the Christian bodies toward indemnities differed. Catholics almost without exception accepted substantial amounts, some of which was used to relieve the sufferings of Chinese Christians. Substantial amounts were used to restore buildings and equipment which had been destroyed. Protestant attitudes varied. Indemnities for personal and property damage were accepted in many cases, although the claims were modest and some societies (notably the China Inland Mission, which had lost by far the largest number of missionaries) refused to accept any indemnity for property damages. One beneficial effect was the United States stipulation that much of its share of indemnity payments be used for education in China and that the balance due be remitted, a decision in which missionary influence had a part. The funds were used for scholarships and to establish Tsinghua University near Peking, one of China's best universities.

The cause of internal reform was strengthened, notably in education. Under the terms of the peace treaty, the outmoded civil service examinations were suspended in many areas, especially where the Boxers had been active, and in 1905 they were abolished. A new educational system was begun—including Western as well as Chinese studies—which afforded new opportunity for the Christian schools. And there was a proliferation of popular magazines and newspapers, which made possible the wider distribution of Christian literature.

The imperial government tried to gradually introduce representative and constitutional government, but it was too late to save the dynasty. In 1911-12 it was overthrown by a Chinese revolution that proclaimed a republic. The divergent elements of the revolutionary movement soon disintegrated in the chaos of factionalism and regionalism.

The years following the Boxer uprising were years of growth and expansion for Protestant Christianity. A number of new societies began work in China, especially from North America, most of them very conservative and separatist. The number of Protestant missionaries continued to grow, reaching a peak in the mid-twenties of more than 8,000. Extremely important in the movement were the Christian schools, especially at the middle school and university level, which provided the opportunity to learn English, the language of commerce, and the science so avidly sought by the young as a panacea for China's problems.

The large number of students in the modern schools led to an increasingly powerful student class which was to have a very important role in the political destinies of China. Missionaries still provided most of the leadership in the Christian movement, but the success of Christian work among students by the missions and the YMCA, the growing number of theological graduates in the service of the church, and the emergence of able Chinese leadership (dealt with in Chapter III) gradually began to alter the pattern of missionary dominance. The financial support of the Christian movement and its institutions still came chiefly from mission sources, but the beginnings of Chinese will to self-support were evident, especially in the formation of a number of independent Chinese congregations in the cities, while an ever larger part of the expenses of educational and medical institutions came from fees.

Chapter Two: Movements
Toward Unity

Early Expressions of Unity

From the earliest days of the Protestant missionary movement in China, there was a keen sense of common cause among many of the missionaries. Two of the major forces in the early years, the London Missionary Society in the United Kingdom and the American Board of Commissioners for Foreign Missions in the United States, were interdenominational and both played an important role in China. This sense was strengthened by the conviction that if the Christian church was to sink roots into Chinese soil, it had to be a Chinese church with Chinese leadership, free to develop its own forms and expressions.

So in the Amoy area of South Fukien we find Reformed Church missionaries from America and Presbyterians from England drawn to form a united presbytery in 1857. Each congregation as it was organized was to be part of an autonomous Chinese church. In spite of objections by the Reformed Church Synod at home, the union was effected, and in 1919 it was joined by the Congregational Union in the area to form the South Fukien Synod of the Church of Christ in China. In 1934 the South Fukien Conference of the Methodist Episcopal Church threw in its lot with the union and brought about the unusual situation of a single church in the area bringing all major Protestant forces together. Irish and Scottish mission work had been united in Manchuria with the formation of a Chinese Presbyterian Church in 1891.

Increasingly, as the years went by, Protestant missionaries held conferences together (Chinese participation was insignificant until well into the twentieth century) to confer on common problems and aims. One of the earliest of these meetings, the China Missionary Conference of 1877, attracted one hundred and forty missionaries from all over China, representing almost all missions. They expressed a desire and a hope for unity and even pleaded that Western denominationalism be disregarded as irrelevant for China. The Reverend Alexander Williamson of the United Scottish Presbyterian Mission is quoted by A. R. Kepler in the 1928 *China Christian Year Book* as saying:

> I believe that denominationalism, as far as possible, should go to the winds. I for my part shall never consent to aid in transplanting the sects and sectarianism of the West into this country.... Be it ours to preach the Gospel and rear a new united and glorious Church in this land—The Church of God in China.

Another such conference was held in 1890, bringing together more than four hundred missionaries. While it dealt primarily with common problems regarding Bible publication and practical matters, a committee on union was also suggested. Such conferences became an accepted part of the Christian movement. Latourette comments, "Beginnings had been made which might in time lead to one organic Protestant Christian Church for China."

In October 1901, fifty-four representatives of ten Presbyterian church bodies, mostly in central and north China, approved the principle of wider union, rather than simply Presbyterian union, and set up a committee to prepare a plan of union representing various Presbyterian bodies around the country and Presbyterians within the nondenominational China Inland Mission. Two resolutions were approved:

> 1. This Conference earnestly desires the unity of the Christian Church in China and cordially welcomes all opportunity of cooperation with all sections of the Church. This conference resolves therefore to take steps for uniting more closely the Presbyterian Churches, hoping thereby to facilitate the ultimate attainment of a wider union.

> 2. The Conference therefore recommends the appointment of a committee to prepare a plan of union, organic or federal as may be found practicable, and submit same to the church courts (native or foreign) concerned.

This meeting also recommended that all new Presbyterian churches be organized as autonomous Chinese churches. These proposals generally received firm support from the mission boards and societies in the West, and by 1905 favorable action on the principle of union had been taken by all related church courts in China and the West. The recommendation was for a federal union with six autonomous synods in which the various bodies would unite. Such synods had already been formed in South Fukien and Manchuria, as we have seen, as well as in East Kwangtung, where Presbyterian and Reformed groups had united. The three other synods were to be North China, Central China, and West Kwangtung.

Kepler, in his article on "Movements for Christian Unity" in the 1928 *China Christian Year Book*, summed up a number of "practical achievements toward Christian unity at the turn of the century." Among them he included the general recognition of the principle of comity, united efforts in Bible translation and the preparation of hymnals, joint efforts in literature (the Bible societies, the Religious Tract Society, the Christian Literature Society), the beginnings of the YMCA, union in theological training and higher education, the Medical Missionary Association (which later merged with the China Medical Association) and the mergers already referred to.

Opposition to Union

Yet, many missionaries conscientiously opposed any kind of church union and in some cases even cooperation with Christians or church agencies other than those committed to their own particular doctrine or polity. These more conservative missionaries were alarmed by what they considered to be unsound theological positions, the blurring of denominational lines, and a tolerant attitude toward Chinese religious practices. The bitter doctrinal controversies between so-called "fundamentalists" and "modernists" going on at the time in the Western churches also had their repercussions in China. In 1920 such dissatisfactions found expression in the organization of The Bible Union. Latourette comments:

> The Union's statement of faith expressed unqualified adherence to belief in the deity of Jesus, his virgin birth, atoning sacrifice for sin, and bodily resurrection, in the miracles of the Old and New Testaments, in the personality and work of the Holy Spirit, in the new birth of the individual as an essential prerequisite to Christian social service, and in "the whole Bible as the inspired Word of God and the ultimate authority for Christian faith and practice". The convictions were not new, but were substantially the position always taken by the great body of Evangelicals and still held by the majority of missionaries in China. (p. 795)

The Union urged upon the home boards that only candidates who subscribed without question to such doctrinal positions be appointed to service in China. By 1922 more than two thousand individuals, mostly missionaries, had taken membership in the Union, and a national convention was held in Shanghai in 1922, apparently in competition with the National Christian Conference held at almost the same time. To quote again from Latourette:

> Many, probably the majority . . . were moderate and irenic, but some were acrimonious, and controversies followed. . . . The result was discord: Protestants were at odds with each other during the years when they were facing the most difficult situation which had yet confronted them in China. (p. 796)

The Growing Sense of Unity
and the Growth of Cooperative Enterprises

On the other hand, there was increasing awareness of the unfortunate effects of division in a land where Christians were few and the obstacles formidable. Consequently, many Protestant missionaries felt their oneness with other Protestants more strongly than their differences. This feeling was shared increasingly by many Chinese Christians as they came into positions of leadership. Many of them found imported denominationalism confusing and irrelevant.

Signs of the growing sense of unity were found even in such groups as the large and important China Inland Mission, strongly conservative but nondenominational, in whose ranks served missionaries from most major Protestant denominations. It assumed greater importance in natural and quite necessary cooperation in the great tasks facing the church. Bible translation was the work of scholars representing different traditions. The work of the Sunday School Union brought together evangelical Protestants from many groups. Christian schools increasingly became union enterprises, especially at the college level and as the small early schools began to develop into institutions of higher learning. This was also true of medical work, especially in the development of a growing number of excellent medical colleges. Even in theological education, limited resources and general agreement on basic fundamentals dictated cooperation, and most of the Bible training and theological schools that developed in all areas of the country were interdenominational or at least nondenominational.

Most of the major theological schools had a long history of interdenominational cooperation. A Bible Training School was formed in Nanking in 1911 by the merger of three institutions, with cooperation by Presbyterians (USA and US) and Disciples. Later, Baptists and Methodists joined in the work of the institution, which eventually became the Nanking Theological Seminary. Union Theological Seminary in Canton began its work in 1914 with the support of eight missions and in time became related administratively to the Kwangtung Synod of the Church of Christ in China with Anglican and Methodist cooperation. The North China Theological College, founded in 1906 by Presbyterians and Congregationalists (the latter related to both the American Board and the London Mission) became the School of Theology of Yenching University, in which the Anglicans also cooperated. The Cheloo University School of Theology in Shantung brought together a wide variety of denominational interests in North China, with ten American, British, and Canadian missions cooperating in support.

Of the thirteen Protestant Christian colleges and universities in China, all but three (Hangchow-Presbyterian; St. John's-Anglican; and Shanghai-Baptist) were interdenominationally supported, and even those of a single denomination had the support of more than one mission society of the same persuasion.

While a national comity agreement was not formally arranged until 1917, under the aegis of the China Continuation Committee, comity was almost always effective at the local level and the various missions were usually very careful to avoid duplicating each other's work. Such cooperation in common causes was made easier by the fact that most of the major missions were related to historic churches which had good relations in the homelands and whose missionaries usually shared a feeling of fellowship and goodwill. Even in the China Inland Mission, somewhat to the right of most of the denominational missions, individuals often cooperated where they found denominational missionaries of kindred spirit, though they shied away from union enterprises.

One of the most important meetings in the series of Missionary Conferences, and the last in which missionaries were overwhelmingly in the majority, was the Centenary Missionary Conference in 1907, held in Shanghai (more than a thousand missionaries were present but fewer than ten Chinese Christians). At this Conference there was proposed a "Christian Federation of China," with a National Council and Provisional Council and membership open to both missionaries and Chinese, but nothing came of this proposal.

In January 1908 representatives of Anglicans, Baptists, Methodists, and Quakers in Szechuan met in Chengtu and proposed a united Protestant Church for West China, closing their meeting with an open communion service in which all joined. A union university, West China Union University, was established in 1910 in which all these groups cooperated, and cooperation continued in a union hymnal and in most areas of Christian work.

Unity continued to grow. Kepler points out that by 1910 there were thirty cooperative enterprises in theological, medical, normal, academic, and collegiate education, most of them organized within the preceding five years. By 1914 the number of such enterprises had grown to almost one hundred. Nurturing this growth, Kepler suggests, were the language schools which brought missionaries from many groups together when first in China; the interdenominational conferences led by John R. Mott of the YMCA in many parts of China following the 1910 Edinburgh Missionary Conference; the work of the China Continuation Committee, especially its annual meeting, which brought together those of different churches; and the growth of seminars and regional conferences bringing together Christians of almost every Protestant group.

The 1910 World Missionary Conference at Edinburgh, Scotland, exercised an important influence in the movement toward unity. One of the proposals of that conference was that regional agencies of cooperation be formed in both the mission lands and the sending countries, all of them represented in the newly-organized International Missionary Council. John R. Mott, one of the great Christian statesmen of the time, was made Chairman of the Continuation Committee set up by Edinburgh to accomplish this purpose. He vigorously devoted his great energy and remarkable powers of leadership to this task in succeeding years.

The China Continuation Committee

Mott went to China in 1913. He chaired five regional conferences, from which delegates were appointed for a national gathering in Shanghai. A marked feature of the regional meetings was the predominance of Chinese participation. Of the one hundred and twenty delegates to the national conference about a third were Chinese. A China Continuation Committee was established to carry out the objectives developed at the regional and national conferences.

From the beginning, the Committee was intended as a provisional structure looking forward to formation of a National Christian Council, but throughout its short span of activity, it was an important instrument of cooperation which dealt with major problems facing the Christian movement in China. It was advisory only, but gave a powerful impetus toward wide cooperation and unity. It emphasized the need for an indigenous Chinese church, and the 1913 national conference suggested that a common name be adopted for all Protestant churches in China. (The preference was for *Chung Hua Chi Tu Chiao Hui,* the Chinese title eventually adopted by and translated as The Church of Christ in China.) The conference also strongly urged the unification of churches of the same ecclesiastical order. Among the important achievements of the China Continuation Committee was a statistical Survey of the Christian Movement in China (published as *The Christian Occupation of China* in English—the Chinese title was *China for Christ*) and the "China for Christ Movement," an evangelistic campaign in which C. Y. Cheng played a leading role.

The Committee was fortunate in its leadership, having chosen as its two secretaries C. Y. Cheng (Ch'eng Ching-yi), the remarkable Chinese leader who did so much for the cause of unity in China, and E. C. Lobenstine, an able Presbyterian (USA) missionary. In 1914 A. L. Warnshuis (who later served with distinction for many years on the staff of the International Missionary Council) was called from his work with the Reformed Church in America mission in Amoy to become National Evangelistic Secretary.

The culmination of the work of the China Continuation Committee came in the important National Christian Conference held in Shanghai in the spring of 1922. The survey already mentioned was part of the preparation for this conference, perhaps the most important of the series which had begun in 1877. Fisher calls it "the first really representative gathering of Chinese Christians," a conference that "may be said to mark the transition period when the Chinese took the leadership in the Christian movement in China." Most of the delegates were Chinese, the Chairman (C. Y. Cheng) was Chinese, the major reports and addresses were given in Chinese as well as in English.

The theme of the Conference was "The Chinese Church," and thorough preparatory papers had been written by five study commissions. To quote from the Conference report volume on *The Chinese Church:*

> The National Christian Conference registered the existence of a Chinese Church and at the same time gave direction to the process of that Church finding itself. Perhaps 1922 will stand out as the date of its declaration of spiritual independence.

Strong emphasis was placed on the need for the Chinese churches to be free from Western denominationalism and to develop along indigenous lines. Chinese leadership spoke strongly in favor of union. A public statement was issued by Chinese representatives in these words:

> We Chinese Christians who represent the various leading denominations express our regret that we are divided by the denominationalism which came from the West.
>
> We recognize fully that denominationalism is based on differences, the historical significance of which, however real and vital to the missionaries from the West, are not shared by us Chinese. Therefore, denominationalism, instead of being a source of inspiration, has been and is a source of confusion, bewilderment and inefficiency.
>
> We recognize most vividly the crying need of the Christian Salvation for China today, and we firmly believe that it is only a United Church that can save China, for our task is great and enough strength can only be attained through solid unity.
>
> We believe that there is an essential unity among all Chinese Christians, and that we are voicing the sentiment of the whole Chinese Christian body in claiming that we have the desire and the possibility to effect a speedy realization of corporate unity and in calling upon missionaries and representatives of the Churches in the West, through self-sacrificial devotion to our Lord, to remove all obstacles in order that Christ's prayer for unity may be fulfilled in China.

The National Christian Council

The most important result of the Conference was the formation of a National Christian Council as the culmination of the work of the China Continuation Committee. The action of the Conference read:

> This Conference, with a view to carrying forward its work, making provision for dealing with matters which concern the Christian Movement throughout China, and promoting cooperation, resolves to appoint a National Christian Council.

Doctrine and ecclesiastical polity were to lie outside the province of the Council. Its functions were to be primarily advisory, but it could "act on behalf of the cooperating churches and missions in matters which concern their common interest" when the cooperating bodies wished such action to be taken. It was "to foster and express the fellowship and unity of the Christian Church in China and the realization of its oneness with the Church throughout the world, and to provide an opportunity for united prayer and corporate thought towards this end."

The findings of the five commissions of the Conference were referred to the new Council "for full consideration . . . and emphasis." Ninety-five members were appointed from the various cooperating churches, missions, and other Christian organizations, in addition to twenty-five "general" members, including many leaders prominent in church or community life.

The National Christian Council was undoubtedly a useful instrument for cooperation through the years. But like similar agencies elsewhere, it was handicapped by being primarily a consultative body composed of representatives of widely divergent views. Most major churches and missions participated at the beginning, the chief exception being the Southern Baptists and the Lutherans, but the China Inland Mission and the Christian and Missionary Alliance withdrew early in its history and by and large the more conservative groups did not participate. Sharp differences of opinion in the early years of the Council on such matters as the registration of Christian schools; ceremonies honoring Sun Yat-sen, the leader of the Nationalist Revolution; and the rise of the Nationalist movement to power and its break with the Communists made it difficult for the Council to speak on such issues. Latourette observes:

> It was looked to by many, especially among the Chinese, for authoritative pronouncements, but the bodies it represented were far from having a single opinion. From time to time it attempted action and as this was usually representative of moderately radical Chinese opinion, many, particularly more conservative foreigners, became increasingly distrustful. (p. 798)

The first annual meeting of the National Christian Council was held in Shanghai May 10-16, 1923. Thirty-eight of sixty-four delegates were Chinese, including a number of women. David Z. T. Yui, the devoted Christian layman who was General Secretary of the YMCA of China, was elected Chairman. The major addresses were given by Chinese (T. C. Chao, T. T. Lew and Peter Chuan). C. Y. Cheng and E. C. Lobenstine were elected General Secretaries. *The Chinese Recorder* commented: "Chinese Christians are now guiding the destinies of the Chinese Church."

Other Cooperative Christian Agencies

A number of other agencies exhibited the will of most Protestants to work together. The work of the major Bible Societies—the American Bible Society, the British and Foreign Bible Society, and the National Bible Society of Scotland, themselves interdenominational in character—was eventually coordinated in China through the establishment of the China Bible House in 1932.

The Educational Association of China was organized in 1890 by missionary educators at the 1890 Missionary Conference. It met triennially and grew in numbers and strength under the ambitious slogan, "The promotion of educational interest in China and the fraternal cooperation of all those engaged in teaching." The Association played an important part in the growing awareness of the need to coordinate the work of Protestant Christian schools. Great emphasis was put on this need in the 1907 Centennial Conference, which recommended a full-time staff for the Association. Regional and local Christian educational associations sprang up, the most successful being that in Szechuan. All major missions cooperated with these associations.

Eventually the Association became the China Christian Educational Association, with subsidiary councils on Christian Higher Education and Primary and Secondary Schools. This became a Commission of the National Christian Council in 1935. Through the years it was a helpful agency of cooperation for the Christian schools and became the spokesman for them in problems arising from increasing government pressures to control them and to minimize religious emphasis.

The China Sunday School Union was another agency of cooperation. The 1907 Centenary Conference appointed a committee to prepare religious education materials such as Sunday School lessons. The World Sunday School Convention in 1910 provided support for a full-time secretary, and the Rev. E. G. Tewksbury, an American Congregational missionary, began a long period of service. Through the preparation of Sunday School material, programs to train teachers, and the organization of local and regional associations, much was done to forward the cause of religious education.

A National Committee for Christian Religious Education was formed in 1931 by the National Christian Council and the China Christian Educational Association, merging the Council's Standing Committee on Religious Education and the Association's Committee on Religious Education. A close relationship continued with the parent organizations. The NCCRE advocated the use of graded Sunday School lessons, while the Sunday School Union preferred the International Sunday School lessons for all ages. The new agency emphasized the need to relate religious education material to life situations, while the CSSU emphasized Bible-centered teaching, reflecting similar disagreements among religious education leadership in the West.

The Christian Literature Society was another organization in which there was wide Protestant cooperation. A Society for the Diffusion of Christian and General Knowledge Among the Chinese was founded in 1887 under the leadership of a Scottish missionary, the Rev. Alexander Williamson. In 1906 this became the Christian Literature Society for China. Timothy Richard of the Baptist Missionary Society, with great visions for the enlightenment of the Chinese people through literature, became Secretary in 1891 and greatly expanded the program. The Society produced a flood of books in Chinese; both translations and original works; not only religious books such as Bible commentaries and theological works, but volumes on history, biography, and functional matters related to health, homemaking, the care of children, etc. Its periodicals included magazines for women and later for children, among the first such to be published in China. In spite of its inadequacies and often inferior quality, Christian literature was undoubtedly one of the most effective instruments in the expansion of the Christian movement in China, especially in the late nineteenth and early twentieth centuries.

Cooperation in Christian medical work has already been mentioned. A Chinese Medical Missionary Association, the first professional society for doctors in China, was established in 1886 and began publishing a medical journal the following year. In 1925 this body merged (at its own request) with the Chinese Medical Association, which had been founded as a wholly Chinese organization in 1915. Membership was then opened to all qualified doctors. A Medical Missions Division of the Association became the Council on Medical Missions in 1932 and in 1935 was invited by the National Christian Council to serve as its Commission on Christian Medical Work.

The Council rendered important service to the many Protestant hospitals in China (about two hundred and seventy in 1937). Dr. K. C. Wong, its Secretary for many years, outlined its functions in an article in *Christian Voices in China* (1948). These included (1) coordinating the work of medical missionaries; (2) advising Christian hospitals on government health plans and programs and in registration; (3) helping to improve hospital efficiency; (4) coordinating and facilitating the purchase of drugs and equipment.

One cooperative organization expressive of Chinese Christian responsibility for mission and the desire for autonomy was the Chinese Home Missionary Society. Founded at Kuling in 1918, it was throughout its life a completely Chinese agency both in personnel and support. C. Y. Cheng, a major influence in its founding, served as its President for ten years. It began its work in Yunnan, where by 1924 there were three stations and six Chinese missionaries. The home missions work of the Presbyterian Church in Manchuria was soon merged with the Society, bringing in work in the far northern province of Heilungchiang, where by the close of 1924 there were seven workers. In the 1934-35 *China Christian Year Book,* the Society reported work in Mongolia and Szechuan, as well as in the areas already mentioned, with a total of twenty-one paid staff members and sixty-four additional workers who were self-supporting. Fifteen types of work carried on by the Society are listed, including dispensaries and clinics, primary schools and literacy classes. Eventually the work in Yunnan was turned over to the local Church of Christ in China mission.

Presbyterian Union

Along with the growth of interdenominational agencies, denominational coordination was proceeding apace. In keeping with the proposals of the Presbyterian meeting of 1901 already mentioned, a Synod of Central China, with five presbyteries, was organized in 1906. This united churches related to the work of the Northern and Southern American Presbyterian missions in the area. In April 1907 in Shanghai, a Federal Council of the Presbyterian Churches in China was formed by Chinese and missionary delegates in approximately equal numbers as a coordinating body for the several synods.

The Federal Council of the Presbyterian Churches in China met in May 1914 at Tsinan (Shantung) with wide representation from the synods. A proposal for a triennial General Assembly was submitted to the presbyteries. In May 1915 in Shanghai, the Council made definite plans for a General Assembly with representation from all Presbyterian and Reformed bodies in China. By this time Chinese leadership dominated, though with the full cooperation and partnership of most of the missionaries. In September 1916 a Committee on a Constitution for the General Assembly met in Nanking and proposed uniform Chinese names for all church courts and regulations for representation at General Assembly. These provided for one Chinese pastor and elder for each 3,000 members, to be appointed by the presbyteries, with an additional missionary representative from each presbytery.

The Federal Council met again in Nanking in April 1918, with invited representation from the Congregational churches. Proposals for wider union were approved and a Committee on the Basis of Union was appointed with representation from both groups. The Committee submitted a proposal for a Federal Council of Christian Churches in China with a committee to prepare recommendations for the wider union. The plan for union was referred to the church courts for consideration and the Council voted to call a First General Assembly of the Presbyterian Church in China and to dissolve the Federal Council.

Although the actual name Church of Christ in China was not formally adopted until later, some Chinese consider the 1918 meeting the beginning date for that church. In October 1958 the Hong Kong Council of the Church of Christ in China, an offshoot from the Kwangtung Synod, observed a "Golden Anniversary" of the Church of Christ in China with five days of lectures and public meetings.

The First Assembly of the Presbyterian Church in China met in Shanghai in April 1922, immediately following the National Christian Conference. The several synods already using that name and Congregational church bodies affiliated with the London and American Board missions were represented. More than 113,000 church members were in the groups represented, of which about 87,000 were Presbyterians. The Committee on Union reported, and the proposed plan of union and doctrinal statement were discussed and adopted.

The question of the name of the church was debated at length. The Chinese were firmly against any denominational name and opposed including the word "United" on the grounds that the new church was to be in its own right a Chinese church and not just a union of Western denominations. They requested that the Chinese representatives be allowed to make the decision, and they unanimously approved the name *Chung Hua Chi Tu Chiao Hui* (translated as The Church of Christ in China), which had been recommended for use by all Chinese churches at the 1913 China Continuation Committee meeting. This name was already in wide use, as we have seen, and (according to this writer's understanding) was first used by an independent Chinese congregation in Peking, of which C. Y. Cheng (later to be first Moderator and first Chinese General Secretary of the CCC) was pastor in the early 1900s.

The meeting then agreed to constitute itself a Provisional Assembly of the Church of Christ in China and adopted the doctrinal basis of union and provisional constitution prepared by the Committee on the Basis of Union, both of which were accepted without change at the First General Assembly of the Church of Christ in China in 1927.

Anglican Union

As the Presbyterians and Congregationalists were drawing closer together and even looking toward wider union, other groups of kindred tradition and polity but of differing national antecedents were quite naturally moving in the same direction. Among the first to seek coordination were the Anglicans.

A number of British Anglican missionary societies, as well as the Canadian Church and the American Episcopalians, were at work in various areas of China by the early twentieth century. Conferences on Anglican union were held in 1907 and 1909. A plan of union was drawn up and the name *Chung Hwa Sheng Kung Hui* (literally "The Holy Catholic Church of China" but often translated "The Chinese Episcopal Church") was proposed. After approval by the related mission societies and the diocesan synods, the First Provisional Synod of the united church was held in April 1912. In a communication addressed to "All Christians in China," the gathering voiced hope for an even wider unity of Christians in China.

Like the Church of Christ in China, this union and other confessional groupings remained loose federations, with the several cooperating mission societies maintaining direct ties with their supporting dioceses. The first Chinese diocesan bishop, Lindel Tseng, was appointed to the Honan diocese in 1934. By 1945 there were thirteen dioceses, three related to American Episcopalians, one related to the Canadian Church, seven with ties to British missionary societies, and two—Shensi and Yunkwei (Yunnan-Kweichow)—created as mission dioceses by the Chinese Church. The reported membership in the 1950 National Christian Council's Directory was 66,651.

Some Sheng Kung Hui leaders were interested in even wider union, and in January 1935, on the initiative and invitation of that church, a Conference on Church Union was held in Shanghai. Twenty-five delegates were present from seven churches: Sheng Kung Hui, Church of Christ in China, Methodist Episcopal, Methodist Episcopal South, English Methodist (later the Chinese Methodist Church), Baptists (American Northern Baptist-related) and the North China Kung Li Hui (the Congregationalists who did not join the CCC). The participants were described as "united in loyalty to Jesus Christ and in an earnest desire to become so united to Christ that the result may be an organic union of all Christian bodies." Fisher reported, perhaps too optimistically:

> In 1937 committees on union were appointed by the Chung Hwa Sheng Kung Hui and the Church of Christ in China. Several conferences were held. . . . When more normal conditions prevail again the great hope is that [a union of] not only the Chung Hwa Sheng Kung Hui and the Church of Christ in China but all the other evangelical churches will take place. (p. 113)

Lutheran Union

Similarly, the Lutherans early sought to bring together the work of the various Lutheran missions in some kind of federation. At the Centenary Conference in 1907, closer cooperation and possible unification of work was discussed by Lutheran delegates but without concrete results. At a summer conference at the summer resort of Chikungshan in Honan in 1908, most of the Lutheran missionaries working in Central China were present and "plans were laid for future cooperation." One result was the organization of the Union Lutheran Seminary at Shekow, Hupei, in 1913. Its work was a strong unifying factor in the training of most of the Chinese ministers of the cooperating churches.

At an April 1915 conference, a temporary Church Council was elected. When the Council held its first meeting in October 1916, committees on organization, church service and hymn books, colleges, literature, etc., were elected. These committees met in 1917 and 1919, and on August 20-24, 1920, a Conference on Union was convened at Chikungshan to which all Lutheran churches in China were invited.

Nine bodies were represented—five European, four American. A constitution, including a confession of faith, was approved, and the congregations in each mission area became synods of the united church. A General Council met annually and a General Assembly formed of representatives of the synods met triennially. The total baptized membership was 14,626. Five other societies (three European, two American) joined the union in the 1920s, which approximately doubled the membership.

By 1949 virtually all Lutheran bodies except the Missouri Synod were working together in the Lutheran Church of China (*Chung Hwa Hsin Yi Hui*). The church was composed of twelve synods, with twelve cooperating mission boards and societies and a membership of 48,140.

Methodist Unions

A number of Methodist societies were at work in China in the early twentieth century—American, British, and Canadian. In 1907 the Central Conference of the Methodist Episcopal Church adopted a memorial to the General Conference of 1908 asking for creation of "a commission with power to originate, receive, consider and consummate proposals looking toward the union of the Methodist Episcopal Church in China with any other Methodist body or bodies in China" (Walter N. Lacy, *A Hundred Years of Chinese Methodism*, p. 245). The several conferences passed supporting resolutions authorizing the Central Conference to receive elected delegates from other Methodist bodies in China with the same rights and privileges as their own. (There seems to be no record of this actually having taken place, however.)

The Canadian Methodist Mission developed a substantial program in Szechuan which became the Mei Dao Hui. In 1925, with church union in Canada, this became related to the United Church of Canada. In 1933 the Mei Dao Hui became the Szechuan Synod of the Church of Christ in China.

In the early twentieth century, when there was strong sentiment for a united Chinese church, Methodist leadership steadfastly rejected that concept in favor of "World Methodism." Quite typical were the remarks of Bishop Bashford in his address at the 1923 Central Conference:

> We believe in a world church; certain that if this, the greatest Protestant church in the world, can remain essentially a unit, organically as well as in spirit, it will be a far more effective instrument of power to our common

Christian hope of a universal brotherhood of men of every race and tongue, than it can be if broken into a sectionalism that may easily tend to emphasize racial prejudices. Organic and spiritual unity are more deeply related than we dream. (Lacy, p. 253)

At the close of the National Christian Conference of 1922, Methodist delegates and local Methodist leaders met to discuss the possibility of bringing together Methodist work in China. Eight groups were represented.

In 1932 a Methodist reunion in England brought together three churches, two of them with work in China. In October 1933, a Uniting Conference of the Methodist Church in China in Ningpo brought together the United Methodists and the Wesleyan Methodists to form the *Hsun Tao Hui*, or Chinese Methodist Church. With seven districts spread widely over China and a strong emphasis on developing Chinese leadership, this Church reported a membership in 1949 of about 45,000.

The Methodist Episcopal Church in China and the Methodist Episcopal Church South were involved in various cooperating programs and planning for union when in 1939 the two mother churches in the United States merged with the Methodist Protestant Church and the work of the three missions in China was united. The 1941 General Conference brought the related Chinese churches into a single body for which the name *Wei Li Kung Hui* (The Methodist Church in China) was adopted. By 1949 this church with four bishops (two Chinese and two missionaries) was organized in ten conferences and reported 102,693 members.

Some Methodists in China were interested in still wider union, specifically in union with the Church of Christ in China. Dr. T. C. Fan of the CCC staff, reporting on new member churches and consultations on church union to the 1932 General Council, said: "The Shantung Methodist churches have sent a fraternal delegate to attend the [Third] General Workers' Conference as an expression of their desire to confer regarding the possibility of union."

A vote welcoming them was taken and "the task of working out concrete plans for such a union was referred to the Shantung Synod Executive Committee to be reported back to the General Council for final approval."

In 1931 the South Fukien Conference of the Methodist Episcopal Church in China, after what Lacy calls "some years of trying to hold it for Methodism," voted to become part of the South Fukien Synod of the Church of Christ in China. Somewhat isolated geographically from other Methodist churches and in an area with strong linguistic and other ties to Amoy, it was quite natural for this conference to ally itself with the neighboring CCC churches. It became a district association in 1934.

At the Eastern Asia Central Conference of the Methodist Episcopal Church in Nanking, April 25—May 1, 1934, a report by the Commission on Program and Policy included the following:

> We deplore the fact that no united front is presented and that to a large number of denominational divisions introduced from the West, there are now being added new names and sects. . . . We believe that the Methodist Episcopal Church has shown the right spirit through the years in entering many union enterprises, and that now one further step should be taken.
>
> Therefore, we recommend that the Methodist Episcopal Church affiliate with the Church of Christ in China . . . and that the Central Conference appoint a committee to confer with the Executive Committee of the CCC with regard to this affiliation.

A commission was appointed "to study this question and report back to the next Central Conference." The commission recommended union first with the Methodist Episcopal Church South, then the union of all Methodist bodies in China, "then the union of the resulting Methodist Church with other Christian bodies in a more inclusive union" (Boynton, *China Christian Year Book*, 1934-35).

The hope of union between the Chinese Methodist Church and the Methodist Church in China was kept alive by frequent consultation. H. B. Rattenbury of the English Methodist Missionary Society quoted Bishop W. Y. Chen of the Methodist Church in China on a visit to London in 1944: "He gave it as his considered judgement that Methodism in China should get together first before looking to the still larger union of which so many dream" (*Let My People Know*, p. 93).

From time to time commissions were appointed to discuss Methodist union, but the union never came to pass. This was one example of denominationalism which seemed unable to work effectively across national lines. Although different national backgrounds did not prevent the establishment of united Anglican and Lutheran bodies, as well as the Church of Christ in China, British- and American-related Methodists and Baptists, among others, went their separate ways.

Chapter Three

The Rise

of

Chinese Leadership

The Growth of National Consciousness

In Chinese history, the end of a dynasty had always been followed by a period of unrest and disorder. This had been true after the revolution of 1911 and the overthrow of the Manchu overlords. Many disparate elements had been involved in the events that culminated in the success of the revolution, but none of them was strong enough to provide competent leadership. The military strongman of the early Republican era, Yuan Shih-kai, failed in his attempt to found a new dynasty in traditional fashion. Civil strife became widespread as regional military leaders fought among themselves for power. So-called "national governments" came and went, while attempts to emulate parliamentary forms of government produced only facades without reality. The "old hundred names" (*lao pai hsing,* colloquial for the masses) were the victims of military struggles, exploitation by the warlords, heavy taxation, and the conscription of their young men.

The Versailles Treaty of 1919 had confirmed Japanese control over concessions in Shantung seized from the Germans in 1915. Chinese opposition, led by students who on May 4, 1919, staged massive demonstrations in Peking, resulted in a national boycott of Japanese goods and gave the students a foretaste of revolutionary power. Hostility towards outsiders and antipathy to new and non-Chinese concepts, typical of a highly developed culture, had frequently found forceful expression in Chinese history. The threat to independence poised by the encroachments of the Western powers and Japan, the disunity and weakness of vacillating Chinese governments, and the pressure for additional concessions now led to an awakening of national consciousness, especially among students.

Dr. Sun Yat-sen, whose ideas had been influential in the 1911 revolution, had resigned as President in favor of Yuan Shih-kai and had little influence with the contending military forces. His ideas, however, continued as a revolutionary force, particularly in the south and among intellectuals, whose resentment against foreign exploitation of China's labor and resources and encroachments on her territory grew ever more bitter. Sun, seeking to regain power and unify China behind his revolutionary philosophy, reportedly sought aid from Western powers. (This must have been done unofficially, as diplomatic relations were maintained by the powers with the ineffective Peking authorities.) Receiving no encouragement, he turned to the Soviet Union, still in its infancy and facing serious internal problems but eager to promote the cause of Marxist revolution. The Soviets provided military and political advisors and funds. The fledgling Chinese Communist Party, organized in 1921, and the Kuomintang, the Nationalist party led by Sun, formed a coalition with the aim of winning control of the country.

An incident of great importance as a catalyst took place in 1925 in Shanghai. On May 30 a demonstration by strikers in a British mill, supported by Chinese students, was fired upon by International Settlement police. A number of the demonstrators were killed and wounded.

This gave fresh impetus to the demands for the recovery of Chinese sovereignty, revocation of the hated treaties forced upon the Chinese since the Opium Wars of the mid-nineteenth century, and the end of territorial concessions and extraterritorial status for foreigners. It was followed by extreme anti-foreign demonstrations, including several bloody incidents in the foreign concessions, and by a national campaign against the British, including an effective boycott, that affected all foreign residents in China. An important element was the growing strength of Chinese Communism, augmented by Chinese students returning from study abroad, especially from France, where many had become convinced that Marxist principles offered the best solution to China's critical needs. The example of the successful overturn of the exploiting classes in Russia also provided a powerful stimulus.

Growth of Anti-Christian Sentiments

As the anti-foreign movement grew, Christianity, especially the foreign missionary, was a prime target. Coming from those nations which were colonial powers in Asia and which had large commercial stakes in China, the missionary was inevitably associated in the minds of many Chinese with Western exploitation, even though he might personally be opposed to such practices. His very presence in China had been made possible by the treaties the Chinese were intent on repudiating. Western governments had on occasion used incidents involving missionaries to bring pressure on the Chinese. Christian work was supported in large measure by foreign funds, even though control over such funds was more and more in the hands of church bodies and institutional boards in which Chinese leadership predominated. The church and its institutions were usually Western in character and often in appearance, and to a considerable degree missionaries were still in control.

Christian churches and institutions were widely scattered throughout the country, highly visible, and altogether vulnerable. So it was not surprising that extreme nationalist and anti-foreign sentiments were frequently vented on them. Opposition to Christianity had always been present in China, expressed most violently in the Boxer Rebellion. Isolated incidents had occurred in many parts of the country. But in the 1920s the antagonism was so serious and widespread as to pose a threat to the very existence of the Christian movement in China.

Anti-Christian Federations sprang up among Chinese students in many places, radically opposed to Christianity and contending that religion and science (the new religion of the Chinese intellectual) were incompatible. In public meetings, Christians were attacked as the agents of imperialism. In 1924 there was a serious and widespread attack upon the Christian schools, in which they were accused of being part of a cultural invasion. In 1925 government regulations were drafted requiring the registration of all Christian schools and the appointment of Chinese principals and of Chinese majorities on school boards, as well as the elimination of required religious courses and religious activities.

As the armies of the Nationalist-Communist coalition moved north from Canton in 1926 in their drive for national power, they encouraged a vigorous campaign against missionaries and Chinese Christians. There was considerable looting and destruction of property, especially in Hunan and Fukien. In March 1927 the coalition forces, largely composed of radical elements from Hunan, triumphantly entered Nanking and soon thereafter proclaimed it as the new capital. Flushed with victory, they were determined to destroy the power of the warlords, eliminate foreign privilege, and unify the nation.

As they marched into Nanking, foreign property and Christian institutions were a major target. Dr. J. E. Williams, Vice-President of the mission-supported University of Nanking, was killed by a soldier outside his home. Five other foreigners were killed (two of them Roman Catholic priests) and many others wounded. The entire foreign community was endangered. After hours of tension, most of the foreigners were evacuated by Western gunboats on the river, which after repeated warnings opened fire as a last resort in order to effect the rescue.

This incident was an element in the increasing friction between conservative elements in the Nationalist forces and the radical leftists which soon led to a complete break and the beginning of a long, costly, and destructive civil war. The radical program of a leftist government set up at Wuhan and numerous violent anti-foreign incidents in the preceding months led to a fear of further attacks on missionaries and Christian work. As the Nationalist armies continued their campaign north of the Yangtze River, most of the foreigners in China, including the bulk of the missionary community, were evacuated. Latourette estimates that of approximately 8,000 Protestant missionaries, 5,000 left China, though many of them returned after a period of furlough; 2,000 took refuge in treaty ports protected by foreign troops, most of whom returned to their work as conditions improved; and only about 500 remained in the interior. By early 1930 there were 5,396 Protestant missionaries at their posts and almost 1,000 others on normal furlough leave.

Growth of Chinese Leadership in the Church

The early part of the twentieth century was a time of remarkable growth in Christian work in China. By 1921 the number of Protestant Christians was about 400,000, approximately four times the number at the turn of the century. There had also been a considerable growth of Christian educational institutions and of students enrolled in them. Even more important was the growth of Chinese leadership. By 1920 there were approximately 28,000 full-time staff workers, about four and a half times the number of Protestant missionaries. Roughly half the total were engaged in church work, more than 1,000 being ordained ministers; the other half were involved in educational, medical, or other institutional programs. For the first time, Chinese ordained ministers outnumbered the ordained missionaries (Latourette gives the figures for 1920 as 1,305 in comparison to 1,268).

There were many indications by the 1920s of the increasing influence and contributions of Chinese leadership in the church. In the early national missionary conferences referred to in the previous chapter, almost no Chinese were involved. In the 1890 Conference, for example, only two Chinese were present, compared to four hundred and forty-five missionaries. In the great Centennial Conference of 1907, with an attendance of 1170, only six or seven Chinese were present. But by 1913, in the organizing meeting of the China Continuation Committee, one-third of the one hundred and twenty delegates were Chinese, as constitutionally required. In the 1919 China Continuation Committee meeting there were as many Chinese as missionaries, and the Committee's constitution required a majority of Chinese from 1920 on. In the highly influential National Christian Conference of 1922, a majority of the 1200 delegates were Chinese, the Chairman (C. Y. Cheng) was a Chinese, the principal addresses were in Chinese, and it was clear that Chinese leadership had taken its rightful place as dominant in the Protestant Christian movement in China.

The impact of growing Chinese nationalism was inevitably felt within the church. Chinese leadership pressed for greater independence for the church and control over funds and policy. At the same time, Chinese churchmen called for greater efforts toward self-support, with the goal of one day completely underwriting the Christian enterprise with Chinese sources, an important emphasis throughout the life of the Church of Christ in China. In general Christians (including most missionaries) were fully sympathetic with the efforts to unite the country and reassert Chinese sovereignty. This unquestionably hastened the process which had already begun of devolving responsibility for Christian work from the missions to the Chinese churches.

Missionary Support for a Chinese Church

Lest there be misunderstanding, we should make clear that almost from the beginning of the Christian movement in China many missionaries, as well as Chinese, wished for a genuinely Chinese church. This can be seen in the early principles adopted by many mission boards. For example, from its inception in 1837 the Board of

Foreign Missions of the Presbyterian Church in the USA stated as its purpose not only the preaching of the Gospel but the establishment of indigenous churches.

We have mentioned the 1901 conference of Presbyterians in China to plan for union, when it was agreed that all churches formed thereafter would be organized as Chinese churches with their own church courts. A similar resolution was incorporated in the 1857 agreement which brought Presbyterian and Reformed work in Amoy into a united Chinese church.

In a statement on "The Chinese Church," the 1907 Centennial Conference, composed almost entirely of missionaries, recommended to the home boards

> that they should sanction the recognition by their missionaries of the right of the churches in China planted by them to organize themselves in accordance with their own views of truth and duty. . . . They should abstain from claiming any permanent right of spiritual or administrative control over these churches.

As early as 1919, the New Zealand Presbyterian Mission in Kwangtung placed its work under control of the Divisional Council of the Church of Christ in China. In 1925 the Kwangtung Synod of the CCC unanimously approved a program policy statement with this preamble:

> In our judgment the time has come when, in the best interest of the Kingdom of Christ and the development of self-supporting, self-governing and self-propagating churches, the direction and control of the work hitherto carried on by the missions in Kwangtung cooperating with the CCC should be committed to the Divisional Council of the Church.

The proposal included full control by the Divisional Council over the assignment of missionaries, property used in the work of the church, all mission funds, and evangelistic, educational, and medical work. (While it took more than ten years to implement fully, by 1937 educational and medical programs were directed by synodical agencies—church and evangelistic work was implemented much earlier.)

More and more Chinese congregations in the cities were completely independent and self-supporting and church buildings were being erected in many parts of China with the gifts of Chinese Christians. We have noted in Chapter II the organization of the Chinese Home Missionary Society in 1918, an assertion of the readiness of Chinese Christians to assume responsibility for mission in their own land. By 1923 Baptists in Shantung and Shansi had turned over responsibility for church work to cooperative councils with equal Chinese and missionary representation. In 1924 the Sheng Kung Hui (Anglican-Episcopal Church) created the missionary diocese of Shensi with a completely Chinese staff, including eventually a Chinese bishop. In 1927 the Methodist Episcopal Church reported that of fifty-one district superintendents, forty-six were Chinese. In 1928 the Honan Synod of the CCC declared itself autonomous. Margaret Brown reports in her manuscript *History of the Honan Mission*: "Full control of the church in North Honan, of its Synod, Presbyteries and congregations would be solidly vested in the Chinese." By 1928 almost all Christian schools were under Chinese leadership, with generally satisfactory results.

The Church-centric Principle

Essential to the development of an indigenous, national church was the concept that the foreign mission was a temporary expedient and that the church was the vital, continuing entity—what C. Y. Cheng and other CCC leaders called the "church-centric principle." The mission as a separate organization existed only as an agency to establish an indigenous church and in the end must wither away. Opposed to this was the concept of mission and church as separate, cooperating agencies continuing along parallel lines. This view was strongly advocated by a pioneer Presbyterian in Shantung, John L. Nevius. "The Nevius Plan" appealed to many Presbyterians and was the basis of the extensive Presbyterian work in Korea.

It was entirely natural for Chinese Christians, especially as they attained leadership in the church with the growth of a native ministry, to press for church control. The Chinese were a proud people with an ancient and rich cultural heritage and an independent spirit. The employer-employee relationship that necessarily had obtained in the early days of missions chafed the spirit of men of ability and was one reason why those missions that continued to work on that basis found it difficult to attract or hold men of good education and independent spirit. Where the emphasis was on indigeneity, and responsibility was turned over to church leadership, a higher and abler type of Chinese leadership emerged.

As more able and better educated Chinese came into positions of leadership in the work of the church, they were not hesitant to express their hopes for a Chinese church. In 1925 we find C. Y. Cheng commenting in the *Wen She Bulletin*:

> The Christian Church as transplanted from the West was deeply dyed with many colors. Some of the colors were merely not appreciated by the Chinese, others were clearly unwelcome. One of the Western expressions of Christianity which from the first has met with disfavor is its denomination-alism.

Such sentiments did not lack support from missionaries. On April 15, 1925, a group of Canadians in the Honan Synod sent a message of greeting to the General Council of the proposed Church of Christ in China which stated:

> Work in China has led us to emphasize less and less those denominational distinctions that characterize our homeland and to emphasize more and more the truth as held by all evangelical churches—thus encouraging the Chinese Christians to unite in propagating a church indigenous to their native country; and we rejoice to see many indications of the growth of a Church of Christ in China, free from denominationalism that has grown up in many lands.

Andrew Weir of Manchuria, writing in the November 1927 *Chinese Recorder,* commented: "Highly though we value the ideas and work and virtues of our ancestors, we must remember that our ancestors were not the ancestors of the Chinese."

Notable Chinese Christian Leadership

Within the church, Chinese more and more gained positions of control and notable figures were coming into prominence. C. Y. Cheng, still a very young man, had impressed the 1910 Edinburgh Missionary Conference by his stirring address emphasizing the need for a united Chinese church and was the leading Chinese advocate of that cause throughout his life. He gave important leadership to the Chinese Home Missionary Society, the China Continuation Committee, and the National Christian Council. Ting Li-mei, a Presbyterian minister from Shantung, who had as a young man barely escaped with his life in the Boxer Rebellion, became the first Secretary of the Chinese Student Volunteer Movement and won many students to Christian commitment. Chia Yu-ming, a well-trained Presbyterian theologian from the conservative Shantung church, was in much demand as a speaker. He eventually founded an independent theological school in Shanghai and produced a number of scholarly commentaries and other writings. Z. T. Kaung (Chiang Ch'ang-ch'uan) had come into prominence as a Shanghai pastor and later became a Methodist bishop. T. C. Chao, a prominent theologian, writer of distinctively Chinese hymns, and dean of the Yenching University School of Religion, and T. T. Lew, a theological teacher, editor, and hymn writer, were also leaders of considerable influence in the church in this period.

A different aspect of the increased leadership taken by Chinese Christians in this period was the important role played by lay Christians in the life of the nation at all levels. Sun Yat-sen was a Christian and Chiang Kai-shek became one after his marriage to Soong Mei-ling, a member of a wealthy and influential Christian family. Neither was ever active in church life and the depth of their Christian experience has been questioned, but the very fact that leaders of such prominence were adherents of the Christian faith somewhat counteracted the forces of opposition.

Feng Yu-hsiang, long called "the Christian General," was a striking figure of impressive physique who had risen from the ranks to become one of the military leaders of the twenties. He was first influenced as a young officer by the spirit of a Congregational missionary, Miss Morrill, who offered her life to save others in the Boxer Rebellion of 1900. Before she was executed, she gave Feng her Chinese New Testament. Later, a strong influence was that of the fiery Calvinism of the Canadian Presbyterian missionary, Jonathan Goforth, who served Feng as an advisor for some years. A powerful and influential leader, Feng enforced exemplary moral standards on his troops, used Christian hymns as marching songs, and conducted regular Christian services for his men, encouraging conversion. But his simplistic beliefs and vacillating loyalties somewhat negated any Christian influence he may have had, though he had warm supporters as well as critics in the missionary community.

Christians were increasingly prominent in various areas of Chinese life. The nursing schools of the Christian hospitals trained a very high proportion of China's nurses, and the Christian medical schools trained a substantial percentage of Chinese doctors. Men such as Dr. F. C. Yen, long associated with Yale-in-China's medical work, were instrumental in developing modern medicine and helped arouse official interest in the improvement of health standards, the development of medical institutions, and the promotion of public health programs. Christians had an important part in the development of modern education in China, not only in the church-related schools, which produced many educators of note, but in government and private school educational programs.

The Young Men's Christian Association played a very important role in developing Chinese Christian leadership, both in the church and in the wider world of Chinese society. Essentially a lay movement, it produced many leaders of note. They included David Z. T. Yui, General Secretary of the Y and Chairman of the National Christian Council during its early years, and C. T. Wang, also a YMCA General Secretary and later a prominent political figure who served in many cabinet posts, including that of Foreign Minister. T. Z. Koo, also a YMCA leader, was a popular and influential speaker to students, both in China and abroad, in this period and later. Dr. Y. C. James Yen worked under the YMCA among Chinese laborers in France during and after World War I. He developed a method of teaching the illiterate to read through the use of a thousand selected characters. On his return to China, he developed the important Mass Education Movement for promoting literacy and improving rural life.

W. W. Yen, the son of an Anglican churchman, served as both Premier and Foreign Minister. Wang Ch'ung-hui, an eminent jurist who was the son of a Christian minister, was presiding judge of the Supreme Court, Minister of Justice, one of three Chinese delegates to the Washington Disarmament Conference in 1921-22, and a member of the Permanent Court of International Justice.

Some indication of the importance of Christian leadership in Chinese life in the Republican period (1911-1949) is found in the selections by the editors of the Columbia University Press *Biographical Dictionary of Republican China*. Out of a total of five hundred and sixty individuals deemed to have been important public figures in that era, seventy were Christians. This reflects primarily the judgment of Western editors, but does indicate the role of Christians in Chinese society in a time of key importance in the development of the modern Chinese nation.

Indigenous Christian Groups

Another indication of the assertion of Christian leadership in Christian work in China was the appearance of indigenous Chinese Christian groups. These included the Ling En Hui ("Spiritual Grace Association"), a highly emotional and strongly anti-missionary revivalist movement emphasizing "spiritual gifts," including speaking with tongues, that swept through the Presbyterian and some other churches in the north in the twenties and early thirties, disrupting church life. The True Jesus Church, founded about 1914 by Barnabas Tung as a Chinese Church, claimed to be the sole preserver of apostolic doctrine. It opposed relationship with other Christian bodies, emphasized tongues, faith healing, and the ministry of the laity, and denounced other churches as apostate. "The Little Flock," the popular name for an anti-church Christian movement led by the able Ni To-sheng ("Watchman Nee"), a charismatic evangelist deeply concerned with theology, also flourished in this period and later, winning many accessions from the membership of the traditional churches. Much akin to the Plymouth Brethren and quite like the groups already mentioned in its practices, its "Christian meeting places" sprang up in many cities. "The Jesus Family" originated somewhat later under the leadership of Ching Tien-ying, a former Methodist evangelist. It was a communal Christian movement organized into "families" in which the members shared all things as the early Christians had done. It offered a refuge from the terrible uncertainties of life in a chaotic society and a genuine and highly meaningful Christian fellowship. Its greatest growth came in the 1940s.

All these groups offered the kind of escape from the hard problems of life and the security of an other-worldly faith that appealed to many Chinese Christians and was a chief object of criticism in Christianity by the Communists. The Ling En Hui had run its course by the mid-thirties, but the other three groups and their leaders encountered serious difficulties when the Communists came to power. For the most part, they drew their followers from Christians who for one reason or another were restless or discontented with the traditional churches. It is difficult to estimate their influence or even to know their numbers, since for the most part they kept no statistics and had no central organization. The True Jesus Church claimed a very large membership in rather vague terms.

Chinese Evangelists

Chinese leadership also came to the fore in the rise of a group of influential Chinese evangelists about this same period, although many of them had their greatest response in the thirties. They were

strongly influenced by the mass evangelism popular in the West in
the late nineteenth and early twentieth centuries, but they were also
motivated by their own deep conviction of the need for repentance
and for Chinese proclamation of the Gospel as they understood it.
One of the best known evangelists was Wang Ming-tao, a largely
self-taught preacher with a powerful, Bible-centered message who
built up a large independent congregation in Peking and was much in
demand as a revivalist throughout the church. The emotional revivalist Dr. John Sung (Sung Shang-chieh) of Amoy was often called "the
Billy Sunday of China." Much in demand in all parts of the country,
as well as in overseas Chinese communities, he was highly critical of
church leadership and of Christian educational institutions. Drawing
deeply on Old Testament themes, he changed many lives and encouraged volunteer preaching bands. But while he enjoyed considerable
success and aroused many dormant Christians, he was often the
center of controversy because of his criticism of church leaders and
programs. Divisions in local congregations frequently followed his
campaigns. Originally associated with the Bethel Band, a Chinese
Christian organization based in Shanghai, he soon broke away to
work independently, as did Andrew Gih, who worked with him in
the early thirties. Eventually the two men found it impossible to
work together and Gih formed his own group. He became influential
in Chinese Christian communities elsewhere in Asia, both as an
evangelist and as the founder of conservative Bible training schools.

There were a number of other independent and popular Chinese
evangelists. In general these men were separatists, highly individualistic, and very critical of traditional church structures. They exerted
considerable influence on the theological attitudes of great numbers
of ordinary Chinese Christians—almost always on the side of extreme
conservatism and literalism—but they represented a genuine element
in Chinese Christian experience.

Summary—Growth in Adversity

In these troubled years many missionary families had been uprooted
and their possessions lost. Some were discouraged by the intense
nationalist opposition and others were affected by the reduced
resources of the mission boards caused by economic depression and
did not return to China. Others rejoiced in the growing strength of

Chinese leadership in the church. The change in the role of the missionary which had been slowly taking place was now clearly revealed. The church was now central, the mission supplemental.

Some missionaries found it difficult to see the change and accept their new status, but its reality was obvious both to Chinese leadership and to the more perceptive missionary. He was now to be the colleague, not the leader; the fellow-worker, rather than the central figure. This concept was set forth clearly in the findings of the Jerusalem Conference of the International Missionary Council in 1928, in which Chinese leadership had an important part.

There was general agreement that the cause of devolution had been greatly advanced by the events of the difficult years of the anti-Christian movement. Frank Rawlinson, editor of the *Chinese Recorder*, commented in the 1928 *Chinese Christian Year Book*, "Recent events have also stimulated the coming forward of Chinese Christian leadership." But he added, "It is nowhere adequate numerically." J. S. Kunkle of Union Theological Seminary (Canton) said in the 1929 *Year Book*, "The Church has had a rebirth. . . . The Church is rapidly taking the place of the mission as the dominant influence in the Christian Movement." C. Y. Cheng, writing in the same issue on "The State of the Church," saw increasing desire by missions and churches for transfer of responsibility to the Chinese church and emphasis on the development of Chinese leadership.

H. T. Hodgkin of the National Christian Council staff summed up the results of the events culminating in the massive 1927 evacuation of missionaries in the 1928 *Year Book*. While admitting that there had been serious defections in church membership and that various weakness in the church had been exposed, he also saw many positive results. These included the desire for a more Chinese expression of Christianity, more readiness on the part of Chinese to accept responsibility, an impetus toward Christian unity, a deeper appreciation of the church's educational function, and a stronger emphasis on character building.

It had become quite clear that no longer was the Christian church in China an exotic import, sustained and nourished by foreign support alone, but that it had sunk its roots deep into Chinese soil. Though there had been serious destruction of church and institutional property, as well as widespread verbal and often physical attacks on Chinese Christians, the reality of Chinese commitment to the Christian cause was clearer than ever before. While there had been some falling away among the more fearful or less well-grounded church members, most Chinese Christians had remained true to their Christian faith and the growth of able Chinese leadership was most encouraging.

Once again, as in the Boxer uprising, the church had survived vicissitudes and opposition which seemed to some to spell its demise, but the obituary notices were premature. The anti-Christian movement which had threatened the very life of the church was an additional stimulus to the healthy growth of Chinese leadership and progress toward the goal of an indigenous church. Like Joseph, the church could say, "You meant evil against me, but God meant it for good" (Genesis 50:20).

Chapter Four

A

Church
United

Organization of the Church of Christ in China

At the close of the important 1922 National Christian Conference, representatives of Presbyterian and Congregational churches were called together in a Provisional Assembly of the Church of Christ in China to consider further steps in the formation of a united church. The plan of union drawn up by the special committee appointed at the 1918 meeting of the Presbyterian Federal Council had been sent out to interested and concerned associations and presbyteries as an overture for their deliberation, and for the most part the response had been favorable.

The Rev. A. R. Kepler (a missionary of the Presbyterian Church USA) was asked to undertake the responsibility for organizing and preparing a General Assembly to formally establish the Church of Christ in China as a national church. He was released by the Presbyterian China Council to give full time to this task. Kepler was a man of remarkable vigor and ability. A high school graduate by age thirteen, he had completed his college and theological education before he was twenty-two. Soon thereafter, in 1901, he went to China as a Presbyterian missionary, one of the first of the new recruits who went out after the terrible events of the Boxer Rebellion. He quickly mastered the Chinese language and displayed the diligence and energy which characterized his lifetime service. In his first term he was organizing secretary for one of the first national Christian assemblies of young people in China, the National Convention of Young People's Societies of Christian Endeavor.

He was deeply committed to the cause of church union and in particular to the proposal for a Church of Christ in China. Through the years of his service to the Church he travelled tirelessly around the country preaching the gospel of a united Chinese church, participating in meetings of church judicatories, and seeking to strengthen the ties of union. Even on his furloughs he was always on the move. After returning to China in 1933, he reported to the General Council of the Church of Christ in China that he had spent ten weeks in the United Kingdom and one month in Canada, in addition to travelling extensively in the United States, and had made two hundred and eighty-two addresses during the furlough year!

Correspondence with the cooperating missionary societies abroad was one of his major responsibilities, and he performed it most effectively, providing a constant stream of reports and evaluations of immeasurable value in interpreting the work of the CCC for the supporting constituencies, especially important in the early years of the Church's life. The depth of his commitment was expressed in a memorial tribute by the Board of Foreign Missions of the Presbyterian Church USA after his death in 1942: "From the beginning of his service, Dr. Kepler had a peculiar singleness of purpose—the upbuilding and strengthening of the church."

On the one hand, it was a courageous undertaking to plan for the organization of a national church body at a time of political disturbance and strong anti-Christian feeling. On the other hand, it was an appropriate time to establish a national Chinese church, which much of the ablest Chinese leadership (supported by many missionaries) had long seen as essential, and when circumstances had again underlined the necessity for a truly Chinese church not dependent on the presence and help of the missionary.

The First General Assembly

The First (and constituting) Assembly of the Church of Christ in China was held in Shanghai October 1-11, 1927, at St. Mary's Hall, an Episcopal school made available for the occasion (a typical expression of the prevailing good will and friendliness between the major Protestant denominations). Eighty-eight commissioners were present, representing eleven synods and forty-six district associations, with over 120,000 communicant members. The great majority of the commissioners (sixty-six) were Chinese. There were also eight commissioners from two presbyteries which had not yet voted to come into the union and twenty-eight fraternal delegates from other churches, many of which later entered the union. Sixteen mission boards were listed as in cooperation with the Church, and approximately one-third of the Protestant Christians of China were represented.

Dr. C. Y. Cheng (Ch'eng Ching-yi), Secretary of the recently formed National Christian Council of China, was elected Moderator. He was certainly one of the ablest leaders to emerge in the Chinese church. His father was one of the early pastors in the Congregational work (London Missionary Society) in North China. His early education, including theological training, was in church institutions in North China. His family was among those who took refuge in the Legation Quarter of Peking during the Boxer siege. He himself served as an interpreter and stretcher bearer with the Allied forces that relieved Peking, narrowly escaping death on several occasions.

He was employed in 1903 to assist the Rev. George Owens of the LMS in preparing a revision of the Chinese New Testament, and went with Owens, who was forced to leave China for reasons of health, to London, where he spent the next three years. He then studied at the Bible Training Institute in Glasgow for two years. Upon his return to China, he was ordained and called as pastor of the independent Mi Shih Street Church in Peking.

He was one of three Chinese delegates to the World Missionary Conference at Edinburgh in 1910. Here he first attracted the attention of the world church with a prophetic seven-minute speech in which he declared: "Speaking plainly, we hope to see in the near future a united Christian church without denominational distinctions. . . . Denominationalism has never interested the Chinese mind." Although not yet thirty, he was elected a member of the continuation committee of the International Missionary Council.

He served as Secretary of a Chinese Advisory Council for the London Missionary Society work in China and after John R. Mott's visit to China in 1913 was elected Secretary of the China Continuation Committee. He was a founder of the Chinese Home Missionary Society and in 1922 was Chairman of the first meeting of the National Christian Council of China, which he then served as General Secretary until 1933. In 1934 he became General Secretary of the Church of Christ in China. He was honored with honorary degrees from Christian institutions in Canada, China, and the United States.

A man of dynamic presence, with a complete command of English as well as his native tongue, he was an eloquent and challenging leader. More than that, he was a man of genuine and convincing Christian faith, deeply committed to the unity of the church, always approachable and having a profound human concern for others. Almost never in robust health, he was frequently unable to do as much as he wanted to do in the service of the Church. Like the Apostle Paul, he could say, "I have cheerfully made up my mind to be proud of my weaknesses, because they mean a deeper experience of the power of Christ. I can even enjoy weakness, suffering, privations, persecutions and difficulties for Christ's sake. For my very weakness makes me strong in him" (II Corinthians 12:9-10—Phillips translation).

Kepler, who had so ably led arrangements for the Assembly, was elected General Secretary of the Church, a natural choice. He worked devotedly in this cause until his death in 1942, but gladly yielded the post of General Secretary to Dr. Cheng in 1934, serving thereafter as one of two Associate General Secretaries (later termed Executive Secretary). The two men worked together harmoniously and spent much time visiting constituent units of the Church, either together or singly. The establishment and early development of the Church of Christ in China was unquestionably due chiefly to the work and leadership of these two men.

The Rev. S. S. Chu was elected Recording Secretary and Dr. T. C. Fan the Assistant General Secretary. Fan, who held a doctorate in sociology, later taught with distinction in both Hangchow Christian College, where he was Dean, and the University of Nanking. He served the Church of Christ for some seven years as Kepler's associate. These four officers, together with four others elected from the commissioners, were to act as an Executive Committee for the Church.

A Call to Unity

The First General Assembly issued a call for Christian solidarity, addressed to all Christians in China. It deprecated the divisions among Christians and expressed the desire for spiritual enrichment through Christian fellowship and cooperation, pleading for dedication to Christian service. It stated that:

> The one important element which we must keep first and foremost is the simple faith of the original fishermen. . . . which needs to be interpreted against the background of Chinese civilization and adapted to the life of the people, so that this universal religion may have its real establishment in this rich soil. When this indigenous Church of Christ is established in China, then we can say that the Christian Church has accomplished her end, at least here in China, as a part of the evangelization of the world.

The Moderator was authorized to "send a letter of greetings and appreciation to all the missionary societies who have been cooperating with the churches connected with the General Assembly."

The desire for wider union had been well expressed in one of the first official statements of the CCC. *What Is the Church of Christ in China?* was a booklet prepared in advance of the 1927 Assembly to explain the plan for union—originally proposed in 1918 and refined in nine years of study and consultation—for the benefit of individuals and churches interested in union. About the purpose of the CCC, the document said:

> It should serve as an adequate point of departure for our ultimate goal—*one indigenous Christian Church for China,* a church which will at one and the same time continue in sympathy and harmony with the Christian life and hope and faith of the Churches of the West and also be expressive in worship, fellowship and service to the Chinese Christian in ways suited to Chinese culture and customs.

So it was quite natural that a broad invitation was issued to other churches to consider union with the CCC. The document states:

> The Church of Christ in China solemnly accepts Christ's holy teachings concerning unity and in order to fulfill the aspirations of the Chinese Church, we are ready and willing to enter into organic union with all other evangelical churches who are of a like mind concerning unity. We extend a heartfelt invitation to all who share this desire with us.

This invitation was renewed at every General Assembly.

Women in the Church

A lengthy statement on the position of women in the Church was adopted which declared that "in the Christian Church men and women have an equal personality and in society they are mutually necessary." The statement, consisting of six paragraphs, noted the efforts of the Christian church in its pioneer program of education for women and in the fight against foot-binding, polygamy, and infanticide. It recognized that women had not been given full opportunity for expression in the church and deplored the high rate of illiteracy among women in China. The document expressed sympathy with "modern ideas on the equality of the sexes" and with the growing woman's movement in China and called upon the Church to support the new spirit of patriotism and provide suitable channels for the expression of the longing to be of service to their country which is animating the best and most capable of the young women of China. No longer will the womanhood of China be content with a position of inferiority and the situation must be frankly faced by the Church.

While this rather advanced position was no doubt honored more in theory than in fact, the author does clearly remember the important part played by many women in the churches of China, not only at the local level, where the proportion of women in the congregational ruling bodies was in general greater than in the West, but in Christian education and medical programs and in the central bodies of the churches. It was not until 1969 that the National Council of the Churches of Christ in the USA elected its first woman president. The National Christian Council of China elected the eminent Dr. Wu Yi-fang, President of Ginling College, its Chairman in 1935.

At the Fourth General Council meeting of the CCC (October 1-7, 1931), the question arose whether women could be ordained to the ministry (the ordination of women elders was already effective in many of the member units). The North China (Hwapei) Synod had raised the question. After discussion, the Council replied that there was no constitutional hindrance to the ordination of women and the synods were free to act accordingly. While this writer has found no record of any such ordination taking place at this time, the right of women to be ordained was accepted long before most Western churches had agreed to it. In the South Fukien Synod there are reports of several ordained women serving the churches by the 1940s, and it is possible that there were others in other areas.

Other Actions of the First Assembly

The Assembly recognized education as a proper activity of the Church with the purpose of "turning out men with the spirit of Christ for church, for country and for society." It also dealt with practical issues related to the relationships of the Church with the mission boards, their missions within China and the missionaries. It acknowledged that the Chinese church should eventually support itself, but asked that the cooperating missions continue their support without decrease for five years and ruled that the district associations fix schedules of increased financial responsibility, with a time limit for complete self-support, to guide the missions in future reductions of appropriations. There was a call for a committee to prepare and present to the General Council a Form of Government, a Directory of Worship, and a Book of Discipline for the Church.

The Assembly recognized the necessity of a full-time ministry for the work of the Church and called for the setting aside of men with special gifts "to give their whole time and strength to leading the Church in thought and worship and service." It approved the principle that there should be freedom within the united Church to use whatever form of Christian baptism was considered suitable by the local church.

It was abundantly clear, as Fisher comments, "that the coming together of the churches which formed the Church of Christ in China was not a forced union but a spontaneous desire for united fellowship, worship and service for Christ, for Church and for country." The Editor of *The Chinese Recorder*, Frank Rawlinson, wrote in the November 1927 issue: "The Church of Christ in China is the biggest actual achievement of Christian Unity yet recorded in China. It has a dramatic significance to the Chinese mind. . . . Out of this rising urge for unity a greater and more inclusive, dynamic fellowship is bound to come." Latourette saw it at the time of its formation as "more inclusive than any ecclesiastical union ever formed in any country."

A General Council was elected as the body with continuing responsibility for the life of the national Church between assemblies. The Council consisted of representatives from each synod and three members at large and was to meet annually or on call.

CCC Membership

Almost all the member churches in 1927 were of Calvinist background and Presbyterian or Congregational polity. These included Presbyterian and Reformed churches related to missions from Canada, England, Ireland, New Zealand, Scotland, and the United States and Congregational churches which had grown out of the work of English and American missions. A small but important group were the independent Chinese congregations, some of them originally mission-related, others the result of the evangelistic zeal of Chinese Christians in Western lands, but now fully autonomous. Included in the union were churches related to the work of the United Brethren, and by December 1927 the Shantung Baptist churches (affiliated with the English Baptist Missionary Society) had also joined, perhaps the first instance of a Baptist group entering a united church. The Baptist churches in Shansi and Shensi later came into the union, as did churches in Central China affiliated with the Swedish Missionary Society (Swedish Evangelical Free Church) and with the American Evangelical and Reformed and Evangelical United Brethren missions.

In 1931 the former Methodist Church in Szechuan, related to the Canadian Methodist Mission and by then part of the United Church of Canada, voted to enter the union and became the Synod of Szechuan. As already noted (Chapter II), a Methodist Conference in South Fukien united with the CCC Synod in 1934 and a Methodist Congregation in Shanghai cast its lot with the CCC churches there about the same time. Kepler reported in his article on "Movements for Christian Unity" in the 1928 *China Christian Year Book:* "The churches affiliated with the China Inland Mission in Lanchow and South Kansu have definitely voted to link up with the united church." There is no clear information that they actually came into the CCC, although an undated publication entitled "Kwangtung Synod" (c. 1929) lists these churches as one of seventeen "church groups constituting the CCC."

Other Interested Churches

The American Church of the Brethren began work in Shansi Province in 1910. The Brethren cooperated rather closely with the Baptists and Congregationalists in the area, and the church which grew out of this work became interested in membership in the CCC. In 1931 A. R. Kepler and T. C. Fan met with church leaders in Shansi. The General Secretary reported to the 1931 General Council meeting: "We found . . . the leadership of the Church of the Brethren not only most friendly, but keen to give the most sympathetic consideration to the question of union with the CCC." And the July 1950 issue of *The Church* reported:

> Six representatives of the Church of the Brethren in Shansi and other representatives of this Church in Peking met with Dr. H. H. Tsui on his recent visit to Peking to discuss the question of union with the CCC. Negotiations are continuing.

There was an effort in 1948 to relocate some of the Brethren missionaries in a Szechuan Synod area, but this did not work out. Some of the missionaries and Chinese pastors did go to Szechuan to begin work in a Methodist area for a short time. It seems quite certain that if the work in Shansi had not been so drastically disrupted during the years of the Japanese occupation and the civil war, the Church of the Brethren would have become part of the Church of Christ in China.

In East China, the Church of Christ (somewhat confusing, since the name in both English and Chinese was very close to that of the CCC) had grown out of the work of the American Disciples of Christ. This was another group which felt close to the CCC and might have taken membership if circumstances had been different. In early discussions regarding the formation of the CCC, the possibility of membership led to a prolonged controversy in the home board on the matter of open membership. The final decision, according to the December 1921 issue of *The Chinese Recorder,* was "that the principle of leaving the Chinese Christians free to settle their own policies was recognized" (p. 869).

This church was deeply involved in a number of union enterprises (the University of Nanking, Ginling College, Nanking Theological Seminary, etc.) including the National Christian Council of China. Although fraternal delegates were sent to several CCC general assemblies and a committee to consider union was appointed after 1945, the union was not consummated.

Continuing Presbyterian Groups

While almost all Presbyterian churches came into the CCC at the time of its organization, there were several exceptions. Two presbyteries in the southern Shantung-northern Anhwei area, related to the Presbyterian US mission, did not join the union, and several strong Shantung presbyteries related to the work of the Presbyterians USA also stayed out. These bodies and the church related to the Canadian Presbyterian work in Manchuria continued to use the name "Presbyterian Church in China." Their chief objections to union lay in their strong loyalty to traditional Presbyterianism and its doctrines. Historically, the missions in these areas had been strongly conservative and Calvinist.

Presbyterian theological training had begun in Shantung as early as 1864, when a school was established at Tenghsien. Early in the twentieth century, Presbyterians cooperated with Baptists in the Gotch-Robinson Theological College at Tsingchow. In the process of merging a number of small denominational colleges into Shantung Christian College (later Cheloo University) the Theological College was moved to Tsinan in 1917. In 1919 some of the Presbyterians, uneasy that Baptists and Congregationalists of more liberal tendencies were involved, established the North China Theological Seminary at Weihsien, under the leadership of Dr. W. M. Hayes. This was moved to Tenghsien in 1922, with support from both Presbyterian missions. Through the years, many students from this area and others received a thoroughly orthodox Presbyterian training in the several courses developed there.

The Canadian Presbyterian work in Manchuria had been started in 1925 by the continuing Presbyterian Church in Canada, a substantial proportion of which had chosen not to enter the United Church of Canada formed that year. Working relations with the major Presbyterian church in the area, established by Irish and Scottish Presbyterians, were harmonious, in spite of the fact that that church entered the CCC at its inception, becoming the Kwantung (later Northeast) Synod.

Canadian Presbyterian missionaries were forced out of Manchuria and Taiwan in the early 1940s by the war, and the question arose of possible service in the missions of the CCC. A. R. Kepler discussed these possibilities at a Canadian Presbyterian board meeting in 1941. The Board of Missions in 1943 recommended to the General Assembly "that we become associated with this work," and the General Assembly voted "to undertake missionary work in Free China by affiliating with the North American Advisory Committee of the Church of Christ in China, particularly with a view to participation in the Yunnan Church-Mission joint project."

Some in the Canadian church were alarmed by the prospect of participating in a united church, citing their own decision twenty years earlier not to join the United Church of Canada. Overtures were introduced by a number of presbyteries, in general opposing cooperation with the CCC (and in some cases other cooperative agencies at home and abroad) on doctrinal grounds. Some of the overtures were critical of the 1943 Assembly action approving arrangements which allowed two women missionaries of the Canadian church to serve with the CCC and urged that no further commitment be made and especially that the Presbyterian churches in Manchuria and Taiwan, where missionaries of the Presbyterian Church in Canada had worked, not be influenced by the 1943 action or "legislated" into union with the CCC.

Actually, as was pointed out by the two mission boards of the Canadian church during this debate, there had been a continuing relationship with the Church of Christ in China since its earliest days. Canadian Presbyterian missionaries had been present at the 1922 Provisional Assembly which considered and approved the wider union. The Woman's Missionary Society had maintained its relationship, as one of its missionaries in Canton, Miss Ethel Reed, elected to remain a Presbyterian when the United Church of Canada took over responsibility for the work in South China and the WMS had continued her support. Fisher comments, "The Presbyterian Church in Canada thus became the first 'sending church' to have direct relationship with a synod of the CCC."

Canadian missionaries were never able to return to the work in Manchuria (except for a brief visit by the Rev. Allen Reoch in 1948). Austin Fulton, in *Through Earthquake, Wind and Fire,* reports discussions between the church and the Northeast Synod of the CCC regarding the possibility of merger. There is no evidence that a union took place, but the 1950 *Dictionary of the Protestant Christian Movement in China* does not include the Manchurian church in the report of the Presbyterian Church in China nor as a separate unit, so a merger may have taken place.

The continuing Presbyterian groups in Shantung-Anhwei did eventually come into the Church of Christ in China. They became the Kianghuai Synod in 1948 and were formally welcomed into membership at the Fifth General Assembly. Dr. H. H. Tsui in a *CCC News Bulletin* (December 1949) reported that the three Shantung presbyteries (Weihsien, Lohan and Shoukwang) which had continued as part of the Presbyterian Church in China "have recently voted to enter the Shantung Synod of the Church of Christ in China." The two Presbyterian synods in Taiwan (related to Canadian Presbyterian work in the north and English Presbyterian work in the south), which in 1951 were united as the Presbyterian Church of Formosa, could not come into the union in the early years of the CCC since Taiwan was under Japanese control until 1945. The synod in the south was definitely interested in CCC affiliation after the war and was represented at the Fifth General Assembly in 1948. If political considerations had not stood in the way, this synod would probably have joined the CCC.

Thus almost all organized Presbyterian churches in China eventually became part of the CCC. It is possible that some individual Presbyterian congregations never affiliated.

North China Congregationalists

The North China Congregational Union, related to American Board work, did not join the union, partly because it thought the CCC too conservative (the Congregationalists related to the London Mission did join the CCC). In 1922 the Union's Council gave its consideration to the Doctrinal Basis and Plan of Union adopted by the Provisional General Assembly of the CCC held in Shanghai in April. As reported in the October 1922 *Chinese Recorder,* the Council voted a five-point statement of its position, based on traditional Congregational practices. "Unless they are accepted, the Council does not express approval of entering the proposed Union." The points included "the right of private judgment, which may not be overruled by any organization"; the right of individual congregations and presbyteries to full authority in matters of "the faith and conduct" of church workers without interference by or appeal to higher judicatories; and "the fundamental authority of church members . . . as central in organization." While there was considerable sentiment for union among North China Congregationalists as the CCC came into being, those who insisted on the incompatibility of the proposals with basic Congregational principles won out. So the North China Congregationalists related to the American Board never came into the union, although their counterpart bodies in the south were actively involved from the inception of the CCC.

CCC Structure and Polity

The organizational pattern common to the Reformed tradition was adopted by the Church of Christ in China. In the local congregation, control lay with a governing body usually composed of elders, though in some churches the term deacon was preferred. District associations corresponded to presbyteries. Synods were based on geographical areas—usually a single province, but sometimes embracing more than one, or where the church was strong or where access was difficult or dialects differed, a region within a province. Thus

Fukien and Kwangtung Provinces each contained three synods because of such reasons. Denominational and mission relationships were also determining factors, and in several instances a synod was composed of a single denominational group which functioned very much as it had before the union, especially in areas where only one church had come into the union. Thus in Hopei Province two synods, one with Presbyterian, the other with Congregational (London Mission) antecedents, continued to exist as separate entities within the CCC until after the Communists came to power, when they finally merged. This continued separation came not only from denominational loyalties, but also because of doctrinal differences and differences on such issues as the use of tobacco and alcoholic beverages. On the other hand, many of the synods represented genuine union and cooperation between groups of varying backgrounds, as we shall see in Chapter V.

The highest court of the Church was the General Assembly, composed of elected commissioners from the synods in proportion to membership, which was to meet triennially. However, during the years of the war with Japan (1937-45), such meetings were impossible, as was the case under the Communist regime. After the First Assembly in Shanghai in 1927, subsequent assemblies met in 1930 (Canton), 1933 (Amoy), 1937 (Tsingtao) and 1948 (Soochow—the final Assembly). An Assembly scheduled for Hankow in 1941 had to be cancelled because of the war. A General Council functioned between assemblies as a continuing committee with considerable power.

Although basically Reformed in tradition, especially in the early years, the CCC never sought uniformity in practice. Although the ultimate aim was complete union, the Church in actuality was a kind of loose federal union, with most authority remaining at the synodical level.

CCC Doctrinal Position

No formulation of doctrine or creed was adopted, although a committee was appointed to prepare a "Statement of Faith"—never completed because of the disruption of the times. A broad "Doctrinal Bond of Union" was incorporated in the Constitution (Part I, Article 3—see Appendix A). In brief, it proclaimed faith in Jesus Christ as Redeemer and Lord, acceptance of the Old and New

Testaments as divinely inspired and "the supreme authority in matters of faith and duty," and a belief in the Apostles' Creed. One of the Church's early statements (*Let Us Unite*—1935) interpreted this as follows:

> The Doctrinal Bond of Union does not contain all that every Christian body of believers should believe. It seeks to express only that modicum of doctrine which all must hold in common if historic Christianity is to be conserved. The doctrinal basis of union, therefore, is an effort to enable those who have gloried in their freedom from credal restraints to unite on the same basis which bound together the Christians of the Early Church.

The First and Second General Assemblies adopted an identical statement: "Although the Church of Christ in China has a commonly accepted Bond of Union, nevertheless she has the sincerest respect for the freedom of the local church in matters of belief." This was difficult for strict constructionists such as the Presbyterians in Shantung and Anhwei to accept. They wanted a doctrinal position clearly spelled out and they wanted assent to it at every level of the church. Thus the Board of Directors of the North China Theological Seminary required signed acceptance of a specific credal statement by each Director at every meeting.

The Church never came to grips with basic issues of theology or polity. This was quite typical of the Chinese churches, which tended to be pragmatic and activist rather than philosophical, though there was also a strong pietistic strain, in part from the missionary heritage. Such theological and political discussion would undoubtedly have occurred if the Church had been permitted to mature more normally, as later happened with much travail but generally satisfactory results in the United Church of Christ in Japan (the Kyodan). There was no prescribed method of baptism or ordination, the decision in such matters being left to the synods (an important concession for Baptists and Congregationalists in such matters as infant baptism, immersion, and congregational ordination). The role of the General Assembly as "confined to such matters only as are essential for the promotion and conservation of true unity" was incorporated in the Constitution, and in practice the leaders of the General Assembly saw themselves as servants of the Church, rather than its masters.

The Church was ecumenical in spirit from its inception. Its beginnings were directly related to the Edinburgh Missionary Conference of 1910 and the emphasis on cooperation and unity which came out of it. It was the first Chinese church to become a member of the World Council of Churches and was represented at the organizing

Assembly in 1949 by the Rev. Li Ting-K'uei of the Northeast Synod. (Incidentally, that membership was never formally withdrawn, in spite of strong Communist attacks upon the Council.) Other Chinese churches which took membership in the World Council were the Chung Hua Sheng Kung Hui, the China Baptist Council, and the North China Kung Li Hui. The CCC was also a member of the World Alliance of Presbyterian Churches and the International Congregational Council.

Summary—a Chinese and United Church

Thus a union had been formed, fulfilling the ardent hopes of many Christians, both Chinese and missionary, and bringing together Christian churches in almost every area of China. While the dominant elements came from the family of Reformed churches, not all churches of that persuasion elected to come in and strong elements from other denominational heritages, including Baptist and Methodist, did enter the mainstream of the united church.

While it never achieved the hope of bringing together the bulk of Protestant Christianity in China, the Church of Christ in China represented a substantial proportion of the whole. It sought to establish an identity as an indigenous Chinese church and with the exception of the distinctively Chinese sects referred to in the previous chapter, came nearer to that goal than any other church in China.

While to some the name Church of Christ in China seemed to claim too much, it was rightly based on the concept of a Chinese church open to all Christians, and was not simply a bringing together of denominational fragments. The presiding officers of the Church were without exception Chinese (a claim which probably no other major church in China could make) and with the exception of its first few years, the top leadership of the Church was Chinese. Representation at official meetings was predominantly Chinese from the first, chosen—whether Chinese or missionary—by the church judicatories and representative of them. The goals of self-support, self-government, and self-propagation, as well as the openness to wider union, were prominent in the pronouncements of its official bodies, and its strong emphasis on the centrality and primacy of the church and its responsibility for mission within its own land validated its intent to be a truly Chinese church.

Chapter Five

The Synods — Their Areas and Characteristics *

Synods—the Basic Structure of the CCC

The synodical structure, while basically Presbyterian, was similar to regional alignments in other denominations and was inevitably related to the mission antecedents of the various church bodies which came into the union. Some synods were strong, others were weak. Some developed into regional churches with a strong sense of unity, able to participate actively in the national church and its programs. Others (such as Northeast, Honan, and Shansi) were cut off from communication with the General Assembly for long periods of time, and some (Shantung and Honan, for example) were even unable to hold synodical meetings during the war and post-war years.

It is difficult to bring the synods and district associations, to say nothing of local congregations, into the story as fully as they deserve. Obviously it was at this level that the basic life of the church went on. With few exceptions, however, records are not available of what was happening in the church bodies, local and regional, that made up the Church of Christ in China.

One of the exceptions is the Kwangtung Synod, one of the best organized at the synodical level. Fairly complete information on its life and work is available in the English-language *Information Service,* which was published regularly for many years. For other areas, some information has been gleaned from reports given at General Assembly and General Council meetings, correspondence to the cooperating missions from General Assembly staff, correspondence from missionaries, and in a few cases Chinese minutes of church judicatories. For the most part, however, the only record is in the memories of those who shared in the ongoing life of the churches at local

---

*See Appendix B for a list of the Synods.

and regional levels. The Chinese leadership is generally not accessible, while few of the missionary participants, especially in the early years, still survive.

For the most part, the life and work of the local churches, the synods, and the district associations of the Church, particularly those cut off by military and political conditions from other member churches for long years, are lost in obscurity. But we may be sure that along with the problems and failures and heartaches there were also achievements. Many humble men and women who sincerely sought God's will in His church, lived lives worthy of followers of Jesus Christ and were lights in a dark world, the salt of the earth.

In effect the Church of Christ in China led a double life. On the one hand it was a national church representing a variety of denominational traditions and carrying on programs in the name of the total Church. On the other hand it was a group of regional churches in loose association with a central staff and not very close relation with each other. The latter aspect of the Church's life was aggravated by a national situation in which invasion from without and civil war within made communication difficult or impossible—in some cases for most of the period of CCC existence as a national church. Some synods were simply regional churches retaining their old denominational character. So the Presbyterian churches in Hopei, at least until 1945, remained in effect Presbyterian churches, following Presbyterian practices and traditions and even in general using the name "Presbyterian." Much the same was true of the Congregationalists in the same province (related to LMS work), who maintained their separate identity in the North China (Hwapei) Synod, and of the Baptists in Shansi and Shensi, the Presbyterians in the Northeast and elsewhere, and the Congregationalists in Central and North Fukien.

Yet, some synods contained a real denominational mix, most notably in Kwangtung and South Fukien, where a number of denominational traditions were merged in CCC synods and the synods were well advanced in the kind of amalgamation that represented a truly united church. In other areas, the process was less advanced, as in Shantung, where political and military upheavals made it impossible for the synod, with member churches of Baptist and Presbyterian lineage, to function meaningfully, even though there was a long history of good will and cooperation antedating the formation of the CCC. In other cases, such as Hunan and Hupei, organizational lines shifted because of the accession of new church bodies, and the period of union was too short to judge whether it would have succeeded in integrating the several participating church bodies.

The synodical structure as it existed at the close of the Nationalist era was recorded in the *1950 Directory of the Christian Movement in China,* reflecting 1948 or 1949 actualities (see Appendix B). At that time the CCC reported twenty-one synods. Of these, eight synods were composed of Presbyterian churches alone (East Kwangtung, Hainan, Hopei, Kiangan, Kianghwai, Malaya, and Northeast); three were composed of Congregational churches only (North China, North and Central Fukien); two were composed of Baptist groups alone (Shansi and Shensi); two were composed of United Church of Canada antecedents (Honan and Szechuan), and only six synods represented a union of churches of differing denominational traditions (Chekiang, Hunan, Hupei, Kwangtung, Shantung, and South Fukien).

Protestant Christian work in China began in the south, and the earliest efforts at union are found there. From the earliest days of Protestant missions, Presbyterians, Congregationalists, and United Brethren cooperated in medical and educational programs, as well as in evangelistic efforts. Following the proposed plan of union and doctrinal statement drawn up by the Committee on Union appointed in 1918 (adopted in 1921 by the General Assembly of the Presbyterian Church in China), the West Kwangtung Synod of the Presbyterian Church in China met with representatives of Congregational churches affiliated with the London Missionary Society and the American Board of Commissioners for Foreign Missions on local union between these churches, which had long experienced close fellowship and cooperation.

Kwangtung Synod

The Kwangtung Synod of the Church of Christ in China was organized in 1919, though the Synod officially dated its inception under the name of the CCC as 1925. It included these churches as well as churches of the Chinese Independent Presbyterian Church (established and supported by Chinese who had emigrated to the U.S. and other English-speaking lands and had become Christians in their adopted lands, many returning to China) and the independent Congregational Association, with similar antecedents. These independent groups were quite strong and had in a number of places developed schools and hospitals as well as churches. Soon thereafter, the churches related to the United Brethren work also joined the union, as did the churches related to what is reported as "the Swedish-American Mission." This seems to relate to the work of the Evangelical Free Church of America, but Fisher reports that these churches "later—under pressure from foreign missionaries—withdrew." About two-thirds of the Synod's work came from results of the Presbyterian Mission program (Fisher, p. 31).

With ten district associations, in addition to churches in Macao and Shanghai, and strong Chinese leadership, both lay and clerical, the Synod was an effective agency of the church from its formation. A Synod office was set up in Canton with a full-time Chinese executive, Dr. Y. S. Tom, who was an able and influential leader for many years and served as Moderator of the Third General Assembly of the CCC (Amoy, 1933). Dr. Fisher served as Associate General Secretary in the early years, as Synod Secretary for Evangelism from 1935, and as Executive Secretary in 1938. Other missionaries who played an important part in the early years of the Synod were the Rev. G. H. McNeur (New Zealand Presbyterian) and the Rev. C. W. Shoop (United Brethren).

On December 2, 1935, the cornerstone was laid for a three-story Synod office building (Kwong Hip Lau), which was officially opened July 1, 1937. The land (the original site of True Light School, the first Christian school for girls in China) was given by the American Presbyterian Mission. One hundred thousand Chinese yuan (approximately $35,000) was given by Chinese Christians. Half was used for construction costs, and half was set aside for upkeep of the building. A strong organizational pattern at the synodical level developed, and the Synod was gradually given responsibility for program and funds. The Synod also issued a Chinese periodical, as well as *Information Service,* and the sense of unity seems to have been very real throughout the synodical area. In its 1937 annual meeting, the Synod reported a communicant membership of 21,300, with two hundred and forty-two organized churches, seven hospitals, seven middle schools, and more than eighty primary schools. The Kwangtung Synod was one of the best examples of genuine union in the Church of Christ in China.

The Synod later developed its own mission program. In the mountainous areas of Kwangtung there were still substantial numbers of aboriginal tribespeople living on a level of bare subsistence. The Yui (or Yu) tribespeople of Lienhsien, isolated from the Chinese and distrustful of outsiders, lived under the most primitive conditions. A Chinese Christian doctor, Ue Hoi Poh, under appointment by Kwangtung Synod, had treated many of these people in her clinic in the town of Saam Kong and their distrust had been eased so that a school was opened for their children and a Chinese evangelist welcomed among them (Fisher, p.172).

Hainan Synod

Protestant Christian work on Hainan Island, the tropical island at the extreme south of China, in the Gulf of Tonkin, was begun by American Presbyterian missionaries in 1885. Their work was among the original inhabitants, the Li people (of Thai origin), as well as among Mandarin and Cantonese-speaking Chinese and Hakka people from the mainland. The Synod was formally organized on June 28, 1932 (Fisher, p. 75), and consisted of three district associations, related to several schools and three hospitals.

East Kwangtung Synod

The East Kwangtung (Lingtung) Synod represented the churches in the Swatow area of Kwangtung, with a different dialect than the Cantonese. The churches there grew out of the work of the English Presbyterian Mission, beginning in 1857, and of the Basel Mission, which began even earlier. The Presbyterian and Reformed churches of the area, both of which stressed the development of Chinese leadership and self-support in their early work, were united in 1907. The first Chinese presbytery was organized in 1881 and soon thereafter organized its own Home Missionary Society, entirely supported by the local churches. There were two district associations, one Swatow-speaking and the other Hakka-speaking, with one hundred and eighteen organized churches reported in 1940. When the CCC was established in 1927, communicant membership was given as 6,972.

South Fukien Synod

The South Fukien (Minnan) Synod was one of the strongest in the Church of Christ in China. Work by the Reformed Church in America began in Amoy in 1842 with the arrival of the Rev. David Abeel, followed soon by the English Presbyterians and the London Missionary Society. By 1857 a united presbytery had been formed by the Presbyterian and Reformed churches. The Reformed Church Synod in the United States opposed the wishes of their missionaries for an independent Chinese church, whereupon all the RCA missionaries submitted their resignations. Synod backed down. Thereafter the policy was that each congregation became part of an autonomous Chinese church as soon as it was organized. In 1919 the Congregational Union in the area (LMS-related) voted to join with the existing merger to form the South Fukien Synod of the Church of Christ in China.

To complete the union, the Methodist South Fukien Conference, centered around Hungchun in the mountains of southern Fukien, voted in 1931 to join the Church of Christ in China, and in 1934 became a district association of the South Fukien Synod. The reasons were largely language and commercial ties with Amoy, though it is worth noting that A. R. Kepler in a letter to the CCC cooperating boards (January 8, 1932) reported that the Methodists were withdrawing support and their missionaries (no doubt because of this action). In another Occasional Letter (January 18, 1934) he speaks of the South Fukien Synod as "one of the rare places in the Christian world where denominationalism has been entirely eliminated."

The Synod's report to the Third General Assembly (1933) mentioned the Synod's Home Missionary Society, established in 1883 by the Presbyterian-Reformed union. Support from local churches provided for work in three counties, with one full-time pastor employed and many volunteers involved. In addition, a Woman's Missionary Society with ten branches and over six hundred members employed several evangelists for work among women.

Mid-Fukien Synod

The Mid-Fukien (Minchung) Synod was one of three synods in Fukien Province, the separate organization being required primarily because of major differences in the spoken language but also because of natural geographical boundaries. The churches here grew out of the work of American Congregationalists begun in Foochow (one of the earliest treaty ports opened to foreign residents) in 1847.

The Synod was organized in 1927 under the Constitution of the

Church of Christ in China and was made the responsible body for the work of Christian mission, with the cooperation of the mission. Requests for missionaries, their work assignments, and full responsibility for the administration of all funds were in the hands of the Synod. An Executive Committee of ten Chinese and five missionaries was selected by the Synod. The General Secretary was a Chinese with a missionary associate. The Rev. Ling Iu-cu (Lin Yu-shu), the General Secretary from 1928, was killed at the time of the Japanese occupation of Foochow in 1944. The Rev. W. H. Topping served as the Associate General Secretary for more than twenty years.

North Fukien Synod

The North Fukien (Minpei) Synod covered the northwest area of Fukien and a small area in the south of Kiangsi Province and was also the result of work by American Congregationalists. With three districts and only eleven churches (plus twenty-nine preaching places), the church was not strong and suffered greatly from disturbances and civil war in the early 1930s when much of the area was under the control of Communists hostile to Christian work. It also organized as a CCC synod in 1927.

East China Synod

The East China (Hwatung) Synod was organized early in the life of the Church of Christ in China to include the churches which had grown out of the work of three missions: the American Presbyterian USA, the American Presbyterian US, and the London Missionary Society. It covered a large area in three provinces (Chekiang, Anhwei, and Kiangsu), including such large cities as Shanghai, Nanking, Soochow, Hangchow, and Ningpo, with seven district associations. At the close of the Sino-Japanese War in 1945, however, it was realized that the area was too large for a single synodical structure, and in 1946 the General Council authorized its division into three synods, chiefly along geographical lines: Chekiang, Kiangnan (south of the Yangtze), and Kiangan (north of the Yangtze). But the Council action provided that action be deferred until the Synod could work out details, and the actual division did not take place until 1948. In the area were a number of important Christian educational institutions in which the CCC cooperated. Hangchow Christian College was essentially a CCC institution, while a number of other denominations also supported such schools as Nanking Theological Seminary, the University of Nanking, and Ginling College for Women. Ten Christian hospitals were directly related to the Synod and the University Hospital at Nanking, in which other churches cooperated as well.

Shantung Synod

Shantung Synod covered the large and heavily populated coastal Shantung Province. Presbyterian work began in 1861. The English Baptist Missionary Society began work in Shantung about the same time.

From the beginning, both groups strongly emphasized the development of indigenous Christian churches and strong Chinese leadership. There was close cooperation from an early date. Baptist and Presbyterian churches in Tsinan, the provincial capital, formed a united church in 1907. In 1904 they agreed on joint sponsorship of three colleges (arts and sciences, theology, medicine) which eventually (1917) were merged at Tsinan to form Shantung Christian University (later Cheeloo University). Ten mission societies (British, Canadian, and American) cooperated, and the school became very influential (Williamson, p. 75). An Inter-Provincial Conference for cooperation was set up in 1912.

With the establishment of the Church of Christ in China as a national church in 1927, the Presbyterians (with the exception of several presbyteries which decided to continue their relationship to a continuing Presbyterian Church in China) went into the union. The Baptists, who had two representatives at the First General Assembly of the CCC, voted to affiliate in December 1927, one of the first instances of a Baptist group entering a union church. At the time, they reported one hundred and twenty-eight churches of more than 7,000 communicant members. In 1929 representatives of the two groups met in Tsinan to form a united synod "to give a united voice for Christ and fulfill the Lord's prayer when He prayed that they might all be one" (Fisher, pp. 95-96). There were seven district associations, but since their territory did not overlap because of early comity arrangements, union was on the synodical rather than on the local level, and the disturbed conditions throughout the province for many years thereafter militated against a complete amalgamation.

In 1933 the Presbytery of Laiyang joined the Synod as a district association (Fisher, p. 96). This is noteworthy because Laiyang was the mission field of the Presbyterian Church of Korea, established at its first General Assembly in 1912, when it was decided that the Church should open a foreign mission field. Work had been established among Koreans and Chinese in this area of Shantung. The Presbytery of Laiyang included five organized churches and eight other places of worship when it joined the Synod of Shantung, with three Korean pastors, as well as a number of Chinese evangelists and a medical clinic with a Korean doctor. The three presbyteries that had remained outside the Synod (Weihsien, Lohan, and Shoukwang) voted in 1949 to join with it.

Liang Hu Synod (Hunan and Hupei)

Moving to the central part of China, the churches in Hunan and Hupei provinces that affiliated with the Church were incorporated in 1924 into a single synod, the Lianghu (two "Hus") Synod. LMS missionaries had begun work in Hankow in 1861 under the leadership of the able Griffith John. Progress was slow in the early days in Hunan because of the strong anti-foreign feeling, but by the 1880s a beginning had been made. The American Presbyterians moved up from northern Kwangtung into southern Hunan about the same period, and a church was organized at Linwu in 1894, probably the first church in Hunan (Fisher, p. 118). Cumberland Presbyterians were among the early workers in Hunan but were united with the Presbyterians USA when the two churches reunited in the homeland. The Reformed Church in the United States (later the Evangelical and Reformed Church) began work in Yochow about 1901. The churches related to these three missions, as well as those related to the Church of Scotland Missionary Society, which began work at Ichang (Hupei) in 1877, joined to form the Lianghu Synod. Again, however, because of the disturbed conditions that prevailed for many years in the area, it was difficult to participate in joint programs, and work was carried on largely at the local level.

In the late 1940s, the churches related to the Evangelical United

Brethren mission (Chung Hwa Tsun Tao Hui) voted to affiliate with the Church of Christ in China, as did the Chung Hwa Hsing Tao Hui in Hupei, related to the work of the Swedish Missionary Society, representing "free church" groups in Sweden as opposed to the state church of Sweden. The 1946 General Council meeting voted to divide the Synod along geographical lines. Just prior to the Fifth General Assembly of the Church in 1948, the Lianghu Synod was divided into Hunan and Hupei Synods, each with three cooperating mission societies. An additional reason for the division was the difficulty of travel between the two areas. The Hunan Synod organized a promising synodical structure with an able young pastor, the Rev. Li Yung-wu, as Synod Executive, but changing circumstances did not permit the development of the kind of strong provincial structure and program that was needed.

Szechuan Synod

In Szechuan, geographically the largest province of China, Canadian Methodist work was begun in 1891. This expanded to ten districts, and at one time some two hundred missionaries were at work. The Mei Dao Hui was organized in 1918 to direct evangelistic work, and eventually responsibility for all programs and distribution of funds was put in the hands of the Chinese church. When the church affiliated with the Church of Christ in China, there were one hundred and twenty churches or chapels, 3,412 communicant members, one hundred and sixty-nine schools, and ten hospitals. The Synod cooperated with four other churches in the West China Union University.

The Mei Dao Hui voted to join the CCC, and at the Third General Assembly (Amoy, 1933) it was formally voted into membership. Formal organization of the Synod as a CCC member did not take place until 1934 because of disturbed conditions in Szechuan which made it impossible to hold the organizing meeting.

Honan Synod

Canadian Presbyterian mission work was begun in Honan Province in 1888 by Jonathan Goforth, famed for his work as an evangelist.

Anti-foreign sentiment was strong and the work developed slowly in the early years, but centers and churches were established at Changteh, Weihwei, and Huaiching. A synod was organized in 1922 with two presbyteries. The synod voted to join the Presbyterian Church in China when it was organized, but was unable to have representatives at the constituting meeting of the Church in 1918 and of the Church of Christ in China in 1927. It was officially organized as a synod of the Church of Christ in China in 1933. A membership of 5,000 was reported in 1925, of which over 1,000 had been added in the previous year.

Honan was a troubled and disrupted area through the entire period from the 1920s through the 1940s. It is somewhat confusing that the Synod used the name "Hopei" Synod (north of the river, i.e., the Yellow River) for some years though it lay entirely within Honan Province and there was a Hopei Synod in the province of that name to the north.

Hopei Synod

Hopei Synod represented the Presbyterian churches in Hopei Province growing out of the work of the Presbyterian USA North China Mission. Presbyterian work began in Peking about 1861, in Paoting about thirty years later, and in Shunteh in the early twentieth century. When the Church of Christ in China was constituted, some opposition to membership was raised, but the final decision was favorable and in 1933 a Provisional Synod met at Paoting and was organized as a constituent member of the Church of Christ in China.

North China Synod

The North China (Hwapei) Synod brought together the churches related to the London Missionary Society and a number of independent churches—three of them in Peking—originally growing out of LMS work but for some years entirely autonomous. The church also worked in Tientsin and the eastern part of Hopei Province (along the Tientsin-Nanking Railroad) as well as in Peking. On September 30, 1931, the Hwapei Synod was organized as part of the Church of Christ in China with Dr. C. Y. Cheng and Dr. A. R. Kepler present at

Ts'angchow to represent the General Assembly. On the same day thirteen evangelists of the Synod were ordained to the Christian ministry. With four district associations, one hundred and seventy organized churches and preaching centers, and over six thousand members, the Synod represented a strong area of the Church.

The Hopei and Hwapei Synods maintained separate identities for many years, even though both were involved in work in Peking. At the close of the war with Japan, however, there were serious negotiations on merging, and this was finally approved by both Synods in joint session in 1947. The actual merger did not take place until after the change of government. On November 12, 1950, the two Synods merged as the Hopei Hsieh Hui (Hopei Union Synod).

Shansi Synod

Shansi, the province west of Hopei, was the scene of the largest loss of Christian lives in the Boxer Rebellion. About two hundred missionaries and their children were killed and many hundreds of Chinese Christians, with destruction of all mission property. Timothy Richard, of the English Baptist Mission in Shantung, went to Taiyuan, the capital of the province, in 1877 at the request of the International Famine Relief Committee, and by 1878 the First Baptist Church had been established in that city (Williamson, pp. 40-41). English Baptists returned to the area after 1900 and work spread to many areas of the province. The Shansi Synod was organized on May 24, 1932, with three district associations and a total church membership of about one thousand.

Shensi Synod

English Baptist mission work began in Shensi Province as the result of the migration of a group of Christian families from Ch'ingchow in Shantung in 1889. At their request Baptist missionaries went to the capital, Sian, in 1891 (Williamson, pp. 43-44).

A unique feature of the work was the establishment of Christian villages by the migrants from Shantung. In 1892 ten families (forty people) built mud houses and named their new town Fuyints'un

(Gospel Village). As George Young describes it in *The Living Christ in Modern China:*

> These Puritan Pilgrims in an alien land determined that the life of their little community should be governed by the principles of the New Testament. They would not follow the customs of the evil society around. None would grow, sell or smoke opium; none would worship the heathen gods; God alone would be worshipped and His laws obeyed. They built a small meeting house, convened a solemn assembly and vowed to their God three things:
> 1. To recognize Jesus Christ as their Lord;
> 2. To follow Christ's laws in their new surroundings;
> 3. To preach Christ's salvation to others.

In 1925 a United Church Council was formed as a responsible agency of cooperation between church and mission, with equal representation of Chinese and missionaries. The church experienced many vicissitudes because of recurring famine and fighting between the war lords, as well as the anti-Christian movement of the 1920s. Though much church property was destroyed and church workers, both missionaries and Chinese, suffered and even died, church membership continued to grow, and on May 22, 1933, the Shensi Synod of the Church of Christ in China was formally organized.

Northeast Synod

The Northeast Synod (Tungpei—originally called Kwantung, both Chinese names for Manchuria) grew from the work of Irish and Scottish missionary societies (the Presbyterian Church in Ireland and eventually—after mergers—the Church of Scotland). The work was begun by the Rev. William C. Burns, a Scot who under the English Presbyterians had twenty years of missionary service in China and who went to Manchuria in 1867. By 1912 a Manchurian Conference had been set up to coordinate the work of the Irish and Scottish missions, and in 1916 this arrangement was amended to provide membership for Danish Lutheran missionaries, who cooperated in a college, a medical school, and its related hospital. The Chinese of Manchuria were chiefly migrants from Shantung, among them many Christians from the strong Presbyterian church there. The life of the developing church was marked by periodic revivals of great intensity. The church became part of the Presbyterian Church in China when it was organized, and when the Church of Christ in China was established in 1927, it became the Kwantung Synod, with three district associations (in 1933 eight were reported) and a membership of more than twenty-one thousand. In 1941 the Synod reported two hundred and eighty-eight organized congregations with a membership of about thirty thousand, one hundred ordained pastors, two hundred and fifty evangelists (men and women), thirty schools, fourteen hospitals, theological and medical colleges, a Bible Training School, and a home for blind girls (Fulton, pp. 156ff.).

Unfortunately, in 1932, with the establishment of "Manchukuo" as a Japanese puppet state, "the Manchurian Church was forced to sever relations with the Church inside the Great Wall" (Fulton, p. 72). Here again a member church of the CCC was effectively cut off from communication with the central structure of the Church for many years.

When the United Church of Canada in 1925 brought together Congregationalists, Methodists, and Presbyterians in that land, the continuing Presbyterian Church in Canada was given northern Taiwan (Formosa) as its field of work. However, many Presbyterians wanted to continue work on the mainland of China, and in 1925, under the leadership of Jonathan Goforth of Honan, an agreement was entered into with the Presbyterians in Manchuria whereby the area of Szupingkai, formerly related to the Irish Presbyterian work, was assigned to them (Fulton, pp. 204ff.).

Fulton reports that a strong church resulting from the Canadian work, with which there had been close cooperation for many years, decided to take membership in the CCC Tungpei Synod after the end of the war with Japan. According to Fulton, the Presbyterian Church in Canada agreed that if the Church wished to go into the union, they would not oppose it.

Other Synods

Two other synods came into the union in the late 1940s. One of these was the Kianghwai Synod, consisting of churches in southern Shantung and northern Anhwei Provinces related to the work of the Presbyterian US mission. Synodical leaders had been divided on membership in the CCC, but finally in 1948 the Synod voted to come into the union and was welcomed at the Fifth General Assembly at Soochow in October, 1948. At the time, it reported a communicant membership of approximately ten thousand.

At the same General Assembly, the Presbyterian Church of Malaya was welcomed into membership as the Malaya Synod. The church had grown out of the work of the English Presbyterian mission but had retained strong ties with the churches in China, particularly those in Amoy, Kwangtung, and Swatow. Later, because of the difficulties in communication and the political situation, the Synod formally withdrew from the CCC and became the Presbyterian Church of Malaysia and Singapore.

Chapter Six

The Church of Christ
in China —
The Early Years (1927-37)

General Conditions in China

The capture of Nanking and Shanghai in 1927 and the assumption of power by the new Nationalist government marked a new era in modern Chinese history, as reported in Chapter III. Soon after, Nationalist armies resumed their march to the north.

Two of the major military commanders in the north, Feng Yu-hsiang and Yen Hsi-shan (the "model governor" of Shansi), declared themselves for the Nationalists, and the combined forces decisively defeated those of Chang Tso-lin, who had controlled much of Manchuria and North China, and Chang Tsung-chang, who had held much of Shantung. Peking was taken by May 1928 and nominal control by the Nationalist government over most of China was confirmed. Its name was changed from Peking (Northern Capital) to Peiping (Northern Peace), though many continued to use the old name until the People's Republic made it the capital again in 1949 and the use of the old name was resumed.

However, large areas, notably Szechwan in the west and Yunnan in the southwest, remained under the control of tyrannous and rapacious military commanders, who officially adhered to the Nationalist cause but actually were a law unto themselves. Other regional military commanders, theoretically loyal to the Central government, were not very dependable. In Kwangtung and Kwangsi, for example, the support of the local military leaders, Li Tsung-jen and Pai Ch'ung-hsi, was highly uncertain. They sometimes supported and sometimes opposed the Central government and occasionally, as in 1929, were at war with each other.

After the Nanking incident of 1927 and clashes between right- and left-wing elements when Shanghai was taken, the left wing, including the Communists, had set up a separate government in Wuhan and challenged the authority of the Nanking government. But serious difficulties among their leaders soon surfaced. Their major military force, the Fourth Army of General Chang Fa-kuei, returned to Kwangtung. An attempted Communist coup in Canton in December 1927 was put down with much bloodshed. Remnants of the Communist leadership were hunted down and forced to retreat into the countryside in Hunan and Kiangsi to regroup.

As Communist strength grew, most of the rural areas of Kiangsi Province and its fringes were reorganized on a commune system, with elimination of the landlords, a redistribution of land, and thorough regimentation. Nationalist armies continued to press against the Communists, and in late 1934 a culminating military campaign, supported by planes and tanks, forced the Communists to withdraw from the areas they held. Thus began the modern epic of "the Long March." Approximately 90,000 Communist adherents started on a trek which took them over mountains and streams, constantly attacking or under attack. They lived off the country, killing and being killed, burning, pillaging, recruiting their strength by impressing men and boys, for close to 5,000 miles. They arrived in northern Shensi, after their hazardous and circuitous route through southwest and western China, almost exactly a year later, making their headquarters at Yenan. Estimates differ as to how many survived, but probably 10% or fewer of those who had left Kiangsi arrived at Yenan.

Gradually the Communists built up their strength again, organizing the peasantry and training themselves in guerilla tactics. By 1936, in spite of frequent attacks by pro-Nationalist forces, a substantial area of Shansi, Hopei, and Chahar was under their control.

The Nationalists were seeking to develop an elite Central government army with modern weapons, trained by German military advisors. Their troops, led by well-trained officers, were disciplined and paid regularly, in contrast to most of the local military forces. They made a favorable impression in areas where they were stationed by their good behavior and by their willingness to help farmers harvest crops and build roads. The Nationalist government was modeled after that of the Soviet Union and was by definition a party dictatorhip, although there was some claim of democratic ambitions. There were reforms in Chinese society, most of which were never put into practice, either because the conservatives blocked them or because of the political and military situation. In the early thirties, major efforts were made in road building and railroad improvement. Currency reform was achieved through the establishment of a Central Bank, a sound national currency, and a stable exchange rate. Strong emphasis was placed on the improvement of the educational system and the building of new schools and there was even talk of land reform. Sporadic efforts were made to control the drug traffic, with stern measures taken in some places against users and sellers. But the sources of raw opium in outlying areas in the northwest and west were beyond Central Government control and in many places controls were not enforced. In some cases officials profited from the drug traffic.

Japanese Aggression and Chinese Response

At the same time, tension was increasing over the open militarism of Japanese policy towards China. In the course of the Nationalists' northern campaign in 1928, the Japanese had sent troops to Tsinan, the capital of Shantung province, on the pretext that Japanese civilians were endangered. They executed a number of Nationalist officials and ordered the Nationalists to withdraw from Tsinan. Chiang Kai-shek, commander of the Nationalist troops, was wisely unwilling to respond to this attempt to provoke hostilities. His armies moved around Tsinan as they went north, but the Chinese smarted over this humiliation.

Since the Sino-Japanese and Russian-Japanese wars of the late nineteenth and early twentieth centuries, Japan had enjoyed special rights in Manchuria and had built up a major commercial stake there. The South Manchurian Railroad was completely under Japanese control and a major Japanese military force, the Kwantung Army, had its headquarters in Mukden, the principal city, and was virtually independent of control by the Japanese government.

Chang Tso-lin, the warlord who had controlled Manchuria and much of North China, was killed when his train was blown up in his 1928 withdrawal to Manchuria. His son Chang Hsueh-liang ("the Young Marshal") inherited his father's army of several hundred thousand troops. He supported a Nationalist effort in 1929 to reassert China's sovereignty over Manchuria by taking control of the Chinese Eastern Railway from the Russians. This led to an encounter with Russian troops in which the Chinese were badly beaten.

On September 18, 1931, the Japanese Kwantung Army, uneasy because of the growing strength of the Nationalist forces and because of failure to win the allegiance of the Manchurian armies under

Chang Hsueh-liang, took matters into its own hands. A fabricated bomb explosion on the South Manchurian Railway served as a pretext for seizing Mukden, followed by military control over all Manchuria. Heavy fighting also took place in a related incident at Shanghai early in 1932, where the Japanese landed marines and met with long and fierce resistance from the famed 19th Route Army from Fukien.

Chiang was not ready to risk battle with the much better equipped Japanese armies and ordered Chang Hsueh-liang to follow a policy of nonresistance. His troops were driven out of Manchuria into North China in 1932. Henry Pu-yi, who as a child had been proclaimed the last emperor of the Manchu dynasty, was placed on the powerless throne of a puppet state called "Manchukuo."

Japanese aggression continued through the 1930s, with incursions into Inner Mongolia and northern Hopei by military action and political pressure on local Chinese officials. Sporadic fighting occurred, but no general resistance. The Japanese smuggled extensively into China, opium and heroin were imported on a wide scale, and copper and silver currency were drained from the mainland. Resentment was rising all over China against the Central Government's avoidance of direct conflict with the Japanese. But Chiang Kai-shek was not ready to take them on and was still concerned over internal dissension.

In December 1936 Chiang flew to Sian, capital of Shensi, to try to bring the mutinous Manchurian troops into line. In a dramatic incident, he was taken prisoner by a coalition of the Manchurians and the Communists and released on Christmas Day after a deal for a united front with the Communists against the Japanese. The threat of expanded Japanese control had brought the opposing Chinese forces together and Japanese arrogance in Manchuria and North China had further swelled the wave of Chinese nationalism and the determination that the time for resistance had come.

The Suffering of the Chinese People

The burden of all this on the people of China was intolerable. They were ground down by poverty, disease was rampant, and disaster commonplace. With almost no medical facilities except in the large cities and those provided by the scattered Christian hospitals, mostly in the smaller cities, life expectancy was less than thirty years. For most of the rural people, their tiny plots of land were too small for adequate livelihood. Taxes were exorbitant, roving military bands took what they wanted, and war or flood or famine often drove thousands, hungry and desperate, from their few possessions as homeless wanderers along the railroads or into the crowded cities in a fight for survival. Beggars were a common sight on the streets of every major city.

China was beset with calamities, natural or man-made. In 1920-21 severe drought in the north took the lives of uncounted people. A terrible earthquake in the northwest in the early 1920s took a toll of several hundred thousand. In a terrible famine in North China in 1928-29, twelve to twenty million were reported to be starving. In 1931 the Yangtze River changed course, as it has frequently, drowning at least two million and inundating vast areas of farmland. Floods in North China in 1933 ruined crops and drove vast numbers from their homes. In the fighting with the Japanese in 1931 and subsequent years, millions were driven from their homes as refugees, and every outbreak of civil war, large or small, affected the lives of large numbers of people. It was a common sight in those years to see freight trains and passenger trains alike loaded to absolute capacity with their human freight, clinging like flies to every available inch of space and burdened down with what they could carry of their possessions. Remarkably, the resilient spirit of the Chinese shone through such awesome tribulations. While there were tears enough, most of the refugees remained cheerful and patient, and it was deeply moving to see the ready smiles and hear long-suffering people who had been driven from their homes joking among themselves and often laughing at their misfortunes.

A Difficult Time for Christians

The lot of the missionary in interior places was not an easy one. No one who did not go through the experiences of the early decades of the twentieth century in China can imagine how trying the circumstances were for the missionary and much more so for Chinese Christians. Human suffering from famine and flood, hunger and disease, civil war and ruthless invading armies was beyond description. Crushing poverty was almost universal, banditry and warlordism were endemic, life was precarious for most Chinese, and the loss of life or health among missionaries and Chinese Christian workers through violence, disease, and privation was great. A substantial number of foreign missionaries were kidnapped and held for ransom in the twenties and thirties, many for long periods of time. Several died in the hands of their captors.

Missionaries were somewhat fewer in number during this period because of the major evacuation in 1927 and because the sending societies lacked funds as a result of the worldwide depression of the late twenties and early thirties. Much-needed furloughs had to be postponed, many were tired and overworked. At least one major board was unable to pay missionary salaries for some months and Chinese Christians generously helped their missionary friends. Some missionaries could return from furlough only if they could raise their own travel expense.

As the widespread animus against foreigners was increasingly re-directed against the Japanese, Westerners came to be thought of by many as friends and allies. A major share of responsibility for relief work fell upon missionaries and their Chinese co-workers. From the earliest days of their presence in China, the missionaries had sought to alleviate the sufferings of the Chinese people. Now in a period of disasters involving millions, the missionary was called upon to play a major role. The missionary was the natural channel for relief resources from outside China, especially as the major source of funds and supplies was the Christian churches.

Refugees crowded into mission compounds and church schools; churches were not infrequently turned into temporary hospitals; feeding stations for the distribution of hot cereal were set up in every available space. It was not uncommon for the mission compounds in interior places to be filled with as many as four or five thousand refugees, crowded into every corner, for long periods of time. The task of feeding and caring for such numbers was heavy and could not have been accomplished without the self-sacrificing and loving labors of Chinese Christians, as well as missionaries. Doctors, nurses, pastors and evangelists, even students, were enlisted in such ministries of mercy. The task grew heavier as the fighting with the Japanese increased and government resources were strained to the limit in the struggle to preserve the nation, and during the years of the Japanese invasion and occupation took a disproportionate share of the time and energy of Chinese Christians and missionaries.

The Life and Work of the Church of Christ in China

In the midst of such great difficulties, the church carried on its work to the best of its ability. A factor in the continued unification of the Church of Christ in China was a series of regional conferences set up to bring church leaders together. The General Council planned such conferences for "integrating the various elements within our Church" and "for spiritual nurture and training of the employed and the voluntary workers of the Church." Seven such regional conferences were held in 1930-31, including one in East China held jointly with the Methodist Episcopal Church (South), at which there were present seventy from the CCC and sixty Methodists. Others were held in South China, Manchuria, Peiping, Hankow, and Shanghai. They were made possible through generous financial assistance given by Dr. John R. Mott. While intended primarily for workers in the CCC, volunteers and workers from other churches were welcomed also.

Dr. Kepler, in his report to the 1931 meeting of the General Council, commented:

> At all of these regional conferences the main emphasis was laid upon the deepening of the spiritual life, on a clearer understanding of the Bible and the message which the church has for China today and on the outstanding immediate tasks which our church is confronting. Judging from the reports . . . we are convinced that these conferences have been of the highest value.

One of the most significant of these meetings was the 1931 Soochow Conference. Major attention was given to the topic of "Youth and the Church." The Christian Student Movement, which had tended to function independently of the Church, had come into better relationships with the CCC in the late 1920s and the slogan "Cooperation with the church" had been adopted.

Present were students from a number of the Church-related universities and middle schools who for the most part supported cooperation with the Church. The student representatives issued a statement deploring the fact that the Christian Student Movement and the Church had in the past each gone its own way and pointing out the need of each for the other. In a rather typically involved and sweeping Chinese statement they expressed the needs of students for:

(1) guidance in matters of life work;
(2) opportunity for expression of their creative life;

(3) satisfaction of their spiritual needs;
(4) a right philosophy of life;
(5) a reasonable religion . . . related to everyday life and in harmony with
      scientific and philosophical truth;
(6) real fellowship;
(7) a place for expression in the councils of the church;
(8) opportunity to share in the responsibilities of the church;
(9) guidance in thought life;
(10) services of worship especially suited for students;
(11) good Christian literature;
(12) religious education adapted to their needs;
(13) home training;
(14) church and student conferences;
(15) guidance by experienced Christian leaders;

The Third General Workers' Conference at Ningpo in 1932 brought together eighty-six delegates. Every synod was represented except North Fukien and Honan, where disturbed conditions made travel almost impossible. In addition, there were Baptist and Sheng Kung Hui (Anglican-Episcopal Church) fraternal delegates, as well as representatives from the Shantung Methodist Conference referred to in Chapter IV and from the United Methodists (British Methodist-related).

The General Council

The Plan of Union drawn up after the 1918 meeting of the Presbyterian Federal Council and approved by the Constituting Assembly of the Church of Christ in China in 1927 provided for a General Council representing the synods which was to meet between assemblies, annually or on call. It was an important agency in the life of the Church, meeting regularly, confronting the crises that arose, especially in the years of Japanese incursions, and providing opportunity for regional leadership to participate in the life of the national Church. Even though travel was usually difficult and occasionally hazardous, attendance was good, and almost all synods were regularly represented at the Council meetings in the first decade of the Church's life.

The General Council held seven annual meetings from 1928 to 1935. For the most part, the Council meetings dealt with housekeeping matters within the Church. The General Secretary reported on the work and problems of the Church and the activities of staff. Through the early years, the secretaries spent much time attending synodical and district association meetings and participating in their conferences. They gave practical and inspirational leadership which helped strengthen the national consciousness of the far-flung member units of the Church.

Two important actions were taken by the General Council in its first meeting (October 26-28, 1928, Shanghai). Affiliation was approved with the World Alliance of Reformed Churches, the Baptist World Alliance, the Ecumenical Methodist Conference, and the International Congregational Council, indicating the intent of the Church to continue identifying with the several denominational strains that had contributed to its life. It is certain that membership was actually established with the first and the last of these world confessional bodies; there is no indication that this was true of the Baptist and Methodist associations.

The Council also acted to register the Church of Christ in China with the recently formed Nationalist Government. Such registration gave it official recognition as a Chinese church and also gave it the right to hold property, a right previously available only to the missions.

At the Second General Council meeting (October 9-18, 1929, Shanghai) the report of the Secretariat, speaking to the issue of centralizing authority within the Church, contained an excellent statement of the philosophy of its early leaders:

> There has been an inclination to criticize our united Church by a few outstanding Christian leaders, both in the West and in China, on the grounds that our organization is too loose and that there is not provided adequate centralized administrative power. We believe that the surest way to defeat this objective of centralized control is to unduly press for it and thus achieve a superimposed organization which will create discontent and misgivings instead of confidence and loyalty among our widely scattered synods and district associations.

The Kwantung Synod in Manchuria had experienced many difficulties since the Japanese takeover there in the fall of 1931. A report was made to the Council of a minor but interesting crisis that had developed over the use of the name Church of Christ in China. The Synod had taken the position that the words "in China" signified only the union of several denominations and had no political significance. (The Chinese name could be translated "Chinese Church of Christ" and so might be understood in an ethnic, rather than a geographical or political sense.) However, this did not satisfy the Japanese, and the Synod in 1934, after an interview with government officials, was told to drop the word "China." For the remainder of the Japanese occupation, the Church was called "The Manchurian Presbyterian Christian Church."

A strong revival movement continued in the Church, even though in late 1935, possibly related to further Japanese incursions into North China and Inner Mongolia, the Church was subjected to renewed pressures. Many pastors and church leaders were arrested, charged with Communist sympathy and activity, imprisoned, and tortured. But reportedly these difficult experiences only strengthened their faith.

At the Fourth Annual Meeting of the General Council (Soochow, October 1-9, 1931), Miss Chen Wen-hsien and Mrs. F. R. Millican (Presbyterian USA) were welcomed to the staff. Miss Chen, formerly a YWCA secretary, gave some years (1931-36) of able leadership to the CCC in student work, as well as to the Christianizing the Home program. She later became Professor of School Administration at the University of Nanking. Mrs. Millican assisted in the Christianizing the Home program for several years.

Church-Mission Relations

The matter of church-mission relationships inevitably came up frequently in church councils and was often discussed. The Church of Christ in China and its leadership genuinely appreciated the help of the missions and the missionaries, and that appreciation was often publicly expressed (e.g., at the First General Assembly and in the last official communication from the Church to the cooperating mission societies).

The churches that had formed the CCC were mainly from the Congregational and Reformed traditions—the former (including the Baptists) stressing the authority of the local congregation, the latter stressing the authority of the presbytery or district association. No doubt because of the strong Presbyterian participation, the CCC generally followed Reformed polity, as we have seen, though always with considerable freedom at the synodical or local level. It is interesting to note that although C. Y. Cheng came out of the Congregational tradition, he felt that central and delegated authority was needed in the Chinese church.

Dr. Cheng frequently emphasized the need for missionary participation in the life of the Church, but on the basis of church decision. The missionary's contribution was welcomed and appreciated, but he felt strongly that in an indigenous church this could only be in partnership, with any office the missionary might hold conferred by decision of the church and never simply by virtue of missionary status. This same openness but firmness on the necessity of church decision characterized the leadership of the CCC throughout its history.

The position of the CCC on church-mission relations was quite clearly set forth in the findings of a joint conference held October 14-17, 1929, in Shanghai and was reviewed and confirmed first by the Second General Council in 1929 and then by the Second General Assembly in 1930. The joint conference brought together fifteen members of the General Council with nine officially appointed representatives of cooperating missions and three other mission representatives without vote.

A preamble expressed gratitude for the work of the missionaries and the firm intent to continue cooperation with the missions. It also made clear that the Church recognized, because of various states of development, that the principles set forth could not be immediately effective in every place. Then followed a statement of principles including the following points:

(1) The "church-centric" principle—church responsibility for administration and personnel—is basic.

(2) Responsibility and control of evangelistic, educational, medical, and benevolent work should be transferred to the church by mutual agreement.

(3) The General Assembly "has the right of direct relationship with the mission boards and church bodies . . . for negotiation of matters of mutual concern."

(4) Assignment of missionaries when they first come and on return from furlough should be the responsibility of the synods in consultation with the missionary and his mission (as long as there remains an organized mission).

(5) Missionaries have the privilege of full membership in the Church. If it is impossible to transfer membership, "cooperative membership" may be arranged by the related synod.

(6) The sympathetic cooperation of the missions is solicited in continuing support and to attain the "church-centric" principle as soon as possible.

Recognizing the need, in view of the growth of the Church as a national body, for interregional and national planning, organization, and administration, the statement also included a set of principles relating to mission subsidies and the goal of self-support:

(1) Self-support must be gradual: first the local church, then the synods, and eventually the General Assembly.

(2) A strong and efficient General Assembly headquarters will expedite self-support at lower levels.

(3) Autonomy and self-propagation are possible even in subsidized churches; they certainly obtain in many subsidized churches in the sending countries.

(4) Subsidies are not necessarily bad and are especially needed in rural areas; a majority of urban churches have already attained self-support.

(5) Many current projects in mission and evangelism could better be operated through the General Assembly. Priority should be given to programs that promise fruitfulness.

Thus at an early stage of the life of the Church of Christ in China there were clearly set forth the principle of the priority of the church and the transient nature of the mission organization. This position was expressed clearly in the statement of the China delegation to the Jerusalem Missionary Conference in 1928, and to the mind of many Chinese and missionary leaders it represented the only path to a truly indigenous and independent church. It was a principle endorsed by many of the Western mission boards or societies but (with a few notable exceptions) was slow of accomplishment. In part this was because Chinese leadership was not strong enough, particularly at the local and synodical level, and because of the chaotic situation within China during much of the period of the Church's life. But it is also true that many missionaries found it difficult to relinquish control and power, often from a conscientious sense of their own stewardship.

The Role of the General Assemblies in the Development of the Church

The General Assemblies of the Church played an important part in the development of the life of the Church and were an instrument for discussion and expression of policy. Total attendance at the CCC

Assemblies was usually little over a hundred, with the number of official commissioners having voting power even fewer (only eighty-eight in 1927, one hundred and fifty in 1948, the largest of the Assemblies). Compared to church assemblies in the West, which bring together thousands, they may seem insignificant. Yet almost without exception, the Assemblies were genuinely representative of the widespread constituency of the Church. The very smallness of these gatherings made for a deeper fellowship and personal involvement than would have been possible in larger meetings.

The Assemblies were a strong unifying force in the life of the CCC and were another factor strengthening the consciousness of a united national church. One of modern China's most serious problems was provincialism, very real in the church as in public life. Chinese found it difficult to be accepted in areas other than their native place. Even in the larger cities, people from other areas tended to seek out their *hsiang ch'in* ("country cousins"), and the provincial guild houses in cities such as Peiping were gathering places of fellow provincials. *P'ai wai* (discrimination against outsiders) was a common phrase, reflecting a common practice.

In the period covered by this history, a good many factors were at work breaking down provincialism and strengthening national consciousness. Among them were the development of Chinese nationalism, the increasing use of the national language, the unifying nature of the intense opposition to Japanese aggression, and the widespread dispersion of people during the war period, throwing people from many parts of China together. The same elements were at work within the CCC, and the General Assemblies were occasions for sharing problems and needs and for grappling with the issues facing the Church. Here too, the national language was used not only for patriotic reasons but because it was the only dialect generally understood.

The Second General Assembly

The Second General Assembly met at Union Theological Seminary, Canton, October 26—November 8, 1930. This was where Protestant Christianity had first found entry into China, and the churches of the area were among the strongest in the country. Church union had come early, and the impetus that led to the formation of the Church of Christ in China had in large part come from the leadership of the church there, where one of the earliest synods of the CCC had been organized. A leading figure was Y. S. Tom (Tom Yuk-sam), long the Executive Secretary of the Kwangtung Synod, later moderator of the Third General Assembly, and still later President of the Union Theological Seminary. Another leader in the Synod and the national church was S. C. Leung (Leung Shiu-choh), a YMCA secretary who later became General Secretary of the National Committee of the YMCAs of China and who throughout his career was active in the life of the CCC both locally and nationally.

Fifty commissioners represented eleven synods. (The difficulties and expense of travel made it impossible for representatives of some of the synods to attend.) Among the visitors were representatives of overseas churches which cooperated with the Church of Christ in China, as well as fifteen fraternal delegates from other churches and Christian agencies in China. Dr. C. Y. Cheng was again elected moderator.

Religious Education

A special committee on religious education, which had met several times prior to the Assembly with a similar committee of the Methodist Episcopal Church, called for the preparation of "a concrete program of religious education for the use of church leaders" and made specific suggestions for local churches. One of the results of this concern was the request for the services of Samuel H. Leger of the American Board Mission in Foochow, a specialist in the field of religious education, to serve the Church nationally.

Leger was given the necessary approval by his church and in December 1930 joined the General Assembly staff. He was the author of *The Education of Christian Ministers in China,* published in 1925 as the report of a national survey and a useful reference work for many years. Exceptionally well-qualified and proficient in both spoken and written Chinese, Leger was a valuable addition to the staff and gave valuable leadership in a discipline much needed by the Church. Unfortunately, because of CCC budget limitations, which grew acute as the depression in the West forced supporting boards to reduce their appropriations, it was necessary for him to leave the CCC after less than four years of service.

Church-Related Schools and Government Pressures

This was a period of tension between the church-related schools and the Nationalist government, which had required the registration of all schools and had banned the teaching of religious subjects. Because of this ban and because of misgivings about ceremonies honoring Dr. Sun Yat-sen, the founder of the Republic, which some felt to be comparable to emperor worship, Christian educators were facing the question of whether to register or to face the probability of being shut down if they did not. Christian schools had made a major contribution to education in China, especially in their pioneer work in the education of women. In 1930 there were more than six thousand Protestant church-related primary schools with about 185,000 students, and in 1932 two hundred and forty middle schools with over 34,000 students, a significant contribution to modern education.

After considerable debate, the General Assembly approved three principles of action: (1) the policies of the Ministry of Education should be observed; (2) religious education should be permitted as voluntary courses in all grades of church schools (voluntary religious courses and activities were in some cases unofficially permitted); (3) all grades of church schools should have freedom of religious exercises. Subsequently most of the church-related schools which had not already done so registered with the government. A number of schools chose not to register, however, and many of them closed. The Assembly also approved the action of the General Council, which had joined thirteen other churches in China in an appeal to the Chinese government to allow all schools to offer elective courses in religion, an appeal that was denied by the Ministry of Education.

Evangelism and Church Unity

The Five Year Forward Movement of the National Christian Council was an evangelistic renewal movement aimed at doubling the number of church members and deepening the spiritual life of Christians. Undertaken at the initiative of C. Y. Cheng, General Secretary of the Council and Moderator of the Church of Christ of China, its motto was "Revive thy church, O Lord, beginning with me." The General

Assembly gave it hearty support, and its purpose gripped the hearts of many Christians, though in the end it was less successful than had been hoped.

The Assembly again voiced the desire of many Chinese Christians for church union, stating, "We believe that nothing short of complete organic unity of the disciples of Christ will satisfy the desire of our Lord, who prayed that we might all be one." Other Chinese churches were invited to enter into negotiation to achieve organic union. The Moderator was asked to send greetings to a number of churches that had already approved union with the CCC or were considering such action. These included the Mei Dao Hui (United Church of Canada-related, formerly Canadian Methodist); the North China churches related to the London Missionary Society; the North China Kung Li Hui (American Congregationalist-related); the Hsing Dao Hui (Swedish Missionary Union-related); the Baptist churches in Shansi and Shensi; and independent churches in various cities in China (many of which eventually affiliated with the CCC). Similar messages were sent to the Methodist Episcopal Church and the China Baptist Council, urging them to consider union.

The Third General Assembly

The Third General Assembly met October 20-30, 1933, on the pleasant island of Kulangsu in the harbor of Amoy, an important port city of Fukien. Seventy-five commissioners were present, representing all sixteen synods of the Church, as well as fraternal delegates and mission board representatives. The national language was used throughout the sessions, and Kepler was impressed by the spirit of unity which prevailed. He quotes the covenant read in unison at the opening session (also used in the Synod's annual meetings) and gives it in translation:

> In the presence of God our Heavenly Father, we enter into a solemn covenant to exert ourselves to the utmost to make this meeting of the General Assembly a sacred, solemn and spiritual fellowship, to be fellow-workers with God and bound to one another by the ties of mutual respect and love. Throughout all of its sessions we will strive in the spirit of cooperation to increasingly strengthen the work of our Church so that the name of God may be glorified and Jesus Christ may be manifested as the Head of the Church and the Universal Church as His body, sharing a

common breath of life and filled with the richness of his abundant life. May the Kingdom of God come to earth even as it is in heaven.

The Assembly was very conscious of the troubled state of the nation. The report of the General Council dealt with this at length and included these comments:

> The last three years have witnessed a great crisis in our national history. From within we have been troubled by the graft of militarists and destruction of communists . . . bandits . . . floods or drought. From without has come oppression and aggression of imperialists. . . . Villages are bankrupt, the people are beggared, merchants cannot carry on trade in peace, scholars cannot give themselves to their study, the army cannot protect the country, the police cannot protect the people. Our soldiers are dead, our land is lost, we are disgraced and ashamed to live; true patriots and men of benevolence can only hide their heads and drink their tears. True bravery has disappeared, discipline is lax. Except we have some great power to strengthen the framework of our national life, how can we hope for a national rebirth, how can we hope for a national revival?

> The message of the Christian Church is based on the adequacy of the Spirit of Jesus Christ to build a healthy personality, to combine the strength of individuals into the strength of a group, to promote the development of mankind and the progress of culture and to bring the Kingdom of Heaven among men. A church with such a mission placed in a time like this—in the China of today—what a responsibility and what a tremendous task!

Self-support

Great Emphasis was given to self-support, expressing continuing concern and determination that the Chinese churches stand on their own feet. Chinese pride was sensitive to the continuing dependence on Western churches, especially in the light of national resentment of Western commercial and political exploitation. "For our church work to look to foreign missionary societies as the source of economic support is not a policy that should long endure." Almost three hundred churches, out of a total of eight hundred, had already achieved full self-support. In 1930-31 the Kwangtung Synod reported an increase in local support from C$99,758 to C$132,917, or about 40%, so progress was being made.

The Assembly approved a plan to raise an endowment fund of

C$100,000 (then about US$35,000) to cover the administrative expenses of the General Assembly. In 1928 the South Fukien Synod, with an annual contribution of nine dollars per capita for more than 10,000 communicants, had not only accepted the $800 annual allotment for the General Assembly budget, but had pledged $1,000 annually to the General Assembly Endowment Fund, and others were responding as well. Unfortunately, the disturbed conditions in the years that followed increased, rather than decreased, the churches' need for assistance from the missions.

The Church had early recommended that each of its constituent units contribute a minimum of 2% of the support received from the cooperating mission agency toward General Assembly administrative costs, but this was often neglected and the administration of the Church had to depend in large measure on the help of the missions. For example, the 1931-32 financial report shows General Assembly income from Chinese sources of $7,597.75 (over half of which came from the contributions of individual missionaries) and $6,048.83 from the missions.

Youth Work

The Assembly expressed a strong desire for coordination of youth work and urged that each synod hold retreats for young people and that youth fellowships be organized in the local churches. It endorsed the intent of the National Provisional Council of the Student Volunteer Movement in China to organize a united Christian Student Movement and expressed its willingness to cooperate. It proposed that the CCC's Secretary for Youth Work, Miss Chen Wen-hsien, work with the Provisional Council for the United Chinese Christian Student Movement. Also, recommendations for strengthening the program of theological education were approved.

Rural-Life Improvement

The cooperation of five synods (Mid-Fukien, East China, East Kwangtung, Honan, and Lianghu) was sought in rural-life improvement centers "to increase skill in production, advance bodily health and thus build healthy personalities inspired by the Christian spirit of service and sacrifice." This was in keeping with the long tradition of Christian efforts to improve the lot of the village people of China which had led to many useful rural programs, notably those sponsored by Nanking and Cheloo Universities and that of the North China Christian Rural Service Union (the CCC was involved in all these programs). Support was also voiced for a plan which called for General Assembly staff to work with the synods and district associations in promoting cooperatives and credit unions.

Orders of Service prepared by a special commission for the various rituals of the Church (baptism, Holy Communion, ordination, marriage, funerals) were approved for submission to the synods and district associations "for voluntary use." Four new communions were voted into membership: the North China (Hwapei) Synod (churches related to the London Missionary Society); the Shansi and Shensi Synods (related to English Baptist work); and Szechuan Synod (Mei Dao Hui—related to the United Church of Canada). A group of independent churches in Peiping also became part of the CCC as members of the Peking district association of Hopei Synod. Kepler commented:

> This infusion of new blood from these new synods and district associations is a real contribution of great value to the whole Church, giving new life and vigor and new powers to us all. Our union is not in form only but in spirit as well, and it greatly enriches the entire life of the Church.

CCC Administration

Important actions were taken in the general administration of the Church. Dr. C. Y. Cheng, the first Moderator and for many years General Secretary of the National Christian Council of China, was elected General Secretary, to take effect January 1, 1934. A. R. Kepler and T. C. Fan were elected Executive Secretaries. It was voted to transfer the General Assembly office to Peiping on April 1, 1934, as a "temporary measure, six to eight years," largely because of high rental costs in Shanghai. (The move actually took place on April 16, 1934.)

Dr. Y. S. Tom, General Secretary of the Kwangtung Synod, was elected Moderator of the Church. It was decided for reasons of economy that the General Assembly should meet quadrennially, instead of triennially, and that the General Council should meet biennially, instead of annually. The boards and committees of the Church were reduced to a single General Board on the Life and Work of the Church, with twenty-four members.

The Seventh General Council Meeting—1935

The Seventh General Council of the CCC (Soochow, 1935) voted that the General and Executive Secretaries' term of office extend over a period of two Assemblies. In line with a growing desire to upgrade the rather informal worship practices of the individual congregations, the Secretariat had been asked to make recommendations on appropriate clerical garb. Their recommendation was approved for a plain black robe in the Chou Dynasty fashion for use by the clergy, together with a red or white stole for appropriate use (red being the Chinese color for rejoicing, white for mourning). The stoles were to bear the cross, crown, and shepherd's crook on one side and the burning bush (symbolic of the indestructibility of the church) on the other. Approved for voluntary use, they came into fairly general use in the congregations of the CCC.

The Church had also been concerned about the preparation of a book of worship and a new hymnal. At the 1935 General Council, the General Secretary reported that both books were ready for publication. Cooperation on *Hymns of Universal Praise* had been initiated by the CCC in 1931, when several denominations were planning new hymnals. A Union Committee of Chinese and missionaries worked together for several years, and in 1936 the first edition was published by the Christian Literature Society for China. The cooperating and sponsoring churches were the Sheng Kung Hui, the CCC, the China Baptist Convention, the Methodist Episcopal Churches North and South, and the North China Kung Li Hui. It contained five hundred fourteen hymns, of which four hundred fifty-two were translations and sixty-one original Chinese hymns, some from ancient sources, while seventy-two original Chinese tunes were included.

By 1946, 361,000 copies had been published in a number of editions. Christian publishers have continued to issue editions in Hong Kong in recent years, and the hymnal is still in wide use among Chinese Christians outside of Mainland China.

A *Book of Common Worship* in two parts, authorized by the Church of Christ in China, the China Baptist Council, the Methodist

Episcopal Church, and the North China Kung Li Hui was first published in 1936 by the CLS. By 1949 a seventh edition was issued. More limited by its nature, it still met a widely felt need and was in general use among the clergy.

General Church Developments, 1927-37

In spite of adversity, the first decade of the Church of Christ in China was a time of growth in numbers, in the assertion of Chinese leadership, and in acceptance by the Chinese people. As one important indicator of widespread interest, the three Bible societies (American, British, and Scottish) reported the sale in 1929 of 35,822 Bibles, 134,876 New Testaments, and 13,750,704 portions, an increase of 20% over the previous high. A. R. Kepler, in his report to the 1931 General Council of the CCC, noted:

> In spite of flood and famine and banditry, we are encouraged by the increasing interest on the part of non-Christians everywhere. . . . In Manchuria especially has there developed a refreshing revival which is most heartening. There has been an ingathering into the church greater than at any time in recent years.

The Canadian Presbyterian work centered in Szepingkai reported nine hundred sixty-six baptisms in 1934. Kepler, present in 1934 at the dedication of the Golden Well church in Amoy, wrote enthusiastically of its growth. Forty years old, this was its third church building, erected with local gifts. Self-supporting for many years, it had developed eight or nine branch churches.

In 1934 the North China Christian Rural Service Union, in which the CCC participated, began publication of *The Christian Farmer,* with T. H. Sun and H. Y. Chang as editors. A semi-monthly, it had built a circulation of about 7,000 subscribers in less than a year. In 1935 the Canton Medical Hospital (the first Christian Hospital in China, founded by Dr. Peter Parker) celebrated its one hundredth anniversary. On the same day, the cornerstone of Sun Yat-sen Medical College (part of Lingnan University) was laid. The South Fukien Synod reported in 1936 that in spite of disturbed conditions in the rural areas, with banditry and skirmishes frequent after the Communist withdrawal, church work was going well.

By 1937 the membership of the Church of Christ in China was reported as 123,043, 24% of the total Protestant church membership in China. Since, however, the membership in 1927 was given as "over 120,000," and a number of new churches had joined the church in the ten years following, bringing in about 13,000 additional members, the 1937 figures would seem inaccurate. The writer can only surmise that perhaps the membership of the Northeast Synod, which had been forced by the Japanese authorities in "Manchukuo" to break its ties with the CCC, was omitted from the 1937 total. The Northeast Synod reported 21,000 members in 1927, and there were many reports of revival and growth in the following years. This means, if the surmise is correct, that there was an increase in CCC membership in the first decade of its life of about 13,000 through the adherence of new groups, and a growth of more than 10,000 within the 1927 member bodies (omitting the Northeast Synod)—a healthy rate of about 10%.

It was an active and productive time of evangelism. The sects and independent Chinese evangelists discussed in Chapter III were very active in this period and had considerable success. There was growing student interest in Christianity and marked progress in the Student Christian Movement. The Five Year Forward Movement begun in 1929 on the initiative of C. Y. Cheng and entrusted by the churches to the National Council was directed by Dr. H. H. Tsui and sponsored meetings and campaigns in many parts of the country. E. Stanley Jones, the Methodist evangelist with a background of missionary service in India and well-known for his devotional books, and Sherwood Eddy of the YMCA, a dynamic speaker who visited Asia frequently and attracted large audiences of students and intellectuals, both came to China several times in this period and travelled widely. After the 1934 Eddy meetings, it was reported that more than 6,000 students had been enrolled in Christian study courses. The Forward Movement sponsored and supported their campaigns and followed them with organized teams of Chinese church and educational leaders who visited and spoke in university centers with notable response. The Forward Movement, with the goal of doubling church membership in its five-year campaign, sought to enlist all churches in its program. The more conservative groups held off, however. Such major groups as the China Inland Mission, the Southern Baptists, and most Lutheran bodies were not affiliated with the NCC.

The 1928 meeting of the National Christian Council, at the request of the International Missionary Council, appointed twenty delegates to the Jerusalem Conference of the International Missionary Council to be held later that year. Fourteen of them were Chinese, six missionaries. They included able laymen, as well as clergy, and made a helpful contribution to the Jerusalem meeting.

The 1933 *China Christian Year Book* reported twenty member churches in the National Christian Council of Churches, representing 70% of Anglican and Protestant church membership.

In 1930-31, Dr. Jesse Lee Corley, General Secretary of the World Sunday School Association, gave a year to a Religious Education Survey in China, with the cooperation of Chinese and missionary leaders. The culmination of the survey process was a Religious Education Conference held at the University of Shanghai on July 31, 1931. The Conference recommended organization of an interdenominational National Committee on Christian Religious Education in China. The Committee was organized as an adjunct to the National Christian Council. It rendered valuable service to the churches for many years under the capable leadership of Dr. Chester C. S. Miao.

A comprehensive Christian Leadership Survey was made in 1934-35 under NCCRE auspices. A team of T. C. Bau (Baptist pastor, later Executive Secretary of the China Baptist Council), C. Stanley Smith (Presbyterian USA-Nanking Theological Seminary), and Chester C. S. Miao (Executive Secretary NCCRE) worked with Dean Luther A. Weigle of Yale Divinity School in a thorough study of theological seminaries and Bible schools. Their report, published as *Training for Service in the Chinese Church,* was of great value in developing theological education programs in China.

In the 1932-33 *China Christian Year Book,* Frank Rawlinson, editor of *The Chinese Recorder* and a keen observer of the Christian movement in China, spoke of signs of encouragement. He noted that the church was in a complex transitional situation "from missionary administrative control . . . to that of Chinese influence and guidance." While he saw "little evidence of creative Chinese theological thinking," he was impressed by the strong trend toward indigenization. Two important indications were the "movements of religious expression"—both "emotionalized individualistic religion and religious practicalism, emphasizing social reconstruction." While Rawlinson's comments described the Protestant churches as a whole, they were essentially applicable to the CCC, which was well along in the process of indigenization.

The National Christian Council shifted from annual to biennial meetings in 1933. At the 1935 meeting, with a majority of the delegates Chinese, Dr. Wu Yi-fang, President of Ginling College in Nanking, was elected Chairman. The Council suffered a major loss in staff personnel at this time. C. Y. Cheng had resigned as General Secretary as of January 1934 to take up his service with the CCC. E. C. Lobenstine, his colleague, who had given notable service to the Chinese Continuation Committee and to the Council in its formative years, retired in June 1935. H. H. Tsui resigned in May 1935 to join the CCC staff. It is of interest to note that the CCC was an important cooperating element in the NCC, as well as in the other agencies of Christian cooperation, and that some of its strongest leadership also played a leading role in the NCC.

Three more commissions were set up at the 1935 meeting of the NCC—one on the Life and Work of the Church, another on Christian Education and a third on Medical Work. The China Christian Educational Association agreed to function as the Education Commission and the Council on Medical Missions of the Chinese Medical Association agreed to serve as the Commission on Christian Medical Work. Because of encouraging results and the desires of many Chinese Christians, the Council decided that the Five Year Forward Movement should continue, with special emphasis on evangelism, training for service, and Christian stewardship. W. Y. Chen, the dynamic dean of Fukien Christian University, became General Secretary of the Council on July 1, 1936. The Council's Chairwoman, Dr. Wu Yi-fang, with Dr. Chester Miao, had at a June 1936 meeting of the International Missionary Council extended an invitation for the 1937 IMC Conference to be held at Hangchow. (Because of the war with Japan, the venue had to be shifted to India.)

General Assembly Staff Leadership

In this first decade of the life of the Church of Christ in China, the staff of the General Assembly had been expanded and strengthened by the addition of a number of Chinese and missionary colleagues. Among the added staff were two men who gave long and wise leadership for many years—indeed, in the eyes of most Chinese churchmen, represented most prominently the Church of Christ in China throughout its history. C. Y. Cheng was its first Moderator and first Chinese General Secretary. H. H. Tsui, his successor, was to serve the Church longer than any other staff executive.

H. H. Tsui (Hiram H. Tsui—Ts'ui Hsien-hsiang) was a Shantung Methodist with a Th.D. degree from Drew University. He had been a pastor and then taught Systematic Theology at Cheeloo University School of Theology for some years. He was Secretary for the Five Year Forward Movement of the National Christian Council of China 1931-34. A man of irenic spirit, cheerful and outgoing, he served first as Executive Secretary with A. R. Kepler (replacing T. C. Fan, who did not want to move with the General Assembly office to Peiping and resigned to go to Hangchow Christian College). After the death of C. Y. Cheng in 1939, Tsui became Acting General Secretary during the war years until in 1946 the General Council voted to confirm him as General Secretary.

Tsui suffered from diabetes, which sometimes limited his activities, but he was never heard to complain about his health. His relations with his colleagues, both Chinese and missionary, were almost always amicable. He gave faithful and devoted service to the Church and was a much loved and respected leader, not only within the CCC but everywhere in the Christian movement. It is worth noting that throughout his many years of service to the Church of Christ in China, he remained a member in good standing of the Shantung Methodist Conference, with no questions raised by the CCC (nor, so far as is known, by his own Methodist Conference).

A number of Western missionaries worked for the General Assembly of the CCC. We have noted the leadership of S. H. Leger in the work of religious education. Another important figure was A. J. Fisher (Presbyterian USA). In the early years of interdenominational cooperation in South China, Fisher was one of several missionaries who supported the cause of unity and union. In the first years of the Kwangtung Synod of the CCC, he was associate to the Reverend Y. S. Tom, the General Secretary. In 1935 he was Synod Secretary for Evangelism and in 1938 Executive Secretary. In 1932-33, when Kepler was on furlough, Fisher was Acting General Secretary of the General Assembly.

Summary—CCC Growth and Promise

In the ten-year period from the first Assembly to the beginning of the war with Japan, the Church of Christ in China had plainly grown stronger in many ways, in spite of the troubled times. It had expanded its membership and added more denominational strains with the addition of the three Baptist groups in Shantung, Shansi, and Shensi and the Mei Dao Hui in Szechuan, as well as a South Fukien group, both with Methodist background. The LMS-related North China Congregationalists and independent congregations in Peiping and elsewhere had also expanded its scope, and the door had been kept open for wider union. Fraternal relations had been maintained with a number of church bodies, some of which later joined the union.

The Church had shown a cooperative spirit, endorsing and supporting the programs of spiritual renewal of the National Christian Council and providing important leadership in its work. It had taken initiative and contributed leadership in the development of an excellent union hymnal containing more adequate worship material than was previously available and in a book of common worship for use by a number of cooperating churches. In literature, Christian education, and other areas of program, the Church had not sought to develop its own denominational programs, but had supported cooperative agencies and their work.

A small but competent secretariat had functioned well and a national program and consciousness were developing. Chinese influence was dominant ar d new and vigorous leadership had strengthened the staff and pror iised effective service for the future.

The General Council meetings, the regional and General Workers' conference, and the General Assemblies had strengthened the cohesiveness of the Church and there was a growing sense of pride of membership in a national Chinese church. Church-mission relationships had been faced candidly and the Church had made clear its conviction that it should have primacy and that control over program, property, and personnel should be vested in the Church and its courts. The Church also stood firmly in its purpose of moving as quickly as possible towards complete self-support.

On the other hand, the general poverty, the civil disturbances of the period, and the deepening national crisis worked against achieving self-reliance, and, with some marked exceptions, local Chinese church leadership was too limited to assume full responsibility. The cooperating boards, though for the most part recognizing the principles set forth by the CCC, continued to deal through mission organizations and channels rather than directly with the church courts.

This was a period of growth and, more importantly, deeper rootage in Chinese society for the Christian church in general in China. The strong anti-Christian manifestations of the early 1920s had almost disappeared, in part because of the concentration of the radical left in Communist-controlled areas, in part because of growing preoccupation with the Japanese threat, along with increased acceptance of the Christian church. The Christian schools had become more Chinese in character and were predominantly under Chinese leadership. The change, already well along at the beginning of this ten-year period, was achieved without too serious difficulties, offset by their increased acceptance as part of the Chinese educational scene. The number of students in Christian primary schools had declined somewhat, while the number in secondary and higher education had markedly increased.

Unquestionably, the Church of Christ in China had grown in strength, cohesiveness, and self-assurance in its first decade. The years of relative peace and order promised continued growth and increased unity. They were to be followed by long years of war and turmoil, years of testing for the nation and the church.

Chapter Seven: The Years of the War with Japan (1937-45)

The War with Japan

The terror and destruction of catastrophes of the past fade away in the glare of today's disasters. But surely the immense destruction and human suffering that almost overwhelmed China as she staggered from the hammer blows of massive Japanese invasions was one of the major cataclysms of history. Refugees were created by the millions, fleeing on foot, by bicycle, by rickshaw, and by trucks and trains weighed down with human freight, carrying on their backs the pitiful remnants of their worldly possessions, often struck down by hunger, weariness, or disease—or more suddenly by fiery death from the air. There was the humiliation of defeat; there were the petty humiliations of standing in queues, of searches and interrogation; there was the arrogance of the conquerers, to whose soldiers Chinese were to respectfully bow; there were the outrages of greedy and lustful soldiers turned loose on civilians after every military victory. There was the terror of planes and artillery pounding towns and villages preparatory to assault, the random torture and shooting of civilians by soldiers, particularly by the feared military police. There was the brutality of the drunken soldier off duty, the rapaciousness of Korean or Formosan camp followers, the pressure to use drugs often sold as medicine. There were the daylight reconnaissances into villages where guerillas ruled by night and there was the questioning at gunpoint, with open graves ready and a bayonet or a bullet the response to unsatisfactory answers. For those who survived flight, or lived in areas unreached by the Japanese, there was deprivation and hunger, long separation from families whose fate was unknown, the economic starvation of uncontrolled inflation, the daily threat of bombs from the air or invasion from the ground.

For the first year and a half, beginning in July 1937, the Japanese

110

continued to overrun the land, taking city after city, sometimes after hard fighting, sometimes with little resistance. By the end of 1939, the situation had stabilized, with the Japanese in control of all major cities in the coastal provinces. As far as the industrial complex of Wuhan in Central China, the invaders were in tenuous control of the railroads and major highways. Frequent forays were made into rural areas by Japanese garrisons that holed up in the towns by night, with frequent harassment and the cutting of communication lines by guerillas. Except for a push in the southwest in 1944, they were never able to penetrate into the mountainous areas of the southwest and west, where the Nationalist government had set up its capital at Chungking. And from the rural areas in the north and northwest, the Communists conducted an intermittent campaign of guerilla warfare, while consolidating their control in preparation for eventual victory.

With the entry of the Western Allies into the war in the Pacific after Pearl Harbor, supplies began to pour in to aid the hard-pressed Chinese, and growing American air power inhibited the bombir.gs of Chungking and other cities of West China that had taken such a terrible toll. The Nationalists and the Communists, theoretically allies, remained wary and hostile, with occasional skirmishes between their forces. In the closing years of the war with Japan, both were more interested in the struggle between them for control of China than in the defeat of the Japanese, who were becoming worn down by their overcommitment throughout Asia and by the growing strength of the U.S. and its allies.

The Impact of the War on Christian Work

Protestant work had continued to expand in the years prior to the war with Japan. Church membership was reported in 1937 as 567,000 (compared to 400,000 in 1921). Ordained workers by 1935-36 numbered about 2,300, double the number in 1920. In 1937 there were 2800 primary schools enrolling about 175,000 pupils. This marked a decline as emphasis shifted to secondary and college level education, in part because of the increase of government primary schools and the ban on religious instruction and activity. There were more than two hundred fifty Protestant middle schools with about 53,000 students. Approximately two hundred fifty Protestant hospitals and about six hundred dispensaries and clinics were served by six hundred medical missionaries (doctors and nurses), five hundred thirty Chinese doctors, and 4,000 student nurses. Six medical colleges annually added to the number of well-trained medical personnel.

As the war progressed, normal church life, like every aspect of life in China, was badly disrupted, especially in the coastal areas most affected, where the churches were strongest and the population greatest. There was heavy damage to church and institutional buildings. Most Christian schools fled westward, some to adjacent areas where the Japanese forces had not penetrated; many, especially the colleges and universities, to the distant West and Southwest. Along with others, a great many church members fled from the invaders, and many lost their lives. Church membership in the occupied areas declined. Many Christian hospitals were left with skeleton staffs. The schools and hospitals that had not evacuated, especially after the Allies were drawn into the war with Japan, were taken over by the puppet government the Japanese had set up.

On August 13, 1937, a group of leading Chinese Christians issued "An open letter to the Christians of the world, on the present Sino-Japanese crisis." This set forth Chinese views on the war, challenged Japanese attempts to justify the invasion and the brutal tactics of the military, and sought to counteract Japanese propaganda.

The National Christian Council was deeply involved in relief programs, as were missionaries and Chinese church workers throughout the areas of military struggle. Through its War Relief Committee, a major effort in which the Church of Christ in China was involved, especially in the early years of the war with Japan, thousands of wounded soldiers were helped. A standing committee of the Council did much to assist European refugees, mostly Jewish, who had fled the Hitler reign of terror and come to Shanghai in large numbers. Through the Christian Medical Council, a number of refugee doctors were placed in Christian hospitals around the country. At the request of the National Child Welfare Association, the Council in early 1939 organized a child Welfare Program with centers in twenty cities and financial assistance from the Association.

A Church Committee for China Relief was organized in New York in June 1938 to combine the China relief efforts of the Federal Council of Churches, the Foreign Missions Conference of North America, and China Famine Relief. This became one of the most significant programs of voluntary relief effort in American history, a major source for relief funds throughout the war and a predecessor of the worldwide relief work of Church World Service following the war.

In spite of the critical situation in China, a Chinese delegation of forty-seven Chinese and ten missionaries was able to attend the meeting of the International Missionary Council in Madras, India. The delegation impressed the conference by the quality of their participation, particularly that of the Chinese lay delegates.

The Christian Forward Movement already planned was launched in 1937 with a three-fold program of relief work, spiritual uplift, and closer cooperation. In June 1939 a Youth and Religion Team of leading Chinese Christians, both lay and clerical, conducted a series of meetings in Southwest China, where 40,000 students were concentrated in refugee universities under conditions of great hardship. An estimated 10% of the total were Christians. In 1939-40 regional conferences for church leaders under NCC auspices were held in Shanghai, Hong Kong, Peiping, Kunming, Kweiyang, and Chengtu. An *NCC News Bulletin* began publication in April 1940 and was widely distributed, providing information on the situation of the churches in China for concerned agencies elsewhere.

Dr. Wu Yi-fang, by now a prominent figure in Chinese political and national life, provided able leadership as Chairman of the Council through the war years and thereafter, while W. Y. Chen continued as General Secretary even after his election as Methodist bishop of West China in 1941. After Pearl Harbor, Council activities and programs were severely curtailed.

Christian literature, always an important element in Protestant Christian work in China, continued to be published and distributed in spite of great difficulties. The South Fukien Religious Tract Society reported distribution in 1937, the first year of all-out war, of 134,584 pieces of literature in the Amoy Romanization, the only truly successful program in phonetic rendering of the Chinese language. Most of the Christian publishing agencies had fled to West China, and in September 1942 the United Christian Publishers were organized as an agency of cooperation and coordination. Members were the Canadian Mission Press, the Christian Literature Society, the Association Press (YMCA), and *The Christian Farmer*. Later the Religious Tract Society, *Christian Youth* (a monthly for middle school students), and the Literature Production Program (a joint enterprise of the National Christian Council and Nanking Theological Seminary for translating the Christian classics into Chinese) also became members.

The Christian Farmer had begun publication in 1934 at Cheloo

University, under the auspices of the North China Christian Rural Service Union. Its officers were moved to Chengtu early in the war period, and under the editorship of T. H. Sun (Sun En-san) the journal had achieved a subscription list of 40,000. H. Y. Chang, after returning from doctoral studies in the U.S., succeeded Sun late in the war as Editor. *T'ien Feng*, a liberal Christian journal that became an important organ of comment and information concerning the church in later years, particularly after 1949, began publication in February 1945. It was the brainchild of Y. T. Wu (Wu Yueh-tsung or Yao-tsung) of the YMCA Association Press, an important figure in the later period, and was intended to be a kind of Chinese *Christian Century*.

Effects on the Missionary Community

The work of the foreign missionaries was of course greatly affected by the war. By and large, the missionaries remained at their posts as the Japanese armies surged into China. The walled mission compound often enclosing schools and hospitals, as well as residences, again became a place of refuge into which thousands poured to seek food and shelter under the protection of a foreign flag. The missionaries and their Chinese colleagues were deeply involved in relief programs and frequently intervened, at considerable risk, between the invader and his helpless victims. A major instance was the "rape of Nanking," when thousands of Japanese troops after taking the city were given three days of liberty and there followed an orgy of killing, looting, and raping almost unparalleled in history. The few missionaries remaining in the city did yeoman service at great personal danger in saving life and protecting Chinese victims, a result duplicated on a smaller scale in many other places.

By late 1940 tensions between Japan and the United States had become so serious that war seemed imminent, and American women and children and nonessential personnel were advised to leave by the State Department. (Similar advice was given to their nationals by other Western nations.) Many did so, but others remained, and when Pearl Harbor was attacked on December 8, 1941 (Chinese time), mission compounds, churches, and Christian institutions in Occupied China were taken over by the Japanese military and missionaries of the Allied nations were put under restraint. A number of Americans were repatriated in the summer of 1942, along with Allied diplomats and other civilians from Japanese-controlled areas, in exchange for Japanese diplomats and civilians from the U.S. and other American lands. Most of those remaining were interned in the Presbyterian compounds in Weihsien (Shantung), Shanghai, and Hong Kong following the arrest and internment of Japanese in the United States about March 1943. A second repatriation occurred in late 1943, but most Allied nationals remained in internment until the end of the war in 1945, although the sick and elderly were allowed to remain in Peiping and some other cities.

Missionaries in Free China, most of them without families because of the war situation, continued to work under difficult and hazardous conditions. Some were frequently forced to move, and all suffered, as did the Chinese, from severe inflation and shortages of necessities.

The Church of Christ in China—Fourth General Assembly

The Third General Assembly of the Church of Christ in China had voted to hold the Fourth Assembly in Tsingtao (Shantung) in July, 1937. On July 5, 1937, General Assembly staff members left Peiping for Tsingtao, as the General Council was scheduled to meet July 7-14, prior to the Assembly. Two days later, on July 7, an incident between Japanese troops on maneuvers at Lukouchiao ("Marco Polo Bridge") south of Peiping and Chinese garrison troops in the nearby walled city signalled the beginning of a long and terrible armed struggle between Japan and China. As a result, members of the CCC staff were separated from their families for months, the General Assembly office in Peiping had to be closed, and the central apparatus of the CCC functioned with limited means and under great difficulties for many years following.

It is a tribute to the importance which the churches gave to the General Assembly and their devotion to the Church that only eight commissioners were unable to attend. Every synod was represented except the Northeast Synod, which had not been permitted by the Japanese puppet government there to continue relations with the Church or any agency within the Great Wall since 1931. There were seventy-six commissioners present, nineteen General Council members (ex-officio commissioners), eleven fraternal delegates from the cooperating missions, five fraternal delegates from other communions, ten invited representatives from national Christian organizations such as the National Christian Council and the Student Christian Movement, and five General Assembly staff executives—a total of one hundred and twenty-six, of whom eighty-eight were Chinese, thirty-eight missionaries.

The Assembly opened as planned on July 15. Sessions proceeded as scheduled, in spite of the tense situation and the growing anxiety of those present. The Japanese, using the pretext of the Marco Polo Bridge incident, mounted a massive offensive in the North and soon moved into Peiping. Chiang Kai-shek refused to yield to a Japanese ultimatum and heavy fighting broke out in Shanghai. A massive landing of Japanese marines backed by strong naval and air forces met with unexpectedly strong Chinese resistance.

Seventeen commissions had met before the Assembly and had prepared reports and recommendations on every aspect of the life of the church. The Rev. C. C. Chen (Ch'en Chi-ching, pastor of the Kulangsu Church—South Fukien) was elected moderator. *The Book of Common Worship* (prepared and sponsored by several denominations) was adopted as the official prayer book of the Church. *Hymns of Universal Praise* (another united effort by a number of churches) was approved as the official hymnal.

The Assembly appointed a ten-member commission to meet with a similar commission of the Chung Hua Sheng Kung Hui (Anglican-Episcopal Church) "to explore ways to effect the organic union of the two communions." The continuing commitment of the Church to unity and cooperation was also emphasized in a statement on union from which the following excerpt is quoted:

> Resolved, that the Church of Christ in China continue to keep the door open to other evangelical churches in China, and to share with others the fellowship of an organically united church, but that until our aim of one united Christian church for China is reached, to cooperate in federal union; in fellowship of worship and service, particularly in new efforts such as the Home Missionary Society, Rural Church Extension Work, United Evangelistic Services, and Educational Work.

> That we continue our close relationship in the sharing of tasks with other churches the world over, in efforts for the evangelization of the whole world.

> That we welcome and give our moral support to the Continuation Committee appointed by the Conference on Church Unity held in Shanghai in January 1937 and accept the invitation to appoint official representatives to

meet together "to explore the possibilities of union and the necessary steps which must be taken to effect corporate union."

The six synods in Kwangtung and Fukien, the areas from which most Chinese emigrants had gone overseas and which to a large extent still provided ministers for overseas Chinese churches, were encouraged to help such churches in their development. It was also recommended that there be interchange of specialized leadership with the Western churches whose missions were in cooperation with the CCC. The desirability of direct relationships between the CCC and "the sending churches" was recognized, with the realization that for practical reasons the cooperating boards and societies would have to deal through their own missions, where they still existed, and directly with the synods for some time to come. A long report on "The Work of the Rural Church" dealt with varied aspects of Christian work in the rural areas of China and listed in an appendix approximately fifty rural service projects of all kinds being carried on by Christian groups in China. The Assembly approved a recommendation that a Rural Work Secretary be added to the General Assembly staff "to further the program of its Rural Service Department," a proposal the Church was unable to implement until after the war.

The staff was instructed to prepare a detailed statement of Church Government and Discipline to be considered by the synods and district associations, with final action to come at the Fifth General Assembly, which was approved for 1941 and scheduled to meet in Hankow.

There was strong support for a program of mission by the Church, cooperating with other denominations if possible. Soon after the conclusion of the Assembly, the Rev. C. K. Lee was called to the General Assembly staff as Church Mission Secretary, a responsibility to which he gave some years of faithful service. It was under his leadership that the Church's first mission was established in Kweichow in 1939. At the closing session on July 29, Holy Communion was celebrated with the use of *The Book of Common Worship* approved and adopted by the Assembly.

Christian Service for the Wounded

One of the most meaningful contributions of Christians to China during the war with Japan was service for wounded soldiers. Left behind as the Chinese forces were overwhelmed and driven back by the better armed and disciplined Japanese armies, their condition was deplorable. Casualties were enormous, limited hospital facilities and military medical services were swamped. Large numbers of wounded lay in railroad stations or boxcars or along the way, often with no care whatever. With a twenty-cent daily food allowance which often did not reach them, many were dying from lack of care.

After a survey of the needs, in which he took a leading part, A. R. Kepler was asked by the National Christian Council, the Chinese Red Cross, and the International Famine Relief Committee to organize help, and the National Christian Service Council for Wounded Soldiers in Transit was founded. Kepler, representing the National Christian Council's War Relief Committee, offered the National government, temporarily located in Hankow, the services of the Christian churches to help meet this need. The government gratefully accepted, and many high government officials contributed to the work from their own means.

After its organization, the Council asked Kepler to be its Director-General. T. C. Fan, former CCC staff member, who at this time was Dean of Hangchow Christian College, was invited to be his associate. Professor W. B. Djang of Cheloo Theological College and George Geng, Principal of the Christian middle school of Hwaiyuan, Anhwei, another former CCC staff member, were appointed Field Directors.

Volunteers were recruited and mobile units of seven to ten persons were stationed along the highways and railroads between the battle front and the hastily set up base hospitals. Council workers cared for the wounded as best they could, bathing them, dressing wounds, providing food, drink, and comfort. Within a few months, one hundred forty-nine full-time workers had been recruited, who received only food and travel allowance, and hundreds of volunteer workers, students, and teachers, men and women, were involved in this ministry of mercy. By 1939, nine hundred seventy-three full-time staff were at work, under the direction of nine regional directors. Almost one hundred of them were women, mostly nurses and teachers. Over 5,000 volunteers were assisting, and in the first two years of war, several hundred thousand wounded men had been cared for in one hundred forty-seven stations.

By 1939 the National government assumed full responsibility for the work of the Council. Dr. Kepler resigned as Director-General and was succeeded by Dean Fan. Throughout its service, the Council was under Christian leadership and the great majority of its workers were Christians.

The Church of Christ in China—Wartime Developments

Two Chinese leaders who made important contributions to the CCC joined its staff in the early years of the war. One was C. T. Tsai (Ts'ai Chi-cheng), called in 1938 to be Secretary for Youth Work. The young and promising pastor of the Second Church in Amoy, he gave many years of helpful leadership to the work of the CCC. After a year of study abroad following the war, he became the Mission Secretary of the Church. The other leader was W. B. Djang (Chang Po-huai—known to his English-speaking friends as "Bill"), a key figure in the work of the Church during the war years. A man of wide experience, he had worked in Rural Education in the Shantung churches, served as Secretary of the Religious Education Department of Shantung Synod, and taught New Testament for some years in the Theological School of Shantung Christian College (later Cheloo University). In 1938, as we have seen, he went to Shansi as Field Director of the work for the wounded, and in the course of that work he became concerned about the aboriginal tribespeople of the Southwest. He became concurrently Director of the Border Mission of the CCC and was largely responsible for the development of that important program. While still continuing his work for the Border Mission, he later became one of the Executive Secretaries and then Chairman of the Provisional Council of the General Assembly of the CCC.

In November 1939 C. Y. Cheng, the much-loved leader of the Church who had done so much to make it a reality, died after a long illness. Coming on top of the calamities that the war had brought to the Church and its members, his death was a sad blow. The principles which he had stated so clearly and his deep commitment to the Christian cause were a continuing influence to those who knew him and to the Church throughout its history.

Miss Y. C. Chi (Ch'i Yu-chen) from the Northeast Synod was appointed Secretary for the CCC Christianizing the Home program, to which she gave able leadership for some years, working closely with a similar program in the National Christian Council.

An Ad Interim General Council meeting was called in Shanghai following the death of Dr. Cheng, and met January 8-9, 1940. Because of the military situation, travel was almost impossible; the only synodical representatives from outside the East China area able to attend were those from Shantung. It took them two weeks to get to Shanghai, compared to the normal two days! Only six of the thirteen cooperating missions were represented.

Correspondence with the synods had indicated general approval for a Missions Cooperating Council in China (proposed by the Third General Assembly in 1933 and the Seventh General Council meeting in Soochow in 1935) and for organizing parallel committees representing the supporting boards and societies in London and New York. The General Council therefore approved implementation of the proposal. The Missions Cooperating Council was not able to function effectively in China, but the counterpart bodies in North America and the United Kingdom proved to be useful agencies for consultation.

A number of missionaries were unable to continue work in their places of assignment because of the military situation, especially in North China, and this meeting of the Council assigned a number of them to service elsewhere. This was the first instance of the assignment of foreign missionaries by a General Assembly organ—done in full consultation with their boards. Victor E. W. Hayward (Baptist Missionary Society) was assigned to student work in Kweiyang, where a number of refugee institutions had fled from occupied China; E. Bruce Copland (United Church of Canada) was assigned to Szechuan (where his board was already at work); and a number of other United Church of Canada and English Baptist missionaries who were unable to get to their stations in Honan and Shansi were assigned to West China work, including in some cases the CCC missions.

As the war progressed and more and more of the coastal provinces, including most of the major cities and railroads, fell to the Japanese invaders, it became clear that the Fifth General Assembly, scheduled for Hankow in 1941, could not be held. It was therefore decided that in the interim a series of emergency conferences should be held with key General Assembly staff visiting accessible synods both in occupied territory and Free China. Fisher states the purpose of such conferences as "to share mutual concerns about the life and the work of our Church in this time of crisis with special reference to the respective regions where each conference was to be held."

The plan was carried out by the two Executive Secretaries, H. H. Tsui and A. R. Kepler; Miss Ch'i, Secretary for Home and Family Life; C. T. Ts'ai, Secretary for Youth Work; and Rev. Sheffield Cheng of Wukingfu (Lingtung Synod). Conferences were held in Sian (Shensi Synod), Chungking and Chengtu (Szechuan), Kweiyang (Kweichow Mission), Yuanling (Hunan), Shaowu (North Fukien), Chuanchow and Amoy (South Fukien), Hong Kong (Kwangtung), Shanghai (East China), and Tsingtao (Shantung). The conferences for the most part dealt with practical issues facing the churches: recruiting university students for the ministry; improving worship services; encouraging and developing better stewardship; strengthening relationships with the General Assembly; church discipline; attitudes toward highly emotional Christian sect groups; and church property and its future status.

Fisher reports on impressions of one of the team members. They included increased interest on the part of students and church members in the ministry of the church and especially an interest in the Border Mission, for which there were a number of volunteers. There was an improved attitude toward Christianity on the part of the general public, especially in view of such humanitarian service as the work for wounded soldiers and the Border Mission. There was evidence of real growth of Christian activity in the schools and of a greater opportunity for witness. On the other hand, the lack of adequate and well-trained leadership in the Church was painfully evident, somewhat counter-balanced by a growth in responsibility on the part of laymen.

On November 5, 1940, the Ad Interim Committee of the General Council appointed W. B. Djang representative of the General Assembly in West China. In the late summer of 1941, A. J. Fisher went to Shanghai to serve as Acting Executive Secretary of the General Assembly during the furlough of A. R. Kepler. In the autumn C. T. Tsai and C. C. Chen (the CCC Moderator elected at the 1937 Tsingtao Assembly) went to the Philippines to visit the Chinese churches there. Generous support for the missions of the church had come from overseas Chinese churches. In a letter to the supporting boards dated June 9, 1941, Kepler reported that C$168,000 had been received from churches in Singapore and the Straits Settlements (Malaya) for support of the church missions. Chinese churches in the Philippines, many of them offshoots from churches affiliated with the CCC, had also indicated their support. It was planned to use these funds to build up an endowment fund for the missions of the Church. The two CCC representatives, Tsai and Chen, were in the Philippines when the Japanese attacked after Pearl Harbor and were imprisoned for some time.

The Missions Cooperating Council met for the first time in Shanghai on June 16-18, 1941. Representatives of five of the cooperating missions were present (the Baptist Missionary Society, London Missionary Society, Presbyterian USA, United Brethren, and United Church of Canada). A. R. Kepler represented the CCC as an *ex officio* member of the Council.

Regret was expressed that the China Mission of the Presbyterian Church US had expressed "inability to participate in the Missions Cooperating Council." A. R. Kepler, who was soon to leave on furlough, was asked to consult with the Executive Committee of the Board of Foreign Missions of the Presbyterian Church in the U.S. concerning membership in the Council. He expressed confidence that "when the purposes and functions of the Missions Cooperating Council are understood the willingness to participate will not be withheld."

A constitution providing representation from each of the cooperating missions was approved and provision made for annual meetings (which would not be held because of the war situation). Note was made of the willingness of the Presbyterian Church in Canada to assign several of its missionaries to work with the CCC and of the reassignment of several missionaries unable to continue in North China.

It was reported that Cooperating Missions Consultative Committees had been set up in London on June 23, 1940, and in New York about June 15, 1940. The Rev. T. W. Douglas James was Chairman of the London Committee, with Dr. H. R. Williamson Recording and Corresponding Secretary. Dr. Wynn Fairfield was Chairman of the Committee in New York and Dr. Lloyd S. Ruland the Secretary.

The entrance of the U.S. and the European allies into war with Japan after the attack on Pearl Harbor greatly complicated the situation for the Christian churches. Missionary colleagues in occupied China were immobilized and the churches were under increased suspicion and pressure because of their historic ties with Western churches. The General Assembly office in Shanghai remained open, with H. H. Tsui in charge, but was able to do very little and was cut off from the support of the missions and from much of its constituency. A. J. Fisher, as a U.S. national, was unable to continue his work for the Church. After Dr. Tsui went to West China in 1943, the Rev. S. S. Chu (Chu Hsin-sheng), for many years the Executive Secretary of the East China Synod, became Acting Secretary of the Shanghai office.

A Provisional General Council of the Church of Christ in China was organized in Chengtu on January 13, 1942, with approval through correspondence of all synods in Free China. According to the October 1944 issue of the Provisional Council's *Newsletter,* the Council met eleven times between 1942 and 1944. Unfortunately, this writer has been unable to find in the board archives and libraries he has seen any copies of minutes of these meetings. Paper was scarce and of very poor quality, communications were slow and difficult, and it is probable that copies were not sent to the cooperating mission boards, while those in China have no doubt disappeared.

The office in Chengtu functioned throughout the war under considerable difficulty. All records and correspondence of the Church remained in the Shanghai office and information on budgets and finances was not available. Administration of the mission work of the Church was transferred to the West China office in 1942, and office space was made available by the Woman's Missionary Society of the United Church of Canada.

W. B. Djang and Gerald Bell (United Church of Canada, Szechuan Synod) were chosen as Executive Secretaries, with Dr. Frank W. Price (Presbyterian US, Professor at Nanking Theological Seminary, relocated at Chengtu) serving as Corresponding Secretary to keep the supporting boards informed. C. K. Lee, Secretary for Missions, and Miss Chi Yu-chen, Christian Home Secretary, managed to slip out of Shanghai and arrived in Kweichow in February 1942. Miss Chi remained in Kweichow for some time and continued her work from that base, while Lee went to Chengtu to work in the Provisional Council office.

A. R. Kepler died of a heart attack in the U.S. in the summer of 1942. Along with C. Y. Cheng, he had worked from the very beginning of the Church of Christ in China and had given wise counsel and unstinted devotion to its development. The Provisional Council, facing the urgent need of finding a successor as Executive Secretary, turned to E. Bruce Copland, a missionary of the United Church of Canada. He had begun his work in Formosa and then had worked for some years in Honan before being transferred to the Szechuan Synod by the General Council of the CCC in 1940. In early 1942 he gave part time to the work of the Provisional Council, but after the death of Kepler he was asked to work full time and with the consent of his board in November 1942 he began a relationship that continued for a good many years. His diligent but unobtrusive service, his excellent relations with Chinese colleagues, and his irenic spirit served the Church well, especially in the critical years during and following the war with Japan.

An October 10, 1942, letter from Djang and Price to the mission boards reported that the *Kung Pao* (Chinese-language periodical of the CCC) was being used to keep the churches informed of the work of the Church. H. Y. Chang of the staff of the *Christian Farmer* was the editor. Encouraging progress was evident in the three missions of the Church, including the appointment of local committees of laymen in each of them and generous gifts from Chinese contributors. On the other hand, rising costs and serious inflation posed great difficulties for the Church, as well as for individuals.

On September 25, 1942, at a meeting of the North American boards that cooperated with the Church of Christ in China, it was voted, in view of the death of A. R. Kepler, to establish a North American Council of the CCC with one representative from each related mission board and to request the services of W. H. Clark, who had returned to the U.S. on health leave, as its executive. After the repatriation of A. J. Fisher in late 1943 and the return of the Clarks to China, Fisher served in that capacity for some time.

At the February 10, 1943, annual meeting of the Provisional Council, it was reported that the Ch'eng Ching-yi Memorial School in Kweiyang had been completed with costs underwritten by the gifts of Chinese Christians. W. B. Djang reported correspondence from a number of individual congregations wishing to affiliate with the CCC. Among them were churches in Shensi and Kansu, probably made up of refugees from Japanese-occupied areas. Others were in Kweichow and Kwantung where "many churches which have been cut off from their European connections have written and applied for admission into the CCC." It was voted to defer action until there could be secretarial visits to the churches applying for membership. Similar cautious action was taken at the 1944 annual meeting of the Provisional Council when the Evangelical Church, at work in Hunan and Kweichow, appointed delegates to confer with the CCC about union. (They were later received as members at the Fifth General Assembly in 1948.)

Dr. H. H. Tsui had managed to slip out of Shanghai and arrived in Chengtu in August 1943. Soon after his arrival, he was appointed General Secretary by the Provisional Council. W. B. Djang then resigned as Chairman of the Provisional Council (and presumably as Executive Secretary) to devote his full time to the work of the Border Mission, which required considerable travel and frequent meetings with government agencies.

The staff was able to carry on a surprising amount of travel, in spite of great difficulties. In most areas of Free China, members travelled by overcrowded and unreliable bus or truck, often exposed to the weather and always vulnerable to intensive Japanese bombing. H. H. Tsui spent a month in Kweichow in the spring of 1944 and, accompanied by Bruce Copland, two months in Yunnan. Miss Chi was in Hunan and Kwantung in early 1943, visited outlying areas of Szechuan and Kweichow later, and then spent some time in Kunming. Copland was in Shensi and Honan in the autumn of 1943, then in Yunnan with Tsui, before leaving for a Canadian furlough in August.

C. K. Lee, oldest member of the staff, left the CCC in 1942 and died in 1946. C. T. Tsai succeeded him as Secretary for Missions, but the date he assumed office is unclear, as is the time of his return to China from the Philippines.

At the January 1944 annual meeting of the Provisional Council, Dr. Tsui was authorized to attend a meeting of the National Christian Council of India as the representative of the Chinese churches, appointed by the NCC of China. He visited many cities in India, speaking on the work of the churches in China and the critical wartime situation. On his return in the spring, a Chungking office was opened and became the headquarters for the remainder of the war, though the Border Mission office remained in Chengtu. Expenses during this period were for the most part undertaken by the supporting boards.

One of the responsibilities of the CCC in this difficult period was relief for church workers. Many of them were suffering great hardships, some were separated from home and family, inflation was a serious problem. From funds which came from the Western churches to the National Christian Council, a share was allotted to the CCC, which distributed such funds through the synodical offices and never directly to individuals.

At the January 1944 annual meeting there was a thorough discussion of church union, which members of the Szechuan Synod, meeting concurrently in Chengtu, attended. As reported in the October 1944 issue of the *Newsletter* of the Provisional Council:

> Some critics have urged that the Church of Christ in China tends to absorb smaller churches, just because of its size. Others have said that in course of time the CCC has just become a denomination, losing its early zeal for union. After a full discussion, the Council issued a statement which emphasized the following points:
>
> 1. The CCC is an organic union church, but it is also a church union movement.
> 2. We have no desire to absorb other churches, but we do desire to unite with other churches, large or small, which desire organic union.
> 3. Real union can only be on the basis of a common faith in Jesus Christ and in a clear understanding of the nature of the Church.

Bishop R. O. Hall of the Sheng Kung Hui asked the Council to appoint presbyters to participate in the ordination of Y. C. Tsai, who had been working in the Yunnan Mission of the CCC. The Council "agreed that it would be a gracious and Christian act to accept the invitation," another example of the good relations obtaining between the two churches.

CCC Synods

The Hunan section of the Lianghu Synod asked the Council to authorize the formation of a separate Hunan Synod, but the Council was unwilling to take responsibility for such action. (The General Council in 1946 did approve the division, and in 1948 the Synods of Hunan and Hupei were organized separately.)

Most of the strongest synods of the CCC were in areas invaded by the Japanese, and throughout the war, many synods found it impossible to hold meetings. Some were split, especially in the South, with the cities and coastal towns held by the Japanese and the rural areas and smaller towns controlled by Chinese guerillas.

South Fukien and Kwangtung Synods, with large areas not controlled by the Japanese, were able to function with some effectiveness. The South Fukien Synod met in December 1942 for the first time in five years. This was the centennial year for Protestant work in South Fukien, and it was celebrated everywhere in the unoccupied areas. A five-year major evangelistic campaign had been undertaken in 1937 with the aim of reaching every person in the area with the Gospel message. Although Japanese air raids were frequent through these years, virtually every village was visited by evangelists or by volunteer preaching bands, which were very active during the war. The communicant membership of the Synod was reported as over 14,000, of which 1238 had been added in 1942. Many new church buildings had been erected in the previous five years. Church and evangelistic work was jointly supported by mission and church giving, and by 1942 church contributions were nine times that of the three cooperating missions. After mission support was completely cut off following Pearl Harbor, there was a marked increase in Chinese giving, in spite of the difficult conditions under which all were living. Considerable support came from Christians who had emigrated to Southeast Asia. One man in the Philippines gave C$100,000 for a Christian middle school in Changchow, conditional on local contributions of C$25,000. In one church three Thanksgiving offerings were taken each year. Before each one, every member was visited by the elders of the church, who urged them to increase their giving. The Synod voted to accept no further mission support except for the two weakest district associations and for new outgoing work.

The South Fukien Synod held its Twenty-Fifth Anniversary Assembly in December 1943 and January 1944 at Changchow, and reported that giving had greatly increased. The total for 1943 (presumably for all causes and presumably in Chinese currency, by then seriously devalued, which makes it difficult to know even the approximate value) was reported as "over $3,000,000" (as compared to $774,740 reported in 1942). Strong sentiment was voiced by a so-called "second-century group," who were pressing for complete self-support and full control by the church of all schools and hospitals, a request which was referred to the home boards of the cooperating missions for their consideration. It was reported that the Women's Missionary Society of the Synod had been very active through the war period. Many of the district associations had employed executives to help in administration and to assist pastors and weaker churches.

In March 1944 the Rev. Ngaw Peng-iau, a pastor for many years in Chuanchow, was installed as the first General Secretary of the Synod at Tungan. A vigorous leader, he visited all seven district associations of the Synod in the following months, walking some hundreds of miles to accomplish his mission. In 1945 the Synod's Board of Domestic Missions was reorganized, and thereafter it concentrated its efforts in the Tingchow area, while responsibility for work on the offshore islands was that of the coastal district associations. All inland districts had their own mission projects.

At the close of 1935, the Kwangtung Synod had reported ten district associations, thirty-six self-supporting churches and one hundred sixty-four other churches, with a communicant membership of 21,000, over half in the self-supporting churches. Canton was under heavy bombing before the Japanese took it, and a number of school and church properties were destroyed. Some relocated in Hong Kong, others in inland towns not yet occupied. A number of the schools were forced to move several times during the course of the war. True Light Middle School was bombed out of Canton in 1937 and reopened at Hong Kong. But in 1941, after Pearl Harbor, many of its students and faculty escaped and the school was reestablished in 1942 in Saam Kong in Northern Kwangtung. Union Theological Seminary was evacuated to Yunnan Province and then, late in the war, to Northern Kwangtung. Union Normal School for Women was moved to Macao in 1937. The synodical office was set up in Kukong but in 1944 had to be abandoned again under Japanese military pressure.

The July 1939 issue of the Synod's *Information Service* reported that work had been severely hampered by Japanese military actions. Six of the ten districts where the church worked were occupied; a seventh had been entered by Japanese troops who had then withdrawn. Nine churches had been totally destroyed. Refugees were crowding into the cities, especially Canton and Hong Kong, and major efforts were being given to relief work.

The Synod held its Fifteenth Annual Meeting in Hong Kong in July 1940, with one hundred and fifty-five delegates representing almost two hundred congregations. Workers were appointed for the concentration of refugee students in the Eighth District (Lin Yuen) and to open up work in Kwong Chau Wan, which had become the chief port of entry for unoccupied areas of South China. In November 1940 Peter Wong, who had returned from two years of graduate study in the U.S., after graduation from Union Theological Seminary, was ordained and appointed the Synod's Secretary for Youth and Student Work. Following the war, he became the Synod's Executive Secretary and later held the same post in the Hong Kong Council of the CCC.

In Shansi the missionaries were forced out in 1939 by the Japanese-sponsored anti-British campaign and Japanese pressure on missionaries and Chinese. Most church property was occupied by the Japanese military and services were perforce discontinued in most churches. Some small groups continued to worship unobtrusively in homes. The Japanese forces did not penetrate as far west as Shensi, except for occasional forays, but because of the heavy bombing and the recurrent threat of Japanese military action, the last of the missionaries had left by the early '40's.

The Canadian missionaries were forced out of North Honan by the Japanese also, and there is only scanty information on the life of the churches of the Honan Synod. However, the Rev. George King wrote from Peiping on May 20, 1941, of a visit by two of the Honan pastors. Conditions in the areas were distressing, with the Japanese in control of the major towns, constant guerilla warfare, much destruction of church and personal property, and the complete disruption of normal life. But the pastors reported that everywhere churches and small groups of Christians continued to meet to worship, with an encouraging number of accessions. Two pastors from the northern presbytery had spent a month visiting church groups in the southern area, which was almost completely occupied by the Japanese. Travelling on foot, often in danger, they had spent their time leading and encouraging the church people and pastors and evangelists, especially in the outlying areas where Japanese troops came only occasionally. Many of the church workers were already in their sixties or even older and keenly felt the need for new leadership in the work of the church.

The End of the War with Japan—Gains and Losses for the Church

The war finally dragged out to its weary close as the Japanese, hard-pressed by the growing momentum of the American campaign up the island chains off Asia, were increasingly unable to mount new offensives in China and could only doggedly hold on to the areas under their control. The Chinese, still divided into two camps, with much of the land wasted and the economy bankrupt, were unable or unwilling to press their advantage, preferring to conserve their strength for the final struggle for control between Nationalists and Communists.

We will not attempt to evaluate the effect of the war on the Chinese nation except to emphasize again the incalculable sufferings and losses that had been incurred. For the Christian church, there were both gains and losses. The institutions of the church had sustained grievous damage. Schools and hospitals had evacuated to unoccupied areas with tremendous loss of buildings, equipment, staff, and students. Some were destroyed and never again became operative. Where they had sought to continue operation in areas of Japanese control, they had done so with a skeleton staff and against great obstacles, and many had eventually been taken over by the government and lost their Christian identity. Complete control by the Chinese government of foreign exchange and remittances, and the consequent unrealistic exchange rate, greatly reduced the effectiveness of funds contributed by American and other churches for religious and humanitarian relief work in Free China.

Many members and leaders of the church fell victims to war violence, disease, or Japanese jails. Theological training had suffered a serious setback, as most institutions had evacuated and carried on limited programs or had been forced to close down entirely. Many church workers in both Japanese-occupied and free areas had been forced by fear or economic pressure to take secular positions. In many cases, church life survived only in minimal programs. A major portion of the missionary community had found it necessary to leave China or had endured years of hardship or captivity. The support of the mission societies in occupied China had been completely cut off and in Free China was inadequate to keep up with the spiralling inflation.

On the other hand, the difficult war period was not without advance for the church. Through relief work, especially that of the National Christian Service Council for Wounded Soldiers in Transit, the courage of individuals, and the identification of the church and its institutions with the Chinese cause, the church had won greater acceptance as a truly Chinese institution. So the *China Critic,* an independent English-language Chinese journal, could say in an editorial in its issue of July 20, 1939:

> One of the many things that have come out of the present war has been the realization that, whatever doubt may have existed in the past, the Christian missions in China fully and indisputably justify their existence. . . . They have preached the gospel not with works but by a practical demonstration of the love of God and the brotherhood of man.

There developed a strong sense of self-reliance and cooperation in both occupied and Free China, and it was made clear that the Chinese church could, albeit on a limited scale, carry on without the missionary or missionary support. Japanese attempts to force a merger of the churches similar to that developed in the Kyodan in Japan as a war measure had only limited success, while enforced cooperation with the military government and its puppets was nominal and limited. The Christian church in China had survived a very difficult period in the nation's history and in its own experience, though not without serious losses, especially in rural churches and in pastoral leadership.

For the Church of Christ in China, unquestionably the breakdown in communications with most of its synods, the impossibility of holding national Church meetings, and the inability of the structures to function except at the local level and in some places not even there, inhibited the process of integration and unification that had been so promising in the early years. The central structure of the Church survived on a limited level, almost completely dependent on the financial support of the missions. Its activities were chiefly the administration of the missions of the Church, an important and cohesive factor in its life which was undoubtedly strengthened through this period, and the distribution of relief, also an important and unifying factor. Self-support at the national level lost ground except in relation to the missions of the Church. The CCC certainly gained in stature as a national church both within church circles and in Chinese society—in part because of its relief work and service to the minority peoples of the Southwest.

There was encouraging growth in Chinese leadership in the missions of the Church. In its central administration, the Church was fortunate in the able leadership given by H. H. Tsui, W. B. Djang, Chi Yu-chen, C. C. Tsai, and others, especially in a time of change when the early leaders had passed from the scene. There was some modest growth in interest in membership by independent congregations and some as yet unaffiliated churches.

Chapter Eight

Ventures
in
Mission

Chinese Christians have almost always had a keen sense of responsibility for mission. This was seen in the work of the Chinese Home Missionary Society, in which C. Y. Cheng played a leading role. A nondenominational effort financed entirely by the gifts of Chinese Christians, it began its program about 1918. It was seen also in the evangelistic zeal of many lay Christians. Evangelistic bands made up of volunteers were an important element in Christian witness in many parts of China and in the growth of Chinese churches among the Chinese communities of Southeast Asia. Lay volunteers often accompanied missionaries and Chinese pastors in their travels to chapels and distant places, rendering great service in the proclamation of the Gospel message. Mention has already been made of the early and extensive efforts in home mission undertaken by the churches in South China.

The substantial growth of Chinese Christian churches in Indonesia, the Philippines, and other lands where Chinese emigration, mostly from Kwangtung and Fukien, was considerable in the early years of the twentieth century, was largely due to the witness of Chinese Christians who brought with them from the ancestral home a deep Christian commitment. Later, the churches that had sprung up were largely served by ministers trained in China, and Chinese evangelists found these prosperous emigrés, especially in the 1920s and later, a fruitful field for their labors—though also sometimes for sectarianism and dissension.

As the Church of Christ in China grew more conscious of its reponsibility as a national church, its sense of responsibility for mission also increased. This growing support for a program of mission work by the Church found expression at the Fourth General

Assembly at Tsingtao in 1937. In spite of the outbreak of war with Japan and the anxiety of delegates over their families and homes, to say nothing of the problem for many of returning to their homes, the need for mission was felt strongly. W. B. Djang, in an account of the Border Mission in *Christian Voices in China* (1948), says:

> One question came up repeatedly in the conversations: "What should the church do to help the nation, if this 'incident' should become a prolonged struggle for national existence?" Out of this query, two major movements were born: (1) the National Christian Service Council to the Wounded, which functioned from January 1938 to July 1945, giving comfort and cure to millions of the wounded; (2) the Border Mission, which came into existence in the summer of 1939.

The Assembly authorized the establishment of a Church Mission. Not long after its close, the Assembly called the Rev. C. K. Lee from Hupei—Lee had been a YMCA secretary, a secretary of the Wuchang Council of Churches, General Secretary of the Hsing Tao Hui (Swedish Missionary Society-related church), and on the staff of the Chinese Home Missionary Society—to the General Assembly staff as Church Mission Secretary, a task to which he gave some years of devoted service. It was under his leadership that the Church's first mission project was established in Kweichow Province in southwest China in 1939.

The Kweichow Mission

Kweichow was chosen because it was a backward and neglected area of the country. Here lived many of the tribespeople—remnants of earlier inhabitants of much of China—who had been displaced by the abler and more aggressive Han people and had retreated to the mountainous areas of the Southwest. Life was difficult even for the Chinese who had penetrated the area, and such amenities as educational and medical facilities were few. As the Japanese armies occupied more and more of the heavily populated coastal provinces, the unprecedented flight of millions of people brought many refugees and refugee schools to Kweiyang, the capital city, and other parts of Kweichow.

The first public worship service of the mission was held in Kweiyang in May 1939. Although every effort had been made to publicize it, only a handful of people were expected. Actually, almost eighty were in the congregation! Many of them were Christians from the occupied regions, and these people formed the backbone of the new congregation. Before long a strong church grew up, and within a year a church building and school had been erected. Chinese Christians and churches all over the nation contributed $25,000 for the erection of the Ch'eng Ching-yi Memorial Church, with a charter membership in 1940 of one hundred and thirty.

The work of the Kweichow Mission was begun by two Chinese staff members. One of them was the Rev. Wu Yik-wan, formerly pastor of the Lienchow Church in Kwangtung and Secretary for Young People's Work of the Kwangtung Synod. The Synod's *Information Service* for September 1939 reported that at the Fourteenth Annual Meeting of Synod in Kowloon, Hong Kong, in July, "Rev. C. K. Lee presented a thrilling account of the first undertaking of the Department of Evangelism of which he is Secretary." There was special interest because one of their own young pastors had been a pioneer in this new venture. The other pioneer appears to have been the Rev. Stephen Tsai (Ts'ai Chih-teng).

By 1942 a church, a school, and a kindergarten had been organized in Tingfan (later called Huishui), and by agreement with the China Inland Mission, which had had a modest program there for the Miao people, responsibility had been turned over to the CCC and a Miao evangelist added to the staff. Work at Tungtze began the same year.

As the war situation released some Western missionaries to work in Free China, several of them were invited by the General Assembly office to join the staff of the Kweichow Mission. The Rev. and Mrs. Victor E. W. Hayward, formerly stationed in Shansi as representatives of the English Baptist Mission, and Miss Jean Sommerville of the United Church of Canada, who formerly worked in Honan, were asked to work in Kweichow in 1939. Mr. Hayward (who later was to serve from 1946 to 1951 as Associate General Secretary of the National Christian Council of China) was appointed first as a student worker. Later he was asked to be Director of the Mission, and served in that capacity until his furlough in 1944. Miss Sommerville, whose work was chiefly with students and in Christian Home Education, worked with Miss Chi Yu-chen of the General Assembly (Secretary for the Christian Home), who escaped from Shanghai to Kweiyang in February 1942 and worked there and later in Chengtu during the war years. Miss Sommerville left on furlough in 1943.

The strongest support came in the early days from the refugees—those who were already Christians and those who were drawn by the fellowship and warmth of the church. Local Chinese were at first suspicious of the "down-river" people. Yet many of them were eventually impressed by the unselfish spirit of the workers and by their willingness to help anyone in need.

From the beginning, the aim was to have the work in Kweichow entirely supported by the Chinese church (with the exception of the salaries of the few foreign missionaries who assisted). To that end, C. K. Lee devoted much of his time to developing support in the established churches of the coastal areas. He reported in 1942 that on the "first Mission Sunday on January 7, 1940, more than fifty cities took part, resulting in a total sum of $1400 as their free will offerings." Eight churches in Shanghai formed a Church Mission Fellowship "to promote and intensify the missionary interest and zeal among the local churches so as to enlist regular intercessors and liberal givers." Two thousand dollars was raised by this group, and the Hop Yat Church in Hong Kong raised an endowment fund of $15,000. Throughout the Church there was warm interest and general support for the work of the Mission and response to the need for workers.

Mr. Lee reported, "Miss Cheng Shao-hwa in Kweiyang was formerly the Bible woman at Changsha. Pastor Stephen Chen at Tingfan was pastor of our church near Hankow and Mr. Hsiao Shih-min in Kweiyang was a worker of one of our churches near Peking." Mr. Li Jui, a Christian businessman formerly from Hankow and a consistently generous supporter of the work in Kweichow, in 1942 underwrote $30,000 for new work at Tungtze and Huangping, in addition to generous gifts for other mission work of the Church.

In 1942 a strong local committee of responsible laymen was formed to administer the work of the Mission, under the general guidance of the Provisional Committee of the General Assembly that had been set up at Chengtu. W. B. Djang reported in a letter dated October 10, 1942, that the Kweiyang congregation had "nearly attained a status of self-support," a church building had been completed at Huishui, "largely due to several special gifts from Chinese laymen," and that new work was to be begun at Huangping and Tungtze with the support of Mr. Li's gifts.

The Rev. Chen Heng, an experienced pastor from Hunan who had been forced to leave his work there by the advance of the Japanese forces, became Director of the Mission in 1944.

Fisher reports in his manuscript history (1946) that at that time the Kweichow Mission was "operating at seven centers, with a staff of fourteen evangelistic workers and seven educational workers.

Two . . . fully qualified nurses are doing clinical work as part of the mission program."

The Rev. and Mrs. John D. Hayes (Presbyterian USA, formerly in Peking) joined the staff in the fall of 1948. Mrs. Hayes went to Hong Kong in the summer of 1949 for reasons of health and for eighteen months assisted Bruce Copland in his liaison work there for the CCC. After the new regime took power in Kweiyang in November 1949, Dr. Hayes severed official connection with the CCC. Realizing that remittances from the U.S. might be cut off, he secured employment as a teacher of English at two government universities. That employment continued until March 1951, when he was put under house arrest by the authorities. In October 1951 he was imprisoned, charged with being an American spy. After ten months of intensive investigation and two lengthy trials, the court did not sustain the charges against him. However, he was sentenced to expulsion from China and deported in September 1952.

In its October 1948 issue, *The Church* (English-language bulletin of the CCC) reported that several workers from the Northeast Synod (including one woman and three ordained ministers) had recently been assigned by the General Assembly office to work in various areas of Kweichow. The August 1949 issue of *The Church* carried a report that the work of the Mission was continuing without interruption and that opportunities among both Chinese and tribespeople were excellent. The same year Stephen Chang, who as a refugee student in Kweiyang had become a Christian, completed his theological training at Nanking Theological Seminary and was ordained as pastor of the Kweiyang Church, which by that time had a membership of about two hundred. Another local convert, Miss Tang Yun-wen, was the director of the excellent kindergarten in the Kweiyang church.

Miss Sommerville had been invited to return to Kweiyang by the General Assembly office in 1947. In a letter to a friend, she wrote about the union Easter morning service in Kweiyang in 1950, after the new regime had taken control of the area. In spite of misgivings, "several hundred were present from our seven or eight little church groups." Seven people were baptized in the CCC that same day.

The Border Mission

A second venture in mission for the Church of Christ in China, and the most ambitious one, was the work of the Border Mission, begun soon after the initiation of the Kweichow Mission and arising from the same felt need to be a church in mission. The Rev. W. B. Djang, whose leadership played an extremely important role in the development of the program, reported on its work on many occasions, most fully in a chapter entitled "An Oasis on a Vast Human Desert" in *Christian Voices in China.*

He visited the Southwest in late 1938 as part of his responsibility for the work with wounded soldiers and became conscious of "vast numbers of minority groups of people in these regions." They were isolated from the rest of the nation, living under primitive conditions with almost no educational or medical facilities. He reported his impression of great need to the General Assembly staff.

Dr. Cheng approached Dr. H. H. Kung, then Premier (they had been schoolmates in their youth), and asked for his help. A tentative plan for a mission effort to help these people was drawn up, and the General Council gave its approval. W. B. Djang "was charged with all preliminary preparations—securing of personnel and exploring possible fields."

As the need became known, a group of six young people, mostly recent university and seminary graduates, volunteered to serve in the new mission. Under Djang's leadership, and with the support of church leaders in Free China and the assurance of Dr. Kung's interest, the six volunteers were commissioned in the Sze Chen Tzu Church in Chengtu the first Sunday of December 1939. They then left for Lifan (Szechuan) to begin the work of the Mission.

Formal organization of the Mission (sometimes designated the Border Service Department, but more commonly called the Border Mission) took place in February 1940, when Djang met with H. H. Tsui and A. R. Kepler in Chungking, a Board of Directors was set up, and the Border Mission became a Department of the General Assembly of the Church. The Board was composed of representatives of the Church, of other major churches in the area, of related government departments (Health, Education, Social Affairs, Agriculture, etc.), and also of community leaders.

It was planned as a service movement in the broadest sense of the term. It was to be useful and helpful to the minority groups in whatever way ... its services were needed. There was no intention of imposing a religion on the minority groups. No church or chapel was to be put up at any place, unless and until the local people desired it. Since the government was willing to give financial help, it was made clear that no public fund would be used for purely religious purposes.

The first group of missionaries agreed upon "certain fundamental principles" which were followed throughout the work of the Border Mission.

(1) *No prejudice*—not to replace the culture and traditions of the people with his own, but to learn to appreciate . . . whatever is good in a given culture.

(2) *No prefixed program*—(because of wide differences among the tribes) the border mission does not attempt to have a uniform program for all fields. . . . The first and still the basic approach in the Tibetan border field is education; and that of the Lolo field is medicine.

(3) *Coordination*—Workers in each department should have a share in the responsibility of every other department . . . to maintain a group spirit . . . essential to an all-round impact on the community.

(4) *Cooperation*—With the local people especially. . . . They must feel that the work is . . . in a real sense their own.

Djang summarized the program as "doing things for people . . . doing things with them, helping them to do things and enabling them to see and do things for themselves."

The Mission was divided into two fields, with work among three minority groups, as well as among the Chinese of the area. The Tibetan Border Mission operated in the vast area on the borders of Sikang, Kansu, and Tsinghai. Work was chiefly with the Chiang and Hsifan people. The Liangshan field was in the mountainous area south of there, in southeastern Sikang, bordering on Szechuan and Yunnan, where the Lolos were the predominant people.

The Chiang people, numbering about one hundred thousand, lived in the Min River Valley in northwestern Szechuan, the "remnant of a once great race who populated western . . . China . . . from the Gobi Desert to the Yangtze River." Often mentioned in Chinese history, they had largely been assimilated by the Han Chinese. West of the Chiangs, on the Tibetan border, were the Hsifans, perhaps a million people in the area. Most were at least nominal adherents of Lama Buddhism, whereas the Chiangs were chiefly animists.

The Lolos (also called Nosu, a different pronounciation of the same word) were more closely related to the Indo-Burmese people than to the Chinese. A warlike people with a very primitive culture, they practiced slavery, and a substantial number of the total (variously estimated as from two to three million) were in fact slaves taken in war or their descendants. Traditionally hostile to the Chinese, with a long history of armed raids and exploitation, they were extremely difficult to work with. In fact, so savage were the Lolos that many people doubted that Chinese missionaries would be able to accomplish anything at all with them. The spirit in which the work of the Border Mission was carried on was well expressed by W. B. Djang in a radio address made March 18, 1948 (probably on the Christian radio station in Shanghai—the report is not specific):

> A real reconciliation (i.e., between Chinese and tribespeople) can only come through a consecrated and well planned program of good will, kindness and long suffering, and never failing love—such as exemplified in Christian missions and supremely demonstrated by our Lord's ministry and His cross.

Suspicious of all Chinese, the Lolos did in time recognize the helpful nature of the Mission's work. Schools, agricultural and industrial programs, and medical clinics were set up at the invitation of and with the cooperation of the chiefs. W. B. Djang, in a 1944 report, attributed the change of attitude to "the loyalty and devotion and skill of our workers who have labored against terrific odds. . . . They have anchored themselves to the hearts of these people by living among them in complete sympathy and understanding" (Joliffe, *The Chinese Church Rides the Storm*, p. 19). Among the most influential programs were a hostel for Lolo visitors in Sichang, the capital city, and a hundred-bed hospital. The need was so great that the mission was not able to meet all the requests from the chiefs for new programs.

In this vast region with over forty million people, the Border Mission sought to cooperate with all concerned agencies. The door was open to other churches to help. There was cooperation, especially in research, both medical and general, with the Christian universities in West China, the National Health Administration, the China Border Research Society, and other organizations. "In teaching the Lolos how to take care of the American airmen who bailed out in their regions, it cooperated with the United States Army in China."

Soon after work began, information about the program was shared with the Christian universities in Chengtu-West China Union and with the refugee institutions in Cheloo, Nanking, and Yenching (Ginling?). A joint committee was set up and very quickly "more than four hundred students from nine colleges and universities applied to join the teams." By careful selection this number was reduced to about one hundred, who were then organized into ten teams and given intensive training. At the end of the school year in

1940, after a religious ceremony, these students went out to help in the program.

They worked for ten weeks, under the supervision of faculty members and Henry D. Tsui, who had been appointed Field Director of the Border Mission. Tsui, an educator from Shantung, had been principal for some years of Cheloo University Elementary School and later of a Christian middle school in Weihsien, Shantung. The students and their supervisors lived and worked under conditions of genuine hardship, with the simplest of fare and accommodations, but with enthusiasm and effectiveness. The experiment was repeated in 1941, but thereafter mounting costs made it possible to send only smaller groups of selected students. Over five hundred students took part in the program during the war period and immediately thereafter. They learned much of the customs of the tribespeople and introduced their folk songs and dances to the campuses.

The first primary school was established in 1940 at Chiashanchai, "the first school . . . for this minority group." The children of this school did so well that they visited a number of towns in Szechuan, presenting programs and impressing those who heard them by their progress. Other schools were gradually set up, as well as clinics, hostels, experimental farms, and rural industries.

By around 1946, according to Fisher, the work on the Tibetan border had resulted in five primary schools ("the first educational advantages ever offered"), three preaching centers, three medical centers, an animal husbandry program, a home industry project, and an agricultural improvement station. The work with the Lolos had produced one organized church and two preaching centers, a very successful kindergarten in Sichang, two pioneer primary schools, a hostel and service center for the Lolos in Sichang, one home industry project in leathercraft, a processing plant for salt and sugar (goiter was extremely prevalent and iodine was added to the salt as a preventative), an agricultural improvement station, and the hundred-bed hospital in Sichang already mentioned.

The circumstances were difficult. Local opposition was sharp, especially from Chinese who were exploiting the minority people, and several of the early Chinese missionaries died from illness brought on by exhaustion and privation. Among them were the Rev. H. C. Geng in Szechuan, the Rev. P. K. Feng, a worker among the Lolos, L. C. Hsu in the Mission office, and Dr. Ma Hsi-shan of the Weichow Hospital. Finances were inadequate and salaries were low. W. B. Djang in the 1944 report mentioned above speaks of having to sell bicycles and other needed items because funds were inadequate, and also of having to cut already low salaries. But by 1941 so enthusiastic was the response of the churches that there were fifty-two Chinese missionaries at work. By 1945 the number was eighty, but for lack of sufficient support this had to be cut back to sixty by 1947.

Throughout the history of the Border Mission, almost all the missionaries were Chinese. Yet there were some exceptions. The Rev. Archie R. Crouch (Presbyterian USA) served as English Language Secretary for the Mission for some years (with responsibility for communicating with the cooperating missionary societies) and did much to make the work of the Border Mission known. Also, several missionaries of the Baptist Missionary Society (British) who were unable to return to their work in Shansi following the war gave helpful service in the Border Mission. They were the Rev. J. Henderson Smith (1945-47), the Rev. and Mrs. W. S. Upchurch (1946-50), and the Rev. and Mrs. Ernest Madge (1948-50).

The Church of February 1948 reported progress in the animal husbandry project at Weichow (Szechuan) with the appointment of a new director, K. S. Wang. Experimental breeding to upgrade stock was going on with cattle, sheep, goats, pigs, and chickens, as well as seed selection of grazing grass. It was hoped to crossbreed cattle with the Tibetan yak, "in order to produce a type suitable for the mountain regions." The child welfare program which had grown out of the kindergarten work at Sichang had been enlarged. The Sichang Hospital had been completely renovated under the supervision of Dr. Ching, and a planeload of vital foodstuffs, drugs, blankets, an X-ray machine, and other supplies had come in January through the efforts of W. B. Djang, working with relief agencies. Much of this material was carried by porters to distant stations on journeys taking as long as two months.

The October 1948 issue of *The Church* reported the appointment of two ordained men from Manchuria. The same issue carried a long report by E. Bruce Copland, Executive Secretary of the CCC, on the visit of a team to the Sichang area in April, 1948. Copland and Djang went on, after the others had left, to visit stations among the Chiang and Giarong tribespeople.

The report speaks in the highest terms of the spirit of the workers. "Our staff is working in remote and lonely places and . . . their task is a very difficult one." They "obviously are living lives of self-sacrifice and self-discipline." The work was in frontier areas where the growing of opium and its sale was a major enterprise among "lawless and uncultured people" and where there was "hostility and misunderstanding between the Chinese and the aboriginal tribes. . . . The program of the Mission is one of service to the Chinese and aboriginal people . . . in a Christian spirit." The religious work, for which government grants were not used, "is basic and recognized as supremely important." A few foreign missionaries were needed, especially medical personnel. Chinese church support, while generous, was inadequate and fluctuating, so aid from the cooperating missions (one-third to one-half of the total needed) would be welcomed.

Dr. W. S. Flowers, a British missionary doctor working with the Chinese Christian Medical Council and a member of the team that went to Sichang, noted in a separate report (typescript) that the Sikang people were heavily afflicted by goiter, opium addiction, and malnutrition. The tribespeople suffered from the same problems, as well as from leprosy and alcoholism. Sanitary conditions, especially for the tribespeople, were appalling. They scorned soap and water. Internecine warfare among the Lolos was common, as were raids on Chinese towns to capture slaves for heavy labor. Flowers proposed an expanded program of preventative and healing medicine in an area where there were virtually no medical facilities for a population of about eight million people.

The August 1949 number of *The Church* reported that in the spring of 1948 community leaders in Zakulao, Szechuan (where there had initially been strong opposition to the work of the Mission), had presented the Mission with "the best site in town" for a hospital, with the promise to furnish all the timber and part of the bricks and tiles for a building. The effort to develop local leadership had had some success in Sikang, as it was also reported that two Lolos were teaching in mission schools and another was preparing to teach at the Union Normal School in Hankow.

The Yunnan Mission

The third mission program of the Church was undertaken in Yunnan, another of the remote and mountainous provinces of the Southwest. Dr. W. H. Clark (Presbyterian USA) had worked for some years with students and intellectuals in Changsha, Hunan. On his return from furlough in the autumn of 1938, the Japanese armies were pushing into Hunan and the General Assembly office asked Clark to undertake work with the refugee students who had flocked into Kunming, the capital of Yunnan.

Kunming, at an altitude of six thousand four hundred feet above sea level, the northern terminus of the Haiphong-Yunnan Railroad, was situated in the midst of mountains and lakes, with a mild and pleasant climate. A backward provincial capital before the war, with limited educational facilities, it was chosen for the relocation of such schools as the National Southwest Union University (made up of refugees from the three great North China universities—Nankai, Peking, and Tsinghua) and Chung Cheng Medical College.

By 1940 it was clear that there was need for some Christian group to assume responsibility for work in southern Yunnan. The Chinese Home Missionary Society had opened work about 1920 in this lawless, remote, and difficult area. By 1924 there were six Chinese missionaries at work, wholly supported, though very inadequately, by the contributions of Chinese Christians. In 1940 only one of them remained at work, a Mrs. Wu, a devoted, faithful, but very tired worker who had reached the age of retirement and wanted to return home.

She urged the Church of Christ in China to come in and shepherd the scattered flock of believers. Other mission and church groups heartily concurred, as this had been virtually the only Christian work in this vast area. Clark visited the main towns, Kokiu, Kienshui, and Shihping, in 1939 and 1940 to study the situation, and two students of Canton Union Theological College (then relocated in West Yunnan) went to south Yunnan for summer work under CCC auspices in 1940.

A. R. Kepler, along with C. W. Shoop and Frank Oldt of the Brethren Mission, visited Yunnan in February 1941 to look into the need. When Kepler reported back, the General Assembly office decided that the Church should undertake this responsibility. Clark was asked to be Secretary of the Directing Committee.

As a first step, it was decided that a church should be established in Kunming. This was begun in late 1941 with the cooperation and encouragement of the YMCA and the Chinese Methodist Church and British missionaries working with it. The Rev. and Mrs. T. K. Chiu from Mid-Fukien began the work in a rented building. Local Chinese support was good, and eventually land was bought and a chapel and manse erected with the gifts of Chinese Christians, many of them refugees from occupied territory. Under the able leadership of the Chius, the congregation grew to almost two hundred.

Mrs. Chiu organized an excellent primary school, and the Yunnan Mission joined with the Chinese Methodist Church in the work of the T'ien Nan Middle School, the only Christian secondary school in Yunnan. In 1947 new buildings for the school were erected outside the city, and the Rev. and Mrs. J. C. Eldon Andrews (Canadian Presbyterian) were assigned to teach there, following language study in Peking. Miss Helena Gibbs (Canadian Presbyterian) served in Kunming for about a year, arriving in 1942, before going to Chengtu to assist in the office of the Provisional General Assembly. The Rev. and Mrs. V. J. Jasper (Baptist Missionary Society, Shantung) also assisted in church work for a brief period in 1942. The Rev. Kenneth J. Foreman, Jr., joined the Kunming staff in September 1949 and was the last of the Western missionaries to leave Yunnan.

The character of the Yunnan Mission was somewhat different than that of the other two missions of the Church. Kweichow and the Border Mission were essentially missions of the Chinese Church, with support primarily from domestic sources and the staff almost completely Chinese. The Yunnan Mission was a unique experiment which sought to begin new work on the basis of a joint effort of mission boards with the Chinese Church. Nevertheless it was to be a "church-centric" (a term central in the thinking of CCC staff for many years) rather than a "mission-centric" enterprise. There was no foreign mission organization, nor were there foreign mission stations. All foreign missionaries were to be responsible to the General Assembly and its agencies for their work and assignments. Through the North American Advisory Committee and the counterpart body in the United Kingdom, the following boards and societies cooperated with the General Assembly from 1941-1952 by the provision of funds and/or personnel:

The Baptist Missionary Society
The Evangelical and United Brethren Church
The London Missionary Society
The Presbyterian Church of Australia
The Presbyterian Church in Canada
The Presbyterian Church of England
The Presbyterian Church in Ireland
The Presbyterian Church in the USA
The Reformed Church in America

The work in southern Yunnan developed only slowly during the war period. Yunnan was still quite primitive and extremely isolated. Bandits were active throughout the countryside, and in the tin-mining center of Kokiu violence was rampant. The Central government, straining all its resources in the war with Japan, had little control over the local situation. Kunming itself, a major center for the transshipment of war supplies coming through Burma, was constantly under Japanese attack from the air, while mounting inflation seriously affected the economy.

However, a beginning was made by Dr. C. W. Shoop (United Brethren), who had been a leader in the Kwangtung Synod and taught at the Canton Union Theological Seminary, and by the Rev. Ralph G. Coonradt (Presbyterian USA), who joined the staff in 1944.

The first work outside of Kunming was begun at Kienshui, an old walled city with a population of more than forty thousand. Set in a rich agricultural valley, the county was populated largely by Chinese, with numerous tribespeople in the surrounding mountains. Mr. Coonradt, who served as Field Secretary of the Mission 1944-46 (Clark had returned to the U.S. on health leave in 1942) opened up the work. He was eventually succeeded by Mr. and Mrs. Everett Teng of Hupei in 1945. A church was established, with good attendance and programs for young people and children.

In 1946 a hospital was opened in a local temple with thirty beds (later expanded to fifty). Mrs. Mildred Gehman, R.N. (Canadian Presbyterian from Manchuria), opened the medical work in 1945, finally leaving on furlough in 1949. Early in 1946 Helen Mackenzie, M.D., and Sister Catherine Mackenzie (Australian Presbyterians) arrived. Together with Irene Watkins and Margaret Cranstoun (also Australian Presbyterians), they worked in Kienshui for some months before going to Peking for a year of language study. Meanwhile, Drs. Hsing and Chow took charge of the medical work for a year (1946-47). Dr. and Mrs. C. H. Chang came in 1947 from Shantung. Dr. Chang was superintendent of the hospital 1947-49. In 1948 the Mackenzie sisters returned from language study and greatly strengthened the medical work. A number of other Chinese medical and evangelistic personnel also came to help in the work of the mission at Kienshui.

The Clarks, who had gone on health furlough in 1942, returned to Kunming in 1946, and Dr. Clark was again appointed Field Secretary of the mission. By this time a strong local Yunnan Mission Committee had been organized, composed mostly of Chinese Christian laymen, with full responsibility for the work, under the General Assembly, including the assignment of all personnel. The Chairman for much of the time was F. C. Lin, Managing Director of the Yunnan railroads.

Dr. Clark frequently visited the cities of southern Yunnan on behalf of the mission in this period. The needs of Kokiu and the mining area in the mountains around the city were especially impelling. Thousands of boys, because of their small stature, were used in the mines under conditions of near slavery (many of them kept in chains until 1940). Most of the mines were narrow, damp, and poorly lighted and conditions were unspeakably bad. A substantial proportion of the world's supply of tin was produced in Kokiu, enriching many mine owners at the expense of exploited child labor.

The Central government opened a modern mine about 1940 which employed mostly men, rather than boys, under much improved conditions. Because the price for tin decreased after the war, many of the privately owned mines closed down. On the nine-thousand-foot peak outside the city, where formerly tens of thousands of workers had lived (mostly boys), only eight thousand or so remained. But some thirty thousand people still lived in the city of Kokiu far below, and their needs were great. Because it lacked personnel, the mission was never able to undertake any major program at the mines, but a preaching center was opened in Kokiu by the Rev. and Mrs. Peter Sun of Hupei in 1945.

Shihping was another city in which Mrs. Wu of the Chinese Home Missionary Society had done some work over the years. The Yunnan Mission was committed to work there, where some twenty to thirty Christians lived and where there were no medical facilities. A Friends Service Unit, invited by the Yunnan Mission Committee for a few months in 1948, helped in a serious epidemic of malignant malaria, with some aid from the Kienshui Hospital. The mission planned to open a branch of the hospital at Shihping, but the *1950-51 Prayer Calendar of the Yunnan Mission* stated "no permanent work yet opened, due to the lack of personnel."

In the church work in Kienshui, the Rev. and Mrs. R. Malcolm Ransom (Canadian Presbyterians) came to assist in 1946. The Misses Margaret Cranstoun (later transferred to Kunming) and Irene Watkins helped in religious education and general church work with the Kienshui Church. Miss C. S. Pai of Manchuria came in 1948 as an evangelist with women, youth, and children.

The Rev. S. S. Sun (Sun Shou-hsin), formerly pastor of a large CCC church in Tsinan, Shantung, arrived in June 1948 and became pastor of the Kunming Church when the T. K. Chius, after seven years of hard work, left for study abroad. Miss Mamie Johnston (Irish Presbyterian formerly in Manchuria) came to Kunming in August of the same year and worked as superintendent of the Kindergarten Training Center of the excellent New Village School, as well as in religious education work in church and school. Dr. Clark left Yunnan in October 1949 for reasons of health and family (his family having left China in June), and on June 1, 1949, S. S. Sun agreed to serve as Field Director of the Yunnan Mission.

The October 1948 issue of *The Church* reported that the Chinese Home Missionary Society was unable to continue its work at Mengtzu. At their request, the Yunnan Mission assumed responsibility and assigned the Rev. Hu Cheng-kuo, an experienced pastor from Manchuria, to serve the church of about one hundred members. The Rev. C. C. Pi from Manchuria was assigned to assist, especially in the country work.

Work had been begun at Kaiyuan in 1947, where Rev. and Mrs. C. S. Wei of Anhwei guided a growing congregation from 1948 and Mr. and Mrs. Coonradt served until leaving for furlough in the spring of 1949. Miss Watkins also served for a period in Kaiyuan. Miss C. F. Chow from Manchuria, after having worked in Kunming for a year, was transferred to Kaiyuan in 1949 to work with women and children.

A chapel was established at Hsiaoshihpa (ten miles outside Kunming) and church services and Bible classes were held there by Kunming staff. As attendance increased, a church building was erected with the gifts of Chinese Christians. Mr. Frank Shu (Hsu Ming-hsien), a Christian businessman, was especially generous in supporting this project and other work of the Yunnan Mission. The Rev. and Mrs. N. T. Wen from Hunan served there briefly, as well as at Kienshui and Kaiyuan, but had to take leave because of a serious health problem. *The Church* reported, "The CCC now has work in the five most important towns in south Yunnan: Mengtzu, Kaiyuan, Kokiu, Kienshui and Shihping, all connected by a narrow gauge railroad."

Kunming was occupied by the advancing Communist armies in December 1949. The other centers where the Mission was at work changed hands about the same time, with sharp fighting in some places, followed by bombing by Nationalist planes. It soon became evident that it would be best for the foreign missionaries to leave. Helen and Catherine Mackenzie, Irene Watkins, and Malcolm Ransom were instructed by the Yunnan Mission Committee to leave Kienshui in June 1950. They were reluctant to do so, feeling that it would be possible to continue work, but yielded to the decision of the Committee. They left by jeep for Burma, arriving there in August. Margaret Cranstoun and Mamie Johnston were granted exit permits in early 1951 and left by way of Chungking. The Andrews family left Kunming on November 1, 1950. Kenneth Foreman was put under house arrest in mid-1951 and held in a Chinese inn for six months before being expelled from China early in 1952.

Dr. Clark, with long experience in the work of the Yunnan Mission, summed up some of its strengths and weaknesses. The Mission was fortunate in the quality of the Chinese pastors and evangelists who served it and in the able laymen on the Yunnan Mission Committee. He speaks with appreciation of the cooperative spirit of other churches in the area, especially the Chinese Methodists and the British missionaries working with them. The sacrificial and enthusiastic spirit of the missionaries who assisted, both those with previous experience and the newcomers, was a valuable asset. The support and contributions of Christian refugees, especially in Kunming, was of prime importance. There were over five hundred communicant members in the Yunnan Mission churches by 1949.

On the other hand, he felt that support from the missions was too great compared to local support, though in 1947 42% of the church finances came from local contributions, while nearly 90% of the educational budget and 61% of the medical budget came from local fees or gifts. As compared with the two other CCC missions, the proportion of foreign missionary staff was large. It would have been better if the Mission had been under a Chinese director at a much earlier date. The missionary imbalance was in part because Yunnan was one of the few places in post-war China where work could be carried on without serious interference and also because of the nature of the program as a joint church-mission project. Finally, although the publicity given the inhuman conditions of child labor in the tin mines helped to ameliorate the situation, no effective work with the miners was undertaken, in spite of the intent of the mission so to do.

Yunnan was certainly a significant venture in mission. It provided an outstanding if imperfect example of a new approach in church-mission cooperation. It opened a field of service for missionary personnel and funds in a difficult period and helped conserve the interest of the churches in the West at a critical juncture. Conserving the work of the Chinese Home Missionary Society and spreading the Gospel to new Christians in five organized congregations and other preaching places was a contribution of some significance. The educational work, particularly at the excellent middle school in Kunming, and the medical work at Kienshui brought learning and healing to many in need of them.

Appraisal

These ventures in mission have been dealt with in considerable detail because they were an important part of the history of the Church of Christ in China. They represented programs which sought to be expressive of the whole church and to enlist the concern and support of all the diverse elements that made it up. They symbolized the Chinese Christian assumption of responsibility for mission within their own country and their willingness to give sacrificial service in distant and unfamiliar situations. They were also an attempt, however modest, to understand the culture of primitive and exploited minorities within their own country and to bridge the gap between cultures.

Other Christian groups were also at work, well before the CCC mission began, in the Southwest and among the tribespeople. These included the China Inland Mission, the British Methodists, and the home mission effort of the Sheng Kung Hui (Anglican-Episcopal Church) in Yunnan-Kweichow, as well as the Chinese Home Missionary Society. But the earlier programs were initiated and administered chiefly by foreign missionaries. Our concern is with mission enterprises conceived, directed, and to a very large extent manned by Chinese Christians. The substantial help given by foreign missionaries, especially in the Yunnan Mission, and the large dependence on the financial support of Western mission boards did not change the basic fact that these were missions undertaken by a Chinese church as their responsibility and an important part of the history of that church.

The three missions of the Church of Christ in China, while each a valid expression of the deep desire of the Chinese leadership of the Church to reach the unevangelized people of their own nation with the Gospel and to minister to the neglected in the spirit of Christian love, differed in their essential nature.

The first venture, the Kweichow Mission, was intended to be solely a mission of the church itself. While a few foreign missionaries were involved, largely because the war situation made it impossible for them to continue in other areas, the intent was for the leadership and support to be that of the Chinese church. During the most difficult of the war years, it became necessary to supplement Chinese support with help from foreign mission sources, but by and large the principle of Chinese support was adhered to.

The second venture, in the border areas, was from the first under able Chinese leadership. It was an attempt to reach neglected people with extensive educational, medical, and social services, as well as with the Christian message. While substantial financial support came from the cooperating mission boards, the personnel of the Mission was almost entirely Chinese. By its very nature it was a joint enterprise with government and secular agencies. The Central government discontinued financial support after 1947, but substantial aid was obtained from relief agencies for the service programs.

The third venture, Yunnan, was still different in that it was a mission of the Chinese church in which a number of missionary societies from the West cooperated by invitation of the church. Therefore the role of the foreign missionary was more prominent, though responsibility and direction for the work of the Mission were from the first that of the CCC itself, through the General Assembly and eventually through a strong local Yunnan Mission Committee.

Were these ventures in mission an important element in the life of the Church of Christ in China? Did their work have significant results in the areas where the programs were carried on? A qualified affirmative would seem to be justified. Judgment could have been much clearer if the programs had been able to continue for a longer period. A span of ten years or less hardly permits a fair judgment. Certainly the development of the mission program of the Church and especially the devotion and commitment of those engaged in it were part of the process of growth and verification of the Church of Christ in China as a Chinese church at the national level. The widespread interest, support, and participation in the mission program were strong unifying factors throughout the Church.

A mimeographed report entitled "The Missions of the Church of Christ in China," issued in June 1950, indicates that at that time there were one hundred and ten workers in the three fields (pastors, teachers, and medical and social work personnel). In the Kweichow Mission there was one city church (Kweiyang), along with five other churches or chapels, and there were two primary schools and one kindergarten. In Yunnan there was one city church (Kunming), along with six other churches or chapels, and there was one middle school, one primary school, one kindergarten, and one hospital. In the border area there were five churches or chapels, ten primary schools, and seven hospitals or clinics, and there was one child welfare center, a hostel for tribespeople, a center for agricultural improvement, a center for animal husbandry, and an experimental station.

While small when compared with the total scale of Christian work in China, this certainly represented a considerable program for the missions of the CCC, developed largely during the war period when communications and finances posed serious problems and in remote areas where living conditions were difficult. The total budget for the mission programs in 1950 was only US$36,000 (two-thirds of the total budget of the CCC General Assembly office—exceedingly modest compared to the total amount involved in the synodical and institutional work of the Church). A third of the mission budget was to be raised in China through contributions and fees. The Kweichow Mission was supported entirely from Chinese sources, the others were receiving support from the cooperating mission societies. While the General Assembly had general oversight, each mission had a local committee, mostly laymen, and a Chinese director.

The appeal of this kind of work to Chinese Christians was seen in the response of students, especially in the Border Mission, and the willingness of a considerable number of pastors, teachers, doctors, and nurses to go to distant and difficult areas, where the pay was minimal and the work hazardous and demanding.

While the total effort of the missions of the Church of Christ in China was modest in the light of the vast areas involved and the great need, it was a valid expression of genuine Christian concern. Success was limited and failures frequent, but within its scope the missions represented a modest achievement and a positive contribution to responsibility for mission on the part of the Church.

There are many incidents that reveal the spirit of the workers. In one Lolo village, work was begun at the invitation of the local chief, in spite of his reputation as a bandit. Three times in the first year the little group of Chinese missionaries had their homes broken into and their meagre belongings, including their clothes and their cooking utensils, stolen from them. As W. B. Djang told the story in his 1948 radio broadcast:

> The missionaries were determined to endure all that may come with patience. In the end the old chief was touched and promised that nothing of the kind will happen again. . . . The missionaries won the final victory. . . . The old man is becoming a new man with a changed heart. Instead of being "the devil's pass" (the popular name for the village) the place has become a welcome stopping place for travellers in that lonely country.

The mission, especially in the Border Mission and among the savage Lolos, often succeeded in winning the confidence of the tribespeople by sacrificial service and self-denying love, where government efforts, often employing force and military suppression, had not. The Christian workers met suspicion with friendship, hostility with kindness, and violence with love. Fisher summarized the accomplishments well when he wrote about the Border Mission:

> It has brought the light of the gospel to those who for centuries have been neglected. . . . It has given friendship to those who felt themselves outside. It has shown love where there was hate, fellowship where there was segregation and, above all, shown the way of eternal truth of the God of love and the Savior from sin.

Chapter Nine

Rehabilitation
and
Renewal (1945-49)

The Political Situation at the End of the War with Japan

The end of the war with Japan in August 1945 found China battered and weary, its cities crowded with refugees. The nation was almost bankrupt, there was a rampant black market, and inflation was so serious that prices sometimes doubled overnight. There had been massive destruction and transportation was completely disrupted, with most of the railroads in the occupied areas non-operative. The nation was divided, with the Communists in control of most of North China outside the major cities. Untra-conservative elements were influential in the Central government, and a demoralized bureaucracy was ill-prepared to assume power in the areas that had been occupied by the Japanese.

On the other hand, China had attained its most prestigious international status in modern times. It was allied with the victorious powers of the West. Territory taken by the Japanese in Formosa and Manchuria had been returned. A permanent seat in the United Nations Security Council as one of the five great powers confirmed China's position of influence.

Soviet troops moved into Manchuria the day after the atom bomb was dropped on Hiroshima, with virtually no opposition from the once-powerful Japanese Kwantung Army, which meekly laid down its arms. Major Chinese Communist forces quickly swarmed into the Northeast and were rewarded by great stores of war materials stockpiled by the Japanese. Enormously strengthened by the acquisition of such equipment, the Communists were given time to take over local police and government apparatus throughout Manchuria, as the Soviet troops moved out a few days ahead of the arrival of the Nationalist armies. The Russians also removed virtually all machinery and tools from this most highly industrialized area of China. Many of the personal effects of the Chinese population had been taken also in a thorough campaign of looting and rape in the short period of Soviet occupation. American planes and ships quickly moved half a million Nationalist troops to the coastal cities and the cities of the Northeast to accept the submission of remaining Japanese troops and forestall occupation by Communist forces.

People in occupied areas generally welcomed the Nationalists back after the hard years under the Japanese. But in many cases they were quickly disillusioned by the inefficiency and rapacity of officials critical of those who had not fled the invaders and eager to make up for the lean years of deprivation and austerity in Free China. Nationalist leadership was in no mood to modify its claim to complete control. Nor were the Communists, confident in their greatly increased power and control of most of the North China countryside, ready to yield in their demands for full participation in national power and their eventual aim of complete control.

Skirmishing between the two factions, which had continued sporadically through the war years, became more serious, despite efforts by the United States to encourage negotiation and to set up a coalition government. General George Marshall was sent to China as a mediator and a three-party headquarters was set up in Peking for negotiations. Leaders of the two factions were brought together, but to no avail. The Nationalist forces moved against the Communist armies in North China with some initial success, but poor planning and overextended lines soon reversed the tide and the relentless pressure of the Communist armies increased and eventually became irresistible.

The Christian Church at the Close of the War

The church and its institutions, as noted at the close of the last chapter, had been seriously affected by the attrition of the war years. Displaced institutions began the long trek back to their original sites, but many buildings had been destroyed and many institutions had disappeared and were never reestablished. The Christian Medical Council reported at the end of 1946 that of two hundred seventy Christian hospitals functioning in 1937 thirty-nine had been closed or destroyed and there was no report on twenty-eight others, which were presumably closed also. Some of the middle schools had been so badly damaged or staff so completely dispersed that they never reopened. But all of the refugee Christian colleges and universities, including the six medical colleges, were soon back in their old locations.

Substantial resources were contributed by the mission boards for the restoration of buildings, and relief funds and materials were made available to alleviate the needs of church workers. Great quantities of medical supplies were purchased by the mission boards from surplus military supplies and shipped in to help the hospitals get under way again. While large numbers of church workers had been forced into secular work in occupied areas to keep their families alive, many had remained in Christian service at great personal sacrifice.

Missionaries trickled back to the areas which had been under Japanese control—some directly from the sending lands, some flown in from Free China, some from Japanese internment camps. Many who had left China early in the war never returned. By late 1946 and early 1947, however, substantial numbers of new missionaries, most of them well-trained and well aware of the changing status of the missionary and the primacy of the church, were moving in.

A number of the mission boards sent deputations of board members and executives to survey the situation and discuss relationships with the Chinese church leadership. For example, such a deputation from the Board of Foreign Missions of the Presbyterian Church USA visited all areas of China where there had historically been relationships and then spent ten days in a Conference on Restoration and Advance in December 1946 in Shanghai, meeting with sixty Chinese and missionary representatives. The deputation strongly recommended that responsibility for evangelistic, educational, and medical work, where it still remained with the mission, be transferred to the synods of the Church of Christ in China, with requests for missionary personnel and assignments handled through the General Assembly office in consultation with the Presbyterian China Council (representing the seven former missions of the Board in China). "The development of the Christian Church as the central and indispensable factor of Christian life . . . [was to be] the ruling motive of all considerations." It also recommended that the "established policy" of transferring property used for church and chapel work to the CCC General Assembly be implemented at once, with the eventual transfer of all institutional property.

In early 1947 a group of fourteen prominent Protestant church leaders, alarmed by the expanding civil war, presented a statement to General A. C. Wedemeyer, who represented the United States in seeking to reconcile the Communists and the Nationalists and bring them into cooperation (among the signers were Samuel K. Ing, a Christian businessman who was Chairman of the CCC General Council, H. H. Tsui, and several other lay members of the General Council). The statement pointed out that China's internal situation was critical, with division and dependence on military measures increasing, and emphasized the desire of the Chinese people for peace and democracy. As Christians, the petitioners expressed their hope that peaceful solutions could be worked out and suggested that in negotiations there be:

1. Full participation of liberal elements in the formulation and execution of national and local programs of reform;
2. Granting and protection of the fundamental rights of the people as citizens of a democracy, such as freedom of speech, freedom of assembly. . . ;
3. Safeguarding the livelihood of the people who have suffered so much through the ravages of the last war;
4. Strengthening of the judicial system to put process of law above personal influence and judgment.

In regard to American policy toward China, the statement suggested (1) that this be a policy designed to assist China become free, united, strong, and democratic; (2) that financial aid be administered honestly and efficiently; (3) that American policy toward China and Japan be such as "to promote peace in the Far East, on which the peace of the world depends."

The National Christian Council held its first postwar meeting in Shanghai December 3-11, 1946—the first full meeting of the Council since the Eleventh Biennial Meeting in May 1937. Bishop W. Y. Chen was still very active in the work of the Council as Honorary General Secretary; George K. T. Wu was the Acting General Secretary (later elected General Secretary). There were eighty-five voting members present, of whom seventy-four were representatives of thirteen member churches and national organizations and eleven were co-opted. Others in attendance included fraternal delegates from nonmember churches, invited visitors, and representatives of missionary societies visiting China.

The theme was "The Church and the Future of China." President Chiang Kai-shek sent a message of commendation and encouragement, and the Council issued a statement expressing concern over divisions and decline in the body politic and a plea for conciliation and cooperation in the rebuilding of the nation. A three-year, nation-wide Forward Movement "which will aim at strengthening the inner life of the Church and at making the service of the Church to the nation more far-reaching and significant" was approved. Reports were given on the work of the Council during the war years and on the postwar relief program. After a vote of appreciation for the long service of Dr. Wu Yi-fang, President of Ginling College, as Chairman for eleven years (1935-1947), Dr. S. C. Leung, General Secretary of the National Committee of the YMCA of China and an active CCC leader, was elected Chairman.

The Protestant Service Department of the American Advisory Committee (major coordinating agency for relief and rehabilitation) reported that in early 1948 there were 1465 students in forty-seven training institutions for Christian work, an encouraging increase since the greatly curtailed program of theological education during the war period. Eleven of these institutions were of middle school grade and thirteen were Bible schools for the lower grades. The Women's World Day of Prayer was widely observed through the churches of China in February 1948 with the help of materials made available through the National Christian Council.

In early 1948 the Yun-Kwei Synod of the Sheng Kung Hui, formerly a missionary diocese, held its first Diocesan Synod, with Quentin K. Y. Huang as Bishop. The Rev. Newton Y. C. Liu was consecrated Bishop of the Sheng Kung Hui missionary diocese of Shensi about the same time. This period was also marked by the development of regional Christian councils as agencies of cooperation in many areas, including North China, Kwangtung, Fukien, Shansi, and Kiangsu.

In 1946 the National Christian Council set up a Committee on Student Evangelism and by the end of 1947 was able to report programs in seven university centers. These were conducted in cooperation with the YMCA and YWCA, and sixteen secretaries were at work (ten men and six women—of whom eleven were Chinese, five missionaries). The Thirteenth Biennial meeting of the NCC was held in Shanghai November 1-9, 1948. A report prepared for the meeting by George K. T. Wu, the General Secretary, spoke of the widespread observance of the Forward Movement, including evangelistic campaigns in many places. Unfortunately, no report on the meeting itself is available.

In the immediate postwar years, it was proposed that the Christian educational institutions in the Shanghai area be merged into a single strong university, the East China Union University, with the constituent units specializing in designated fields, thus eliminating duplication of the basic educational requirements of the first two college years and using faculty and equipment to the best advantage. Involved were St. John's University (Sheng Kung Hui), which included an excellent medical school; Soochow University (Methodist) with a strong emphasis on law training; and Hangchow Christian University (Presbyterian) with a strong emphasis on engineering. (Shanghai University, related to the American Baptist and Southern Baptist Conventions, chose not to participate.) A Board of Directors for the proposed union university had been set up and had begun functioning, and specific plans for specialization had been completed (arts and medicine at St. John's; law and science at Soochow; engineering and business at Hangchow) when the changing political scene made it impossible to proceed further.

The China Christian Educational Association celebrated its seventieth anniversary at Union Church, Shanghai, in October 1947. Delegates from one hundred and twenty institutions and organizations attended, and thirteen provinces were represented. Among the speakers was Dr. J. Leighton Stuart, formerly President of Yenching University, who had recently been appointed the American Ambassador to China. The Christian Literature Society celebrated its seventy-fifth anniversary in 1947. The National Christian Council's Christian Home Committee held its first postwar meeting in Shanghai on December 1947, with sixty attendants. A statement on the work of the Committee included these words:

> The universal breakdown of family life, especially among the educated people, is a cause of great concern. The old Confucian ethics are not being taught in schools and we have a correspondingly greater responsibility for teaching the Christian Way of life.

CCC Program and Activities

In the Church of Christ in China, the General Assembly offices were moved back to Shanghai soon after the close of the war. Living conditions were difficult, prices were high, and inflation was serious. Workers were exhausted after the tensions and privations of the war years. But there was also pride that China had survived as an independent nation, a sense of accomplishment that the church had maintained its identity and carried on meaningful programs, and a determination and hope for a better day for China and its people.

The Standing Committee of the General Assembly met (apparently for the first time after the war) on February 11, 1946. A

Committee on Coordination of Relief Activities was set up to handle the considerable sums that were coming, chiefly from the cooperating missions, for the relief and rehabilitation of war-weary Chinese church workers. The Rev. C. S. Chu (Chu Chen-sheng), from Shensi Synod, who was active in the work for wounded soldiers during the war and later became editor of the CCC's *Kung Pao* (Chinese-language periodical), was asked to join the staff as Rehabilitation Secretary.

A. J. Fisher had come to Shanghai at the request of the CCC for a special year of post-retirement service to "assist in setting up the post-war program of the Church." W. H. Clark had returned to the work of the CCC mission in Yunnan, and the Standing Committee at its April 18, 1946, meeting expressed its welcome to these two men. It was proposed that W. B. Djang visit Formosa with C. C. Chen, the Moderator of the General Assembly, "to discuss church cooperation there." In June 1946 Bruce Copland returned from furlough in Canada and resumed his responsibilities as Executive Secretary.

Conditions were still too disrupted to permit a meeting of the General Assembly, but on October 7-11, 1946, an enlarged meeting of the General Council was held in Nanking. This was the first General Council meeting since 1937 (the regular biennial meetings could not be held during the years of the war with Japan). All but five synods were represented by thirteen synodical representatives. Twelve others were co-opted, while fifteen representatives of the cooperating missions (including members of deputations from several home boards) were also present. The Yunnan Mission was represented by two staff members and its Chairman, the Kweichow Mission by its Director, and the Border Service Department by the Director and a staff member, as well as a church member.

Reports were made on the wartime services of the CCC. These included (1) relief and refugee work; (2) the ministry to wounded soldiers through the National Christian Service Council for Wounded Soldiers in Transit, formed under the leadership of A. R. Kepler and T. C. Fan; (3) Christian literature work, continued and extended when new presses were acquired by the Canadian Mission Press in Changtu; (4) the establishment of the three missions of the Church.

H. H. Tsui was elected General Secretary, confirming the 1943 action of the Provincial Council, with provision for a period of rest after his years of strenuous service. The action of the Provisional Council electing E. Bruce Copland as Executive Secretary was also confirmed. It was recommended that the C. Y. Cheng and A. R. Kepler Memorial Fund "be further augmented" in providing scholarships for students in theological schools and training institutions. A separate A. R. Kepler Memorial Scholarship Fund had been set up by the National Christian Service Council for Wounded Soldiers before it was dissolved after the close of the war. The modest proceeds from sale of the Council's property in Chungking were used for this purpose, and W. Y. Chen, General Secretary of the National Christian Council, was elected Chairman and George Geng Executive Secretary of the fund, which was converted into U.S. currency because of inflation and is now administered by the Chinese Christian Fellowship of New York. The Council approved the Provisional Council action of August 1945, recommending full support of the General Assembly work from Chinese sources within eight years. For the next five years, support was to be sought one-third from the Chinese churches, one-third from other Chinese gifts, and one-third from the cooperating missions.

A Missions Cooperating Council had been organized in Shanghai in 1941 but had been unable to function because of the war. The General Council now recommended formation of a joint Conference of Representatives of Cooperating Missions as an agency of coordination and cooperation.

An important step forward in church-mission relations was taken at this meeting. Recognizing that there were still many areas in China unreached by Christianity, the Council saw the task of evangelizing the unoccupied areas of China as a first duty of the Church, but also as a responsibility of the missions. Therefore it urged that any such outreach be a joint project and that the boards establish no new mission work except in consultation with the Church and in the pattern of the three existing missions of the Church. Growing out of this discussion was the recommendation that a Board of National Missions be organized "as recommended by the Fourth General Assembly" and that each synod and district association organize a committee on national missions to promote this work and educate the whole membership of the Church.

Church workers and church property had suffered greatly during the war years. Substantial relief funds were made available by the Relief and Rehabilitation Fund of the Board of Foreign Missions of the Presbyterian Church in the USA and other cooperating missions. The General Assembly staff, having worked out equitable principles for the distribution of such funds, was able to help pastors and other church workers in most areas of the Church. (It was impossible for the Northeast, Shansi, Shantung, and North China Synods to provide the needed information because of disturbed conditions in the immediate postwar period.) Families of a substantial number of church workers and lay leaders who had been killed during the war were also given assistance. In order to further help war-weary church workers, grants had been made to Hopei, Lianghu, and Shansi Synods to hold retreats, and provision was made for short-term refresher courses at Nanking Theological Seminary.

General Assembly staff had travelled widely in the postwar period, providing leadership for retreats and discussing rehabilitation with local churches and judicatories, reaching all the synods except Shansi, Shantung, and Hainan. The General Council also gratefully accepted the offer of the Union Church of Shanghai (which ministered chiefly to the British community) for the use of the church building for General Assembly offices and a meeting place, with payment of nominal rent and responsibility for repairs, thus providing the staff with much-needed office space at minimal cost.

The Standing Committee met frequently in the following months. On October 26, 1946, at the request of the Northeast Synod, it voted to ask the General Assembly's legal department to investigate the possibility of securing the release of Japanese church property in Manchuria for use in religious purposes, with the understanding that it would be held in trust for future use by the Japanese church owners. This was intended to save church property from confiscation and secular use.

In response to a request from the East China Synod, it was resolved to ask all CCC-related schools to give special consideration in the matter of fees to the children of church workers and to seek to provide scholarship aid for such purposes from available relief funds. The cooperating missions were asked to consider grants for this purpose and the synods urged to raise funds.

The Rev. W. B. Djang submitted his resignation as Director of the Border Service Mission. After careful consideration, the Committee expressed its appreciation for and confidence in his leadership of the Mission and asked him to withdraw his resignation and continue as Director.

At the Standing Committee meeting of November 8, 1946, a committee appointed at the previous meeting to consider the administrative relationship of the Border Service Department to the General Assembly, with Dr. S. C. Leung, General Secretary of the YMCA of China, as Chairman, reported back: "The nature of the work, the sources of financial support . . . and the magnitude of the task make clear that this work is different in many ways from our task in Kweichow and Yunnan." Additional staff was needed to carry on the program. But though the participation of "other missions" had been invited, thus far only the CCC had taken responsibility. Direct relationship to the General Assembly should continue, the report stated, every effort should be made to raise needed funds for medical, educational, and social service programs from the government and other sources, and the synods and cooperating missions should assist the work with funds and personnel. The possibility of other churches participating should be investigated.

Dr. Tsui, in conformity with the action of the General Council, was granted six months leave of absence. He spent most of that time with his family in Peking, from whom he had been separated for years. He had been found to be a diabetic, which posed a serious health problem for him for many years. C. T. Tsai returned from study in the United States in December 1946 and after a visit with his family in Amoy resumed his duties with the CCC General Assembly office in March, 1947. During Dr. Tsui's health leave, Bruce Copland was Acting General Secretary. In a "Memorandum on the Work of the General Assembly" reported to the Standing Committee on April 3, 1947, he pointed out that while some synods were now functioning well, others were not yet organized and looked to the General Assembly staff for guidance. The relationship with the synods had been strengthened in recent years by the substantial distribution of relief by the General Assembly office.

Through the early postwar years, the General Assembly staff was responsible not only for distributing sizeable relief funds to workers and institutions, but also for helping to plan and to provide leadership for synodical conferences and retreats. A widespread program of visitation and consultation by General Assembly staff to synods and district associations was carried on—a strong unifying factor in the life of the CCC. Virtually every synodical meeting had a General Assembly staff representative present.

It was reported at the June 5, 1947, meeting of the Standing Committee that the United Church of North India had offered to send an Indian missionary to help in the work of the CCC. The Committee expressed its warm welcome for such an arrangement and the Acting General Secretary was authorized to take responsibility for such an assignment in consultation with Church leaders. (There is no further record of this proposal and presumably because of the changing situation it was never effectuated.) At the same meeting, the Rev. Wu Yik-wang, one of the pioneers in the Kweichow Mission and for some years on the staff of the Kwangtung Synod, was invited to join the General Assembly staff as an Executive Secretary after his return from study in the United States. (Apparently he served for only a few months in late 1948.)

Church-Mission Relations

The Joint Conference of Representatives of Mission Boards Cooperating with the Church of Christ in China (one of those awkward titles to which church bodies seem prone) was set up by the General Council meeting of October 1946. The Joint Conference met only three times, however: November 27-28, 1947 (Shanghai); October 20, 1949 (Soochow); and November 22, 1959 (Hong Kong). There was also one ad interim committee meeting on September 30, 1948, and an unofficial meeting with eleven cooperating missions represented in Hong Kong on March 9, 1950, to discuss the situation of the CCC in China. Representation of the mission boards was not complete at any of the meetings, but in each case a majority was present. For the most part, discussion concerned the budgets of the CCC and mission support for them and matters related to responsibility for assigning missionaries.

At the 1947 meeting it was agreed that the missions of the Church should be supported from Chinese sources (including contributions from Chinese churches abroad) but that until conditions became more normal, the mission boards would continue to assist with funds and personnel except in Kweichow, which was to be solely a Chinese church venture. It was agreed also that the most pressing need of the Chinese church was for training in leadership. Since the Church was as yet unable to assume full financial responsibility, the missions would give needed assistance. It was decided that all funds given by the missions for evangelistic work should go to the synods and that where there was more than one society at work, evangelistic funds should be pooled, with the synod having administrative responsibility.

For the first time, the General Assembly had prepared a personnel list of needed missionaries (for university evangelism and the General Assembly office, as well as the Yunnan and Border missions). Twenty-nine missionaries (of nine boards) were listed as working under General Assembly assignment. Staff had prepared a memorandum on "Christian Work in Communist Areas" which, after reviewing the actual situation, challenged Christian workers to continue work in such areas even though the risks were considerable. The 1948 Conference recommended that all evangelistic missionaries receive work assignments from the synods, rather than from mission bodies, and "that all other Western missionary workers should be effectively related to the Chinese church."

The February 1948 issue of *The Church* (Vol. II, No. 1) included a supplementary chart of church-mission relationships. It indicated that of the fifteen missions cooperating with the CCC in 1947 (several were added later), most evangelistic missionary work assignments were made by the synods or in consultation between synods and missions. However, two missions, the Evangelical and Reformed and the Presbyterian US, retained control of missionary assignments. In reply to the question whether the executive responsibility of the General Assembly should be enlarged, three missions answered no and four suggested that the role of the General Assembly staff should primarily be inspirational. The need for coordination of the mission programs and strengthening relationships between the synods and the General Assembly were mentioned by others.

The Work of the Synods

In the immediate postwar years, the work of the synods varied enormously. Those in the south generally were able to resume a fairly normal program of activity and rehabilitation, while the northern synods were greatly affected by the accelerating civil war.

H. H. Tsui was present at the first postwar meeting of the Northeast Synod in September 1946, when the Synod's ties with the Church of Christ in China, severed for so many years because of the political separation of Manchuria, were reestablished. In July 1947 Dr. Tsui returned for a meeting of the Enlarged Executive Committee of the Synod. The February 1948 issue of *The Church* reported: "The work of the church is greatly restricted because of political conditions. In some places churches have been destroyed and Christians are not able to meet even in homes for public worship." Many Christians had moved into the cities because of disturbed conditions in the countryside.

The same issue carried extensive reports on a number of the synods. In Shensi, Christian work had been hindered greatly by political unrest. The civil war had disrupted communications. The capital city of Sian could be reached only by air or roundabout overland travel. Yet, a conference of church workers was able to meet in the summer of 1947 with C. S. Chu present representing General Assembly staff. "For the first time in many years representatives from North Shensi were able to be present."

Honan was reported to be "the one synod which at the present time is completely disorganized." Ninety percent of the area was under Communist control and missionaries had been forced to leave. "A few of the Chinese congregations can carry on church services but the presbyteries are not able to function." The mission compound outside the walled city of Weihwei had been occupied by government and Communist forces in turn, with looting and much damage to the hospital and other property. Szechuan Synod "is perhaps less affected by present political disturbances than any other area in China." Missionary staff had been augmented by returns from furlough, additions from Honan, and some new appointees. In Lingtung Synod, Swatow suffered great destruction in a typhoon in October. Miss Chi had visited all the churches in the Synod in the autumn.

It was impossible for staff to visit Shantung until the autumn of 1947, when Dr. Tsui went to Tsinan and Tsingtao. He reported that conditions were difficult because of the continuing civil war, with ninety percent of the rural churches unable to carry on. Tsui visited the Mid-Fukien Synod in December and reported on the Shantung situation, whereupon C$5,000,000 was contributed in relief for the Shantung churches (not as great a sum as it would appear to be, because of the serious inflation of Chinese currency, but a genuine expression of concern).

The Lianghu Synod was divided early in 1947 into the Hunan and Hupei Synods because of the difficulty of communication between the two provinces and the addition of new member churches. "The churches in the Hankow area perhaps suffered more than any other part of China. During the . . . occupation, much church property was destroyed and the Japanese were very oppressive." Ichang hospital was destroyed by fire in the autumn of 1947.

"With the exception of one group [presumably North Fukien, where the church was weakest and conditions had been badly disrupted by the early civil war and then by the Japanese occupation], all the churches in Fukien are growing and in a healthy condition." The South Fukien Synod had grown during the war years and had added seven new churches. One reason suggested for the strength and growth of the church was "the development of Christian life through small groups."

In 1946 agreement was reached between the South Fukien Synod and the cooperating missions giving the Synod control of all work, not just church work, which had been under synodical control for some years, and responsibility for all missionary appointments, not just those of evangelistic missionaries as in the past. Evangelistic funds had been administered by the Synod for some years; now *all* funds were to be channeled through it. In 1948 it was agreed that communication between the Synod and the three cooperating boards of mission should be "direct and not through any intermediary" (i.e., mission organizations in the area). In further discussions in 1949, reports to the Reformed Church in America Board by their missionaries indicated that the synodical representatives had made the CCC position very clear—"they were an indigenous Chinese church—always had been, always will be."

Kwangtung Synod was able to develop an extensive program soon after the war ended. The Synod's *Information Service,* now edited by Peter Wong, reported many activities. Lois Armentrout, a Presbyterian USA missionary who was involved in the Synod's Women's Work program, commented on her impressions two months after return from the U.S. (June, 1946 issue):

> First is the fact of God's care for His people during their time of greatest need and extremity. Second is the fact of the heroic witness of the church's leaders during the years of war and the resultant hearing which now awaits the Christian message. Third is the necessity of dealing with a multitude of the many inter-related problems caused by undernourishment and the depletion of physical, mental and material resources.

Damage to church and institutional property had been substantial, and many Christians had been killed in the war or by the Japanese policy of retaliation. The Synod held its first annual conference since 1940 in Canton in June 1946 and at the same time also brought together church workers for a retreat. It was still not possible to hold a youth summer conference for the entire Synod, but one was held in mid-summer for the Canton area. In June 1946 the Sik-on Church, an independent Chinese Methodist Church, joined the Kwangtung Synod.

The Women's Work program of the Synod, which had long been an important part of its work, had been continued on a limited scale during the war but now developed new vigor. It suffered a serious loss, however, in the death in late 1946 of Mrs. Law Lau Sam Tsz, long its leading spirit. A graduate of the True Light School, she taught there for many years. Active in her local church, she was a founder of the YWCA in Canton and had addressed the First Provisional Assembly under the Nationalist government on behalf of the women of Kwangtung.

The report of the General Assembly for 1947 was issued as a supplement to the February 1948 issue of *The Church*. Almost every synod of the Church had been visited by members of the staff in 1947. It included reports of the work of the three missions of the Church, with over sixty at work in the Border Mission and promising new openings. Additional staff, both missionary and Chinese, had joined the work in Yunnan and new work had been opened in Kaiyuan. Relief and rehabilitation had been a major responsibility in 1947. Circulating libraries had been provided for each of about one hundred district associations. Scholarship grants had been made to children of church workers, aid given to workers who had withdrawn from areas under Communist control, and grants made to assist synodical meetings and district conferences for Church workers.

The Fifth General Assembly

It was not until October 1948 that the Church was able to bring together the scattered representatives of the synods in a General Assembly, the first since Tsingtao in 1937. Long months of planning were involved: the civil war was continuing and transportation was a serious problem for many. The railroads in North China were unreliable—in many places destroyed—but the new airlines made travel possible from the major cities.

The site of the Fifth General Assembly was Soochow, where the participants met from October 18 to 27 in spite of many problems. The political situation was changing rapidly and some commissioners from the North had to leave before the meeting was over because of the Communist victories in Manchuria and the rapid advance toward North China. Rice was difficult to obtain and feeding the delegates was a serious problem as the Assembly opened. But the strenuous efforts of local church people surmounted every difficulty.

One hundred and fifty commissioners represented every synod but Honan, where the civil war made communication and travel impossible. In addition, there were a number of fraternal delegates from interdenominational Christian agencies, and representatives from interested Chinese churches in Java, Formosa, Malaya, and Singapore. Dr. Tsou Ping-I, a professor at Nanking Theological Seminary (soon thereafter elected President of West China Union Theological College) was elected Moderator.

An impressive memorial service honored more than three hundred leaders who had died since the Fourth Assembly (Chinese and missionaries, including the two most prominent early leaders of the CCC, C. Y. Cheng and A. R. Kepler). Three evenings were given over to presentations on the missions of the Church and the Assembly voted to appoint C. T. Tsai as full-time Missions Secretary and to set up an Assembly committee to oversee the missions program. Much time was given to reports from the various synods, whose representatives had not been able to come together for so long. On the whole, these were optimistic, even in the Communist areas, where many churches were at least able to carry on in small group meetings.

It was announced that the General Assembly office was now prepared to accept any property the mission boards wished to turn over to the Church. Deep concern was expressed over the need for help to aged workers and others in need, and pension and disability plans developed by the Kwangtung and Szechuan Synods were commended as models. The Assembly recommended that middle school (i.e., high school) graduation be the minimum requirement for entrance into theological college and urged that more scholarships for theological students be sought. It also recommended that missionary work assignments be the responsibility of the synods, which were to keep the General Assembly office informed, but that transfers between synods be the responsibility of the General Assembly office.

There was discussion of the problems of good relations between church bodies and the church-related institutions. The latter, as they had grown stronger, tended to drift away from church relations, and local church or district association ties were weak and often irksome. It was felt that such relationships would be more effective at the synodical level, and it was recommended that each synod set up a medical committee and that the hospitals have voting representation in the district associations. Church-related institutions were urged to have the needs of the rural areas in mind and to train workers to help meet such needs. The Church was called upon to cooperate in the Forward Movement of evangelism being coordinated on behalf of its member churches by the National Christian Council. One of the major addresses, by T. H. Sun of Cheloo University, outlined the contribution of Christianity to Chinese civilization and culture, with a realistic appraisal of the current situation and the serious problems faced by the Church.

Four new churches were accepted into membership: the Malaya Synod (related to English Presbyterian Mission work); the Kianghwai Synod (churches in the Shantung-Kiangsu-Anhwei area related to Presbyterian US work); the Chung Hua Hsing Tao Hui (related to Swedish Missionary Society work in Hupei, long in fraternal relationship with the CCC); and the Chung Hua Tsun Tao Hui (Hunan, related to the Evangelical-United Brethren). It was reported after the Assembly that the Chinese Church in Java had decided to enter the CCC, official action to be taken by the Standing Committee, and that the Presbyterian South Synod on Formosa was also ready for membership.

Near the close of the Assembly, a draft statement was presented on the attitude of the Church toward the national crisis, which led to extended debate. It was decided to accept the statement in principle, but to refer the text to the Standing Committee for revision. The statement was issued under the title "Statement on the National Situation," dated October 1948, and was reported in full in *The Church* for August 1949. It began with a six-point statement of "our convictions." Included were claims about the rights of the individual; the importance of spiritual values; the validity of Christian teachings, especially the sacrifice of self as the standard of personal relations; the church's mandate to serve society "as a manifestation of love and truth"; and the judgment of God on war, retaliation, and special privilege.

There followed four points on "our attitude":

1) The Church should maintain its integrity, not committing itself to any particular political program, not taking sides with any party, but preaching the truth with boldness.

2) Where confronted with misunderstanding or persecution, the Church should examine herself. . . . History tells us that whenever the Church is persecuted, it is the beginning of a period of flourishing. Therefore there is no reason for being discouraged or disheartened, but only for patience and obedience, waiting for the realization of the will of God.

3) When persecuted wilfully, remember the teaching of our Lord . . . of loving our enemies. This is the most effective weapon for conquering the world; show the greatness of love in our times of difficulty.

4) "All things work together for good to them that love God." We must rejoice at all times. Whether conditions are favorable or not, remember that it is our duty to preach the Gospel, to preach the Gospel, to minister to all of humanity, to minister, to minister, to minister!

The statement was obviously influenced by the fears of many churchmen, based on past experiences of strong anti-Christian attitudes and the repression of religious activity in Communist-controlled areas. It was worded cautiously but courageously, and while touching on the basic human values and Christian convictions concerning them, seems primarily to have been addressed to the church, admonishing Christians to display, in difficulty and adversity, the patient love and abiding faith that have always been the marks of true Christianity.

The Deepening Political Crisis and Its Effects on the CCC

As the civil war grew in intensity, conditions in the northern synods became more difficult. At the July 20, 1948, meeting of the Standing Committee, eight workers from the Northeast Synod, where it was impossible to carry on normal church work in the rural areas, were assigned to the three missions of the Church. At this meeting, W. B. Djang submitted his resignation as Director of the Border Mission and from all CCC responsibilities. His resignation was accepted with regret and Liu Ling-chiu was appointed Acting Director. The Border Mission office, which had been moved to Nanking after the war, was moved back to Chengtu in December 1948. In March 1949 Henry D. Tsui returned from study abroad and assumed the Directorship of the Border Mission. W. H. Clark left Yunnan in October 1948 for health reasons and on June 1, 1949, the Rev. Sun Shou-hsin, who had been pastor of the Kunming church since June 1948, was appointed Director of the Yunnan Mission.

The December 1948 meeting of the Standing Committee voted unanimously that the General Assembly office should remain in Shanghai. But Bruce Copland was asked to go to Canton to keep in touch with the missions and synods in areas not yet taken over by the Communist forces. In early March 1949 he represented the General Assembly office at the Second Assembly of the Hunan Synod at Changsha. The disturbed conditions cut attendance in half, but more than forty delegates from district associations, hospitals, schools, and the Synod Executive Committee were present. The Tsun Tao Hui was welcomed into membership as a symbol of the growing unity of the Church.

Summary-Evaluation

The period after the war during which a degree of normal life became possible for some areas of the Church of Christ in China was very short, brought to an end by another upheaval in the political scene. While there were some encouraging signs, there were few solid indicators of what the future might otherwise have held for the life and growth of the Church.

The accession of several new bodies further supported the Church's claim to be a national, unifying Chinese church. Continued support for the missions of the Church marked its continuing commitment to mission. The growth in self-support and self-dependence that had characterized the stronger and less disrupted synods during the war years was sustained and gave hope of increasing strength. Able Chinese leadership at the General Assembly level and in the Church's missions were hopeful signs. So was the rise of young leadership in many of the synods, in spite of the difficulties of the war years, much of which would begin to assert itself in the early years of the new political regime. But the Church had hardly had time to catch its breath before it was thrown into a new era of trial and testing.

Chapter Ten: The
New Day
in China

This account will not try to relate in any detail the growing military success of the Communist armies in 1948-49 or the collapse of the Nationalist government and its military forces. Suffice it to say that the total defeat of the best trained and equipped Central government divisions in Manchuria in the closing months of 1948 made the inevitable result clear. When the new government was officially proclaimed as the People's Republic of China on October 1, 1949, the entire country, with the exception of the Southwest, Taiwan, and a few small offshore islands, where the Nationalist government and its remaining troops had taken refuge, was under the effective control of the Communists.

The Christian Church and Political Change

In mid-1947 there had been strong pressure for a public endorsement of the Nationalist government by Protestant leaders, in line with such a statement by Roman Catholic leadership. But Protestant leaders were unwilling to take such a position, in part because of the traditional Protestant position of noninvolvement in political issues, but also because of a lack of confidence in a failing regime which by this time had demonstrated its inability to deal with the issues confronting the nation. They strongly felt the need for a peaceful resolution of internal difficulties. The National government was unable to secure this by military means and unwilling to seek it by political means. Support of the National government would mean continuation of the civil war, with further suffering and destruction.

The mood of the Christian forces in China in this period of transition was troubled. The dangers, anxieties, and sufferings of the past several decades had left Chinese Christians and missionaries exhausted and uneasy. The general populace had been increasingly disillusioned with the ineffectiveness, mismanagement, and growing corruption in government and the appalling condition of the country, crippled by the destruction of the long war with the Japanese and the savage civil war that had followed. The cities were full of refugees, destitute and near starvation.

The Communists had favorably impressed many, especially during the early years of the war with Japan in North China, by their orderly government, lack of corruption, and generally equitable use of land for the public good. On the other hand, harsh treatment had been used to bring about cooperation and ruthless measures taken against any who failed to cooperate. They were openly anti-religious and memories were still fresh of the violence with which Christians and Christian institutions had been treated, especially in the twenties. Churches had been forbidden to carry on their work in many rural areas under Communist control and there had been a number of incidents in the postwar period in which Christian hospitals and schools had been destroyed and also some incidents in which Christian workers had been brought to trial and even executed.

Because of such uncertainties and on the advice of consular authorities, who were aware of the anti-Western animus of the Communists and feared the kind of violence that had been directed against foreigners in past times of unrest, many of the Protestant missionaries had already left the country by the time the new government was officially established on October 1, 1949. Most of those who remained felt it wise to leave after the Korean conflict began in June, 1950. Anti-American propaganda became increasingly bitter and it became clear that their activity would.be severely circumscribed and that they were an embarrassment to the Chinese church. The U.S. and Chinese governments mutually froze assets in late 1950, which made the problem of missionary support acute. Accusations of espionage and hostile activities were made against some missionaries, a number were placed under house arrest, and a limited number were imprisoned, usually for short periods, but several for extended terms.

The Church and the New Regime

By and large the Chinese, who had endured so many political upheavals in the twentieth century, accepted the need for change, but were fearful of what the change would mean for them, though others, especially students, eagerly welcomed it. The Communist forces were well-disciplined and efficient. Before long the disrupted economy began to right itself, exemplary currency control and food distribution measures were introduced, and order began to emerge out of the chaos of the civil war. From the first, the new regime proclaimed a policy of religious freedom, or to translate the Chinese term literally, "freedom of belief." But it soon became quite clear that church activity would generally be limited to worship.

Many thought that when the Communists came to power the churches would be closed but such Christian institutions as hospitals, schools, and orphanages would be permitted to continue. Actually, the institutions were soon taken over by government agencies for one reason or another, service to the people being conceived as a governmental function, while churches were permitted to remain open, at least in the larger towns or cities. In most rural areas the churches were closed, generally on the grounds that no public meetings were permitted during the period of land reform. Even in the cities, competing activities in schools and on public occasions with virtually compulsory attendance made it difficult for the churches to carry on even their normal worship services.

All elements of the population were subjected to reform in their thinking and to intensive study and confession processes intended to bring about thorough conformity to Marxist-Maoist thought. Under the guidance of Christian leaders committed to cooperation with the new government, a "Three-Self Reform Movement" (during the Korean War called the "Three-Self Patriotic Oppose-America Aid-Korea Movement") was formed and became the chief instrument of Christian activity. (The "Three-Self" came from the traditional church goals of self-support, self-government, and self-propagation.)

Church leaders were aware of the great changes taking place, and in the spring of 1950 a group of Christian leaders addressed a message to the mission boards which stated: "From now on, a new political concept, a new philosophy, a new creed and a new mode of living will be instilled into the masses of the people with a vigor that is hitherto unknown."

The "Christian Manifesto"

In May 1950 a group of several Christian leaders, including Dr. H. H. Tsui, General Secretary of the Church of Christ in China, visited

Peking and along with local church leaders met with government officials, including Premier Chou En-lai, on three separate occasions. Out of these discussions came a draft statement which, after extended debate by church leaders in Shanghai, and with at least tacit approval by high government officials, was made public as the "Christian Manifesto" in July 1950. Originally signed by forty well-known Christian leaders, it was widely publicized, and in an energetic public campaign the signatures of about 400,000 Protestants were obtained.

While recognizing Christianity's "not unworthy contribution to Chinese society," the document charges that since most missionaries came from imperialistic countries, Christianity "became related with imperialism." Such countries "may also make use of Christianity to forward . . . internal dissension and . . . [create] reactionary forces in this country." Christians and the churches were urged to support the new government's "Common Political Platform," oppose capitalism and imperialism (especially American imperialism), and help in building "a prosperous and powerful China." They should "purge imperialistic influences from within Christianity . . . participate in the movement opposing war and upholding peace," and support the policy of agrarian reform. "Self-criticism should be advocated, all forms of Christian activity re-examined and readjusted . . . so as to achieve the goals of a reformation in the church." The churches "should work out concrete plans . . . within the shortest possible time" to discontinue reliance "upon foreign personnel and financial aid." They should "emphasize anti-imperialistic, anti-feudalistic and anti-bureaucratic-capitalism education, together with such forms of service to the people as productive labor, teaching them to understand the new era."

In the October 1950 issue of *The Church*, the Manifesto is called:

> A document of historical significance. In this declaration . . . Chinese Christians condemn all imperialism and aggressive designs in China, announce their patriotic support of the "Common Program" and set before themselves the goal of self-support in the near future.

In spite of the comment in the same issue that "In no sense is the statement considered a denial of ecumenical Christian fellowship and love," the implications were clear. When in December 1950 the United States and Chinese governments mutually froze assets, and remittances to China from the U.S. were permitted only by license, financial support had virtually ceased, though some funds from other than the American boards trickled in. With a few exceptions, in the early period of the new regime visas were not granted to missionaries seeking to return to China.

The CCC and the New Day

In January 1949, E. Bruce Copland, as Executive Secretary of the CCC, went to Canton to ensure communication with CCC churches and synods in areas not yet "liberated," and in April he moved to Hong Kong. Although this was not considered an official CCC office, he was able in this period, with the secretarial help of Mrs. John D. Hayes, who had left Kweiyang in 1949 for reasons of health, to serve as a liaison for the Church. His function was that of sharing with the cooperating mission agencies available information on the situation of the churches in China, and his objective reports were of great value during this critical period. He was also of assistance to the remaining missionaries related to the CCC as they trickled out of China.

We shall attempt to trace concisely the effects of the tremendous changes that took place in the life and work of the Church of Christ in China in the ensuing years. Information was plentiful in 1949 and 1950, but increasingly meagre thereafter. The 1949 issues of *The Church*, a chief source of information at this period, had been published in Hong Kong. Publication resumed in Shanghai with the April 1950 issue (Volume IV, Number 2). Two more issues appeared in 1950 (July and October-November), but apparently those were the last. *Kung Pao*, the Chinese periodical of the CCC, continued publication somewhat irregularly until about 1954.

Early Optimism

Cautious optimism characterized the early reactions of the CCC leadership to the new situation. An editorial on "The Chinese Church in the New Age," in the April issue of *The Church*, points out "new trends" (mostly in an approving vein) and expresses confidence "that the Church will be stimulated and purified by the new situation into which it is plunged." Referring to the call for church reform:

This is all to the good. If this social revolution can help to strengthen the faith and witness of Christians, raise the standard of Christian living and service, hasten the day of independence and self-support in the Chinese Church, make the Church more democratic, bring Christians closer to the working masses, and further the cause of church unity, we may all thank God.

How far the Church should go in adapting to the new social environment, when it should take a stand for essential Christian beliefs, what the Word of God is for this time, are questions Chinese Christians must decide.

Religious liberty has been officially promised in China. With this guarantee the Church should have the right and the courage to preach, to teach, and to demonstrate in life the complete gospel of our Lord and Saviour Jesus Christ. The world, including China, cannot do without Christianity.

A second editorial on "Missionaries under the New Democracy" points out that a considerable number of missionaries still remained in China. Their work is limited in the "liberated areas." They are under suspicion because of a century of Western imperialism and misunderstanding of their purposes and motives. But "missionaries are still needed for their contributions" and "as personal links with the ecumenical church."

The same issue carries a number of "Important Statements on Religious Liberty" from Communist sources, including one by Chairman Mao. The July issue carries a long report of conferences in May between the "Christian Visiting Team" of national leaders, together with Peking church leaders, and government officials, including Premier Chou En-lai.

His attitude was one of tolerance and sincerity. . . . Mission funds may continue to be received for a time but they should be free from any political connection or control and they should decrease in amounts from year to year. . . . Missionaries not under political suspicion may stay on in China until their periods of service end or their passports expire, following which it would be better for them to return to their own countries.

A long article on the "Attitude of Government Leaders" credits high government officials with having a generally sympathetic attitude toward the problems of the churches:

It would appear that much of the difficulty has been with those of lower administrative levels, often . . . young and inexperienced people. . . . At present there seems to be no need for any change in the relationship between the CCC and the cooperating missions. Present arrangements should continue, but thought should be given to possible future developments, especially in view of . . . withdrawals of Western missionaries . . . with little prospect of return or reinforcements. . . . If there comes a time when readjustments are necessary, the General Assembly will certainly have to take more responsibility than in the past. . . . It seems desirable that ultimately all requests for personnel and funds should be channeled through the General Assembly.

The July 1950 issue of *The Church* reported a statement by missionaries working in the Mid-Fukien Synod reflecting the hope that missionaries could continue their work: "All churches, schools and hospitals have been able to live and work much as before. . . . Missionaries are still wanted and needed."

A report on the Fourteenth Biennial Meeting of the National Christian Council (October 18-25, 1950, Shanghai) was carried in the October-November issue of *The Church.* Church leadership was well represented, with over one hundred in attendance (including government "observers") from all over the nation.

> The most regrettable and noticeable part was the absence of missionary friends at the meeting. . . . The deliberations . . . clearly indicated that the leadership and services of the NCC were very widely appreciated. There was a very genuine desire on the part of non-member churches and local Christian councils . . . to cooperate more closely with the NCC. This broadening of the basis of the NCC will greatly strengthen the future usefulness of the Council.

These were hardly prophetic words, in view of the fact that the Council never met again! Important actions included support for the "Christian Manifesto" and the government's land reform program; a recommendation for a "Conference on Theological Education" to determine the direction the Church should take; a proposal to revise the Constitution "in accord with actual conditions"; authorization for an NCC Peking office and for a five-year plan for full support of the council. Program and staff withered away in the next few years. The writer of the report, George K. T. Wu, had resigned as General Secretary of the Council early in 1950 and no mention is made of a successor.

The enlarged Standing Committee of the CCC General Assembly met in Shanghai October 27-28, 1950 (the last meeting for which records are available). Taking advantage of the presence in Shanghai of many Church leaders for the NCC meeting, nineteen representatives of various CCC synods around the country, including a number of synodical executives, were co-opted to meet with seven regular members of the Committee available in or near Shanghai. Eight staff members were present, including the directors of the three missions of the Church. No missionaries were present. Not many still remained in China, foreigners were no longer permitted to travel freely, and for obvious reasons their presence would have been an embarrassment.

The theme of the meeting was "The Future Direction of the Church of Christ in China." Dr. Tsui, in introducing it, emphasized:

> (1) We should understand the new relationship between the government and the Church. (2) We should understand the ecumenical relationship between the Church and Mission. (3) We should actively and sincerely promote self-government, self-support and self-propagation in the Church. (4) We should strive to serve and win the masses to the Church. (5) We should earnestly cooperate with all other Church bodies. (6) Our fundamental task is the nurture of the spiritual life of believers.

The churches were urged to move forward to self-support within a target period of five years. The General Assembly was also to achieve financial autonomy within that period, and the synods were urged to appoint and support workers in the missions of the Church. The members of the Committee must have realized how unrealistic these objectives were, in the light of past history and present circumstances.

The Committee voted that "all former personnel and work programs of the missionary societies" be transferred to the synods. (Some of the missions had maintained programs of their own for which they directly employed Chinese staff, though in the more advanced synods all work and personnel were under church control.) A plan was approved "for administration of grants-in-aid from missionary societies to the CCC." This provided for (1) agreements for proportional decreases; (2) General Assembly and synodical authority in the use of mission funds, with due regard for "the wishes of the donors"; (3) the possibility of mission grants directly to the General Assembly for national church programs.

A ten-point plan was adopted "as a tentative measure pending the promulgation of government regulations regarding administration of property of foreign nationals in China whereby term agreements could be made by missions with synods for their custodianship of property." Staff was "to proceed as rapidly as possible with negotiations for registration and incorporation of the General Assembly of the Church of Christ in China with the Central People's Government."

At this meeting, probably the last which brought together wide representation from the outlying synods, the Standing Committee made a final appeal for the kind of self-support that would enable the Church to stand completely on its own feet, for which the leadership had been calling throughout the short history of the united Church. But the end of the road for aid from the missions was already clearly in sight and it must have been obvious that a new kind of society would make increased support from the laity an economic impossibility.

The appeal was incorporated in an "Open Letter to Fellow-Workers and Fellow-Christians in China." The letter begins with a reminder that great changes were taking place and that the Church "must re-study its own responsibility and determine anew its future direction." The contributions of the older churches in bringing the Gospel to China were mentioned appreciatively but the consistent goal of the CCC had been autonomy. "Moreover, the situation today enables us to see very clearly that unless the Church speedily achieves self-support it cannot possibly maintain its existence." Careful thought must be given to the need for cutting programs, remembering that the apostolic church was even poorer and yet built a viable church. The Manifesto "clearly indicates the direction in which the Church must now struggle."

> God is indeed using the problems before us to test again His chosen church and make it as refined gold in the fire. May we all with hearts that are fearless and on fire for reform become instruments with which God is well-pleased. Let us lift up our heads and look at the great Leader of the Church Jesus Christ. Trusting in His great power let us carry out the holy will of God.

Conditions in the Synods

In these early days of the new regime, the situation of the churches and their work varied greatly. The March 1950 statement on the work of the CCC reports the situation in Manchuria as "very difficult." Only forty-seven churches were able to function (out of two hundred and sixty-nine).

> Five-sixths of the total Christian work has been wiped out . . . due partly to the destruction . . . during the fighting, partly to the departure of some of the church leaders, and partly to the mistaken idea that the church was a

superstitious and capitalistic body and the consequent closing down of its work. Hospitals have been reduced from fourteen to four, middle schools from four to two.

On the other hand, in Shantung the situation had improved. "Two years ago, all pastors and evangelists suffered persecution and often imprisonment" but now officials welcomed pastors, and workers were requested to return to hospitals and churches. Shantung Synod met in November 1949 for the first time in eleven years. In Hopei "the rural church is still suffering severely and in some places cannot carry on at all, with frequent physical persecution and investigation." In Fukien and Anhwei "mission property has in many cases been borrowed without formal notice by local authorities."

In many places there were church activities of a relatively normal nature. A Religious Education Institute for East China held in Shanghai April 18-20 brought together forty-one delegates from four synods. At the annual meeting of the Board of Directors of Nanking Theological Seminary on May 5, 1950, Dr. Andrew C. Y. Cheng (a younger brother of Cheng Ching-yi) was elected President. The Hangchow Christian University Board ("the one Christian University entirely sponsored by the CCC") met, with H. H. Tsui as Chairman, and elected Dr. Usang Ly as President. A Round Table Conference of Christian Universities and Colleges met in Nanking in April with all but two institutions represented.

A number of the synods were able to hold meetings. Chekiang Synod met in May at Hangchow and elected the Rev. Peter Tsai (Ts'ai Wen-hao) of the Soochow Lay Training Center as Synod Executive Secretary. Kwangtung Synod held its twenty-fourth annual meeting at Canton on May 23, with representation from churches, district associations, and church-related institutions. Kiangnan Synod, meeting on May 16, reported "hopeful growth" with a communicant membership of 8,471. Rev. Z. H. Tong was Executive Secretary of the Synod. "A few missionaries were present, but did not take part in the discussions." Mid-Fukien elected J. M. Tan (Tan Jen-mei) of Fukien Christian University as General Secretary. Szechuan voted to reduce financial grants by 20% annually. An interdenominational evangelistic meeting was held in Sian (Shensi), and Wang Tao-sheng was elected Synod Executive. Synodical and district associations met in Shantung under the leadership of Chang Su-ching as Executive Secretary. Some rural churches in the Paoting (Hopei) area reopened and Shao Feng-yuan was elected Synod Executive. A new church building seating four hundred was dedicated at

Kiangmen (Kwangtung). Chuanchow Presbytery (South Fukien) reported 4,358 communicant members, an increase of fifty-four. Kiangnan Synod's Executive Committee met in May for the first time since "liberation" and elected Timothy Lee (Li Cheng-ch'ung) as Executive—5,455 church members were reported. Church attendance was larger and youth work active in Nanking. In general, then, reports from the churches were encouraging. On the other hand, some churches were closed and at Hwaiyuan all property except the church building and an orphanage had been occupied by government agencies.

Hopei and Hwapei Synods united on November 12 with a special service of commemoration in C. Y. Cheng's old church in Peking, with C. T. Tsai present to represent the General Assembly. On November 1, four East China synods (Kianghuai, Kiangan, Kiangnan, and Chekiang) set up a "joint committee for business purposes with an office in Shanghai" and Dr. Philip Peh-chun Chang as Executive Secretary (son of the first ordained pastor in North Kiangsu). Shensi Synod met in July in Sanyuan, with H. H. Tsui present. All mission property and finances were transferred to synodical control. Mid-Fukien Synod accepted the resignations of missionary staff members and elected Li Hsueh-yuan as Synod Executive (apparently J. M. Tan had resigned). Kwangtung Synod reported encouraging progress in the churches.

A number of ordinations of new ministers were reported in Chekiang and North Fukien. Hunan Synod reported a Medical Insurance Plan for church workers in cooperation with the seven hospitals of the Synod. A revival under the leadership of Shantung Synod evangelists was reported in August in Tsouping, where the church had long been without pastoral leadership and had become disorganized. Kianghuai Synod, where the churches had suffered heavy losses, reported a similar experience under the leadership of a new pastor. CCC Religious Education institutes were held in Shensi, North China, Lingtung, Mid-Fukien, and other synods.

The Missions of the CCC

Communications from the missions of the Church in late 1949 and early 1950 reported work going on and virtually all workers at their posts, in spite of heavy fighting. The April 1950 issue of *The Church* reported optimistically on all three missions: Kienshui Hospital (Yunnan) had added forty beds—sixteen staff members were at work in Kweichow, twenty-two in Yunnan, seventy-one in the Border Mission. In Yunnan encouraging evangelistic work went on under Chinese leadership, particularly that of Pastor Hu in Mengtze-Kienshui and Pastor Sun in Kunming. It was reported that in one area there were more baptisms during the first year under Communism than in the previous year. A neighborhood school for poor children and a clinic with simple, free medical care had been opened by the Kunming Church in 1949 and continued under the new regime. The October-November issue of *The Church* reports, however, "The work of the Border Mission has had its up and downs in recent months," though no details are given.

Church-related Schools and Hospitals

Early in 1950 reports on church-related schools were mixed. In most schools enrollments were holding steady, but others reported serious financial difficulty and fewer students with considerable pressure against religious activities. "In all schools, the control is in the hands of a committee consisting of students, teachers, and servants." Late in the year, a government official (T. L. Shen, Vice-Minister of Education for East China, formerly principal of a Christian middle school, Medhurst College in Shanghai) is quoted as outlining government policy toward Christian education as "to maintain positively, to reform gradually, to subsidize centrally. . . . If Christian schools operate in conformity with the Common Program and obey government laws the government will show no discrimination against them." But, there must be "elimination of feudalistic and undemocratic practices" and of the "culture which is linked to capitalistic society and colonial . . . ways of life" (such terms were, of course, susceptible of varying interpretations by those in power). Hangchow University reported "an active religious program." In general, "It is possible to have chapel services . . . provided attendance is voluntary." Szechuan Synod reported its six middle schools were all open with decreased attendance. The theological schools noted increased enrollment.

The CCC March report referred to above states that a government committee had indicated policy on Christian hospitals as:

1. No government support . . . let them die a natural death.
2. Limitation of the scope of Christian hospitals.

3. Moving of Christian hospitals . . . as need arises.
4. Taking over of Christian hospitals if necessary.

Szechuan Synod reported in the July issue of *The Church,* "So far our eight hospitals and the University Hospital, in which we cooperate, have had the most difficulties, whereas we thought they would be the least affected." A chief problem was financial, partly because the new government had imposed heavy taxes on the hospitals, but there were serious internal difficulties as well.

The Goal of Self-Support Reaffirmed

On February 21, 1951, a letter was sent from the General Assembly "To the Secretaries of all Cooperating Missionary Societies" (probably the last official communication sent abroad). Referring to the Enlarged Standing Committee resolution of October 1950, it stated: "All grades of church organization . . . and all forms of work . . . shall strive to attain the goal of autonomy—self-government, self-support and self-propagation—within the shortest possible time."

The aim was complete self-support within five years. However, the situation had changed with the freezing of assets and Chinese government requirements that all bodies receiving foreign subsidies register and "redouble their efforts in the movement for self-government, self-support and self-propagation." The Enlarged Standing Committee, meeting again on January 22, 1951, had taken the following action:

> The present situation does not permit us to hesitate any longer. We have decided, from the beginning of 1951, to receive no further financial aid of any kind from abroad. We call upon all grades of church organization . . . immediately, of their own accord, to plan to maintain with their own strength the various forms of work in the Church of Christ in China.

Recent events had challenged the Church to financial independence sooner than anticipated and posed great difficulties. But faith was expressed that it would be possible to maintain the essential program. In view of the strength of anti-Western sentiment under the new regime, the final words of this communication are worthy of note:

Our spiritual bonds can never be broken. We assure you that the Church of Christ in China will always be true to the faith once for all delivered to the saints, to the Word of God, to the teachings of Christ and to the eternal Gospel of our Lord. Will you pray for us that through this great period our Church may be made a more fitting instrument of God's holy purpose for China and the world. You know, without our saying it again, how greatly we appreciate the contributions of your China Mission to the establishment of the Christian church in China. Christian memories and influences abide, and in Christ no thought or labor or prayer of love is ever lost.

At the Standing Committee meeting in February 1950, the resignation of E. Bruce Copland as Executive Secretary was accepted with appreciation for his eight years of service. The committee then voted to ask him on return from furlough to serve as Corresponding Secretary. In the October meeting, the resignation of Frank W. Price, who had been serving as Rural Work Secretary, was accepted with a vote of appreciation to him and his mission (Presbyterian US) for their "help in the past to the CCC."

In April 1951, one hundred and fifty-one Protestant Christian leaders met in Peking. For more than a year before this, the government had put tremendous pressure on people everywhere to denounce their associates and even their neighbors. On April 24, eighteen of the church leaders present joined in accusations against "the obviously evil-smelling agents of imperialism." The accusations were directed specifically against four Chinese and one missionary. The Chinese were Methodist Bishop W. Y. Ch'en, subsequently imprisoned for some years; S. C. Leung, former General Secretary of the YMCA and a CCC leader, who had gone to Hong Kong; Ku Jen-en, a former actor who had become a Christian evangelist and who also suffered imprisonment; and Bishop Y. Y. Tsu of the Sheng Kung Hui, who had reached the age of retirement and joined his family in the U.S. It is worth noting that two of the accused had already left China and that the other two were already under suspicion and detention.

Five of the leaders spoke against Dr. Frank Price, "agent of American imperialism for cultural aggression." Among the accusers was H. H. Tsui, who is quoted as saying "angrily":

Formerly we suffered poisonous harm from imperialism and fell into their trap. But today the Chinese people stand erect, the Chinese church stands erect. We will thoroughly cut off forever our relations with imperialism and establish the Chinese people's own church.

CCC Staff Members

From this period on, the chief source of news on the Christian movement in China is *T'ien Feng* (*The Christian Weekly*), for most of this time published twice monthly and then somewhat irregularly until 1963. There are occasional references to the activities of Dr. Tsui and other CCC staff members.

In 1953 the Three-Self Movement published *The Record of a Revival,* with a major chapter by H. H. Tsui. This was an attack on the "Jesus Family," a largely indigenous Christian communal movement which had attracted many followers in North China, and especially on its leader, Ching Tien-ying. The publication charged that Ching was "a criminal of first rank," adulterous and tyrannical. He was sentenced to twenty years imprisonment and the movement was banned by the authorities.

At a "Unity Conference" in Shanghai in April 1955, under auspices of the Three-Self Movement, Dr. Tsui was the major speaker. He urged support for the Movement and criticized the "illegal activities of the church," such as the activities of those who "openly opposed church unity," or of the independent evangelists who spread reaction by saying "I belong to the Kingdom of Heaven; I obey Jesus, not Mao Tse-tung." Tsui was the author of an article in the July 1955 issue of *T'ien Feng* attacking the position taken by Wang Ming-tao, an independent Chinese evangelist in Peking opposed to cooperation with the Communist regime who suffered long imprisonment because of his views. This was part of a concerted attack on Wang by Three-Self Movement leaders.

At a National Christian Conference in Peking in March 1956, Dr. Tsui spoke in refutation of an article in *The Christian Century* (November 4, 1953) by Wallace C. Merwin, asserting that the government was not guilty of coercion in church matters, especially in the accusation meetings, and asserting the full freedom of the church:

> In the past three years, the membership of the Chekiang Synod has increased by 18%, of the Shantung Synod by 22%, and of the Kiangnan Synod by 40%. Where did these new members come from if we had no freedom of evangelism? . . . Lastly, we want seriously to inform the imperialists; the Chinese Church has risen to its own feet; the Chinese Church is irrevocably against imperialism; the Chinese love their own fatherland deeply; the Chinese Church united with the Chinese people and all the peace-

loving people of the whole world will fight for the maintenance and defence of world peace.

In 1959 Dr. Tsui was reported to have resigned as General Secretary. He had been classified as a "bad element" because of his having corresponded with missionaries and mission societies in 1950-51 and especially because of a visit to Hong Kong to meet with an American mission board secretary. He was assigned to a Committee on Research of the United Protestant Publishers. This Committee, with twenty members, was commissioned to seek out all historical evidences of corrupt activities by Protestant missionaries and churches and report them to YMCA Secretary Kiang Wen-han, who as editor-in-chief was to prepare this material for publication. A publication date of October 1, 1959, had been set, but it is not known whether such a document was ever published.

In 1962 *T'ien Feng* reported that Dr. Tsui was present at a New Year reception of the Three-Self Movement in Shanghai. "His current work on compiling a history of the imperialist use of religion was noted." However, at the December 1962 meeting of the Board of Directors of Nanking Union Theological Seminary (a number of institutions had been merged under this name), Dr. Tsui was listed as a member of the Board and as General Secretary of the CCC. (Other CCC leaders listed were Wan Fu-lin of Wuhan and Shao Feng-yuan and Yin Chi-tseng of Peking.)

In 1953 it was reported that Dr. Y. S. Tom, Moderator of the CCC from 1933 to 1937, for many years General Secretary of the Kwangtung Synod, and after 1945 President of Union Theological Seminary (Canton), had been imprisoned in Canton. It was rumored, but not confirmed, that he had committed suicide.

Local CCC Activities

In 1953 the Hopei Synod's General Committee held an enlarged meeting with representatives present from nine cities. The CCC church at Changshu (near Shanghai) dedicated a new church building seating six hundred. Building materials were obtained from the government at a "low rate" and church members supplied most of the labor. A small CCC country church at Chiassu (near Hangchow) reported two hundred members at the close of 1953, with fifty inquirers (compared to ninety-three members in 1949). In 1956 the Wanshan Church (CCC) in Canton celebrated its forty-fifth anniversary and reported one hundred forty-seven baptisms in the 1950-55 period.

In 1956 there began a process of reorganizing CCC structures in accordance with recommendations of the Executive Committee of the General Assembly. It was charged that the former lines of demarcation were determined partly by language, partly by fields of mission board responsibility—"another example of the mission boards' 'divide and rule' strategy." In late 1956 the three synods in Fukien met in Foochow, with almost a hundred delegates present, and reorganized as the Synod of Fukien. A governing committee of twenty-eight members was set up with Wang Tsung-ch'eng as Chairman. Five candidates for the ministry were ordained, three from the Foochow area and two from Amoy. (One of the latter was a woman, reportedly the first ordained in the Amoy area—but many women had held important positions in South Fukien in earlier years, including at least one who served as pastor of a strong church in Amoy.)

At a meeting on September 4-7, 1957, in Nanking, the former boundary lines were set aside and the Synods of Kiangsu and Anhwei set up coinciding with province boundaries. Shanghai, with a substantial number of CCC churches, was set up as an independent district directly responsible to the General Assembly, paralleling government classification of large cities as separate political entities.

In early 1957, Y. T. Wu and Cora Deng (former General Secretary of the YWCA), as representatives of the Three-Self Movement, visited churches in Anhwei. They reported that in a CCC church at Pengp'u, Pastor Chu had baptized two hundred persons in the past few years. Francis James, editor of an Australian Anglican periodical and part of a delegation from that Church visiting China, was told that the CCC membership was 160,000 (1949—176,983) and that of the Sheng Kung Hui just over 40,000 (1949—76,731). However, William Kinmond of the Toronto *Globe and Mail* talked with Dr. H. H. Tsui the same year and was told that the CCC membership was 120,000, with seventeen synods. A delegation of Japanese Christian leaders also visited China in 1957 and said later that they had talked with Dr. Tsui and were given 106,000 as the CCC membership, with 1,457 churches, 437 ordained pastors and 777 unordained evangelists. They also reported more than seven hundred congregations where Sunday attendance exceeded one hundred.

Also in 1957 the Kiangyin District Association (Kiangnan Synod) reported "steady progress." Representatives of twenty-three churches (including nineteen pastors) were meeting monthly for extended periods of political study. Membership in 1953 was 2,402; in 1955 it was 2,933 (with 2,069 inquirers). Chu Pei-en, a YMCA secretary in Nanking, was elected Executive Secretary of the Kiangsu Synod. A CCC church in Yunnan for Miao tribesmen had been closed for several years after liberation. But the elders called the people together monthly for communion, and in 1957 the church was reopened with congregations of more than one hundred and fifty. At a service on May 5, one hundred and fourteen were baptized and six hundred took communion.

Other CCC Staff Members

There were occasional reports on the activities of other members of the CCC staff. In 1957 Dr. C. T. Tsai, Missions Secretary, was reported as being present at the meeting establishing the Fukien Synod, at reorganization meetings of the Anhwei and Kiangsu Synods and the Soochow District, as visiting the churches in the Northeast, and as participating in railroad construction on the Yingtan-Amoy Railroad (part of the labor program in which everyone, including government officials, took part).

C. S. Chu, a member of the CCC staff who had been Editor of *Kung Pao,* was denounced in July 1958, along with a number of other Christians in Shanghai. He is also mentioned the same year as helping in the organization of the Anhwei Synod and as a member of the Christian Endeavor National Board. In 1957 Sun Shou-hsin, Director of the Yunnan Mission, was reported as making a visit to the tribal churches in Yunnan under Three-Self auspices. In 1959 Sun was listed as Chairman of the Kunming Three-Self Committee and as one of a number of pastors working with Roman Catholic priests in a paperboard factory. The pastors were also engaged in raising chickens and rabbits and growing vegetables. In 1960 both C. T. Tsai and Sun Shou-hsin were listed as members of the National Committee of the Three-Self Movement. In 1962 *T'ien Feng* again reported a visit by Sun (linked with the YMCA as well as the CCC in Kunming) with Ma Chung-wen to southern Yunnan. They were sent by the Three-Self

Movement, and Sun reported at the National Christian Conference in January 1962 that they were "enthusiastically received." He said at that meeting that the majority of the Lahu people in Lan-ts'ang County were Christians.

The "One Hundred Flowers" Period and Its Effects on the Church

In early 1957 the tight control over public expression that characterized the new regime in its early stages was relaxed. Chairman Mao, quoting the well-known Chinese saying, "Let a hundred flowers bloom; let a hundred schools contend," seemed to be encouraging criticism. A flood of critical comment and opposition resulted—leading to a prompt and sharp reaction by the government.

A number of Christian leaders joined openly in criticizing both the general situation and the Three-Self Movement. In November one hundred and thirty Protestant leaders were summoned to a conference in Peking. At this meeting six church leaders were denounced by fellow-Christians. One of them was Liu Ling-chiu, who in the late 1940s had been Assistant Field Director of the Border Mission and later Editor of *The Christian Farmer.* Delegates received instruction in dealing with obstructionists, and when they returned home organized similar meetings all over China in which many Christians who had been critical during the "Hundred Flowers" period were denounced. Details are lacking, but apparently most of those denounced lost their church positions.

The year 1958 saw the "Great Leap Forward," an intensive effort at "instant-industrialization" of the entire nation, and the massive development of the agricultural communes. Pastors and other church workers, like everyone else, had to engage in "constructive labor" in farm or factory, many being sent to the expanding communes to work. Church attendance declined sharply, and in early 1958 a consolidation of congregations began. Rural churches had ceased functioning by this time. In the cities union services were encouraged and only one or two churches remained opened in each of the smaller cities. In Shanghai, where there had been more than two hundred Protestant churches, only twenty-three were reported as open (actually there were probably even fewer); of sixty-five in Peking, four remained. Unused church or mission property was turned over to the government, though in some instances, through the oversight of a government agency, the property was rented out and the income used in part to subsidize the few churches still open. Theological education had declined, and by 1965 only one school was still open, with eighty-five students.

Christian Visitors from Abroad

Through the 1950s Christians from Asia, Europe, Canada, and Australia occasionally visited China and talked with spokesmen for the Christian churches, mostly younger men who had recently come into leadership. Most of these new leaders enthusiastically endorsed the government, without necessarily accepting its Marxist ideology. They said that the government had been generous and open-minded in its treatment of the church. They universally categorized missionary activity in the past as imperialistic and reactionary and were highly critical of the world church and the ecumenical movement. All ties with churches and church agencies outside China were repudiated.

Decline in Church Activity

News of church activities was scanty after 1958. So far as is known, denominational programs and meetings simply ceased. There had been some doctrinal controversy in the early years of the new regime, mostly between Three-Self leaders and dissenters within the church, chiefly conservatives who repudiated the Movement, but even that seems to have come to an end. Thus it appears that all denominational activity was gradually choked off, and it is probably fair to say that by the late fifties, at least, the Church of Christ in China had ceased to function as a national body, even though some congregations were able to maintain minimal activity.

With the Great Proletarian Cultural Revolution in 1966, another major change came in the life of the church. The Red Guards, young students, fiercely attacked everything and everyone with ties to the West or to the past in their crusade against the "four olds" (old culture, old thinking, old habits, old customs). Many Christians, as well as others, suffered cruel personal indignities. Churches were vandalized, hymn books and Bibles burned, windows broken, religious symbols destroyed or defaced, buildings taken over as dormitories or warehouses. While there have been occasional reports of Christians meeting in homes for prayer or Bible study, it seems that public worship and other church activities have virtually stopped.

Since the Cultural Revolution there has been little evidence of organized Christian activity in China. Chinese visitors from the United States in 1972 were told by relatives in several places that churches were open, though they did not themselves attend services. There also have been a number of reports of small groups meeting for worship and Bible study in homes.

On Easter Sunday 1972, worship services were resumed in the Mi Shih (Rice Market) Street Church in Peking, described by a foreign correspondent as "the first public Protestant worship in Peking since the Cultural Revolution." This is the former independent church of which C. Y. Cheng was pastor in the early 1900s, where the name Church of Christ in China was first used. Reports by visitors and correspondents indicate that Sunday services continue in this church in the Chinese language but are attended chiefly by foreign diplomats and correspondents, with few Chinese worshippers.

The Hong Kong Council of the CCC

One unit of the Church of Christ in China has been able to continue a separate existence. This is the Hong Kong Council of the Church of Christ in China, formerly a district association of the Kwangtung Synod. Hong Kong, although contiguous to China and populated chiefly by Chinese people, has been a separate political entity, as a British crown colony, for over a hundred years. The CCC there was an outgrowth of the work of the London Missionary Society in the early years of the colony. However, through migration to Hong Kong of Christians from almost all parts of China in times of political crisis (in some instances whole congregations moved), almost every denominational tradition in the CCC on the mainland is represented in the Church in Hong Kong today.

In 1951, because of the political situation and the virtually complete breakdown of communications with China, the Hong Kong Council declared itself an autonomous church. As such, it has continued a life of its own and exhibited considerable vitality. It considers itself a "daughter church" of the Church of Christ in China.

Mission boards in Great Britain, Australia, New Zealand, Canada, and the United States cooperate with it.

By 1971 this church claimed more than twenty thousand members, a growth of about 100% in fifteen years. There were thirty organized congregations and significant educational and welfare programs. In 1971 there were fourteen kindergartens, and forty-five primary and secondary schools related to the Church, with an enrollment of forty-three thousand students. The Council sponsors a medical clinic, a school health program, children's summer camps and youth programs in the resettlement areas, and a coffee house for young workers.

The Church in China in the Future?

At a time when a more conciliatory attitude seems to prevail in China, certainly in regard to relations with the rest of the world, is there hope for renewed life for the Christian church in China? It is very difficult to know. While the stock assurance of "freedom of belief" is still maintained, one certainly sees few signs that religious activity is being encouraged.

Even if the government of China should tomorrow publicly take the position that the church could resume at least its worship services, the obstacles would be enormous. Congregations have been scattered and surviving leaders diverted to other occupations. Many church leaders will undoubtedly have passed from the scene and there has been no theological training in recent years and very little for more than a generation. Church buildings have been converted to other uses and probably would be unavailable for church use.

It is very unlikely that financial aid from churches outside China would be permitted. Indeed it is almost inconceivable that in the current climate Chinese Christians would seek such aid. The spirit of self-reliance and independence so marked in recent years would no doubt prevail among Christians, as among other Chinese. Without outside assistance, the development of even a very simple form of theological education, so necessary for the training of theologically qualified leadership, would be very dubious. The major institutional programs in education, medicine, and social service could certainly not be revived, not only because of costs but because of the Socialist position that such functions are the responsibility of the state.

If the organized church should again be permitted to function, it would be a long struggle to get back on its feet unless there was a great change in the whole atmosphere, which does not seem likely. But God's miracle of grace cannot be contained and we may yet see a living and vital Christian church arise in China, calling the faithful back to devotion and service. If and when that happens, we may be sure that it will be a Chinese church, possibly with new forms and expressions that will be peculiarly Chinese. The old denominations would not likely be revived without outside encouragement.

In other words, the church will quite certainly be what the Church of Christ in China was intended to be—indigenous, autonomous, a unifying force within the nation—even though it may not bear that name. The mission-church relationship of the past is forever gone, and it seems certain that the foreign missionary, certainly in the old pattern, will not be welcomed. Hopefully, such a church, as it grew in strength and maturity, would be in constructive, ecumenical fellowship with other Christian churches in Asia and around the world, making its contribution as an independent Chinese church to the work and mission of the world church.

Chapter Eleven: The Church
of Christ
in China — Goals and Achievements

We have sought to describe in the preceding chapters the desire within the Christian movement in China for unity expressed in a Chinese church transcending the denominational traditions of the Western missions and bringing together many Christians of varied doctrinal inheritances in a Church of Christ in China. The only true union church in China, going beyond denominational lines, did the CCC claim too much? Was the very name, *the* Church of Christ in China, presumptuous and pretentious, as charged by some who opposed or criticized it?

Certainly the concept of a truly indigenous church was attractive to many at a time of national crisis when the Chinese people were seeking to establish their independence and identity. Its growth coincided with a time of growth in national consciousness and of Chinese leadership within the church. The Chinese who chose the name in 1922 rejected the use of the word "united" in the title, hoping to establish a church that was Chinese from its inception and not simply a bringing together of Western denominations. It did express the conviction of many dedicated and determined Chinese Christians that the need for a union of the Protestant churches of China far outweighed denominational considerations.

In the "Bond of Union," the closest thing to a doctrinal statement of the Church, it was stated:

> The Church shall have as its object to unite Christian believers in China, to plan and promote with united strength the spirit of self-support, self-government and self-propagation, in order to extend Christ's Gospel, practice His Way of Life and spread His Kingdom throughout the World.

Was that goal achieved in reasonable measure? Were the chief

195

objectives called for by the Church and its leadership reached? In this closing chapter, we will look at some of those objectives and try to evaluate the extent to which they were accomplished.

A Truly United Church?

Was the Church of Christ in China truly a united Church at the national level? Probably that can be claimed only to a limited degree. Circumstances did not permit the full achievement of that goal—war disrupted normal functioning of the Church at national and regional levels; political and civil circumstances did not permit development to continue; economic difficulties made continued dependence on outside support necessary; the mission agencies were slow in accepting the church's claim to autonomy and authority.

Certainly the direction in which the Church of Christ in China was moving was right. We can hardly question the concept of a church with Chinese leadership uniting Christians throughout the nation, with a sense of community with the nation, seeing its role as a servant church, an instrument of God's will for the redemption of Chinese individuals and society. The goal of mission, accepted by most of the cooperating mission bodies, was an indigenous church, truly controlled, supported, led by nationals.

The kind of unity that was espoused by the leadership of the Church of Christ in China certainly included such purposes. Those missions in China that did not seek to establish an indigenous and autonomous church, either because they had little concept of that as a goal or because they did not trust national leadership, developed neither strong churches nor an able national leadership.

A church such as the CCC envisioned would need to develop its own theological thinkers, using Chinese terms and Chinese concepts. It is true that theology must be universal in concept if a church is to be truly catholic and part of the universal church. But a truly indigenous church ought to have within it those who are giving serious thought to the interpretation and application of the Gospel message to its own people and its own age. This seems to be the case in the Japanese church, where the relevance of Christian thought to the needs of twentieth-century Japan is under constant discussion.

The Chinese churches produced few serious theological thinkers. They tended to be pragmatic rather than philosophical (though China historically has produced its share of philosophical thinkers).

This was in part due to the missionary heritage, for missionaries tend to be doers, rather than thinkers, concerned with action, rather than thought.

Union (and specifically the Church of Christ in China) was opposed by many—both missionaries and Chinese—on doctrinal grounds, forgetting that no denomination has ever been able to maintain doctrinal unanimity. The divergences within denominations (at least in the major denominations in the West) are about as great as they are between denominations. Unity and church union are far more important in areas where churches are young than in areas where the church is strongly established. This was strongly felt by many Chinese and Western leaders. The Western denominational heritage was not their own except in a second-hand way. The small membership in churches in China argued for union to provide a wide basis of support for the essential services of a church—leadership training, including theological education, and denominational literature, including Christian educational material and a viable mission enterprise. Such pressures were inevitably strengthened by nationalism and the natural demand for control of their own institutions by nationals.

Unquestionably, the concept of a truly Chinese Church had enormous appeal to many Chinese Christians. We have seen that as far back as the early years of the twentieth century there was a strong desire on the part of able Chinese leadership for such a church. C. Y. Cheng, as he voiced insistence on a truly Chinese Church at Edinburgh and Jerusalem and in his own land, epitomized that desire and spoke for many of his fellow Chinese Christians. The Chinese were an able people with a proud history, and in the long years of humiliation and exploitation by alien and often arrogant outside powers they were especially mindful of their own heritage and eager to be masters again in their own house and in the house of the Lord.

The appeal of a Chinese church was seen also in the strong interest of Chinese Christians in Southeast Asia in the CCC. Links with the mainland churches were strong for many of these Christians. Most of their churches were the fruit of Christian witness on the part of Christian emigrés, and their pastors were drawn from the home churches. A substantial number of these churches were related by many such ties to churches that became part of the CCC in Kwangtung or Fukien and were related to missions (such as the English Presbyterians in Malaya and Formosa) whose work on the mainland united with the CCC. National pride, increasingly stronger among Chinese in the twentieth century, drew many overseas Chinese Christians toward the CCC. The Presbyterian Church of Malaya actually became a synod of the CCC in 1948 (but later withdrew), and the Presbyterian Church in southern Formosa was preparing to take membership. Churches in Java and the Philippines, which had given strong financial support to the CCC, especially its mission programs, were represented at the 1948 Soochow Assembly and interested in membership.

Within the synodical structures of the Church, the degree of unity attained varied considerably. Where only one mission or church tradition was represented in a Synod, it often continued its life as though the church were still a denominational body, rather than part of a united church. Thus in Hopei Province, as we have noted, two synods went their separate ways for almost twenty years; and in Hopei Synod, at least, many Chinese and missionaries thought of themselves and talked of their church as Presbyterian, rather than as a unit of a national Church of Christ in China. But a change did take place after the close of the war with Japan, when there was serious consultation on coming together, and union was finally effected in 1950, though in view of the breakdown of normal church procedures with the growth in power of the Three-Self Movement and the decline in church activity that followed, it is impossible to say how much meaning the union had.

It was also true that there was a growing sense of participation in a national church in the late 1940s, related in part to a growth in national pride and consciousness forged by the suffering of the long struggle with Japan. Many Christians, especially the younger leaders, began to drop the old denominational tags and refer to their churches as the Church of Christ in China.

The period following the war with Japan and well into the years of the People's Republic of China was marked by a growing consciousness of the need for strong leadership at the synodical level. Synod after synod elected General Secretaries, many from the most promising younger leadership of the area, in order to crystallize the growing sentiment of unity within the regions, as well as within the nation as a whole.

A mimeographed report entitled "The Church of Christ in China" (undated, about 1948—probably written by E. Bruce Copland to mission boards and others outside China interested in the CCC) included the following statement:

> The common life of the church in China has undoubtedly been much affected by the formation of the Church of Christ in China. There has been a gradual and steady development in church consciousness during the years

since church union so that most church members have a sense of belonging to a great fellowship, not just to their local church. . . . There is no doubt that the CCC, small as it is in numbers, has helped to develop a . . . healthy national loyalty.

Where there were several denominational traditions involved in a synod, the sense of a united church was much stronger. This was particularly true in the South Fukien Synod, with its long history of union between Presbyterians and Reformed, joined later by Congregationalists and Methodists, and where the church was strong in membership and Chinese leadership. Another area where true union seems to have taken place was in the Kwangtung Synod, where the history of cooperative and united effort by most of the churches in the area went back further than the organization of the national church. Chinese nationalism developed early in the area, and the work of at least six mission boards, along with a number of strong independent Chinese church groups, was coordinated at an early stage. A strong synodical consciousness developed, and responsibility for work and finances was early turned over to the Synod. Through the Synod's periodicals (both Chinese and English) and its programs in many areas of work (Youth, Relief, Women's Work, etc.), with Chinese staff giving full- or part-time service, there developed a synodical consciousness and a strong sense of unity lacking in many of the weaker synods.

In some areas chaotic conditions and difficult communications made participation in the life of the national church or even the synod virtually impossible. In the Northeast Synod, for example, composed entirely of churches of the Presbyterian tradition, a relatively strong area-wide program was built up even before there was affiliation with the CCC. There was close cooperation with the Presbyterian churches which grew out of Canadian Presbyterian work, though it is not clear whether this latter group actually came into the Synod. But the Japanese occupation of Manchuria in 1931 and the establishment of a separate political regime meant that virtually all communication between the Synod and the CCC General Assembly office was cut off for more than fifteen years. Although the Synod was represented by its Moderator and its Executive Secretary (Ma Ch'ing-hsuan and Liu Huai-yi) at the 1948 General Assembly at Soochow, both men were killed in an airplane crash as they returned to Mukden on January 5, 1949. Nationalist armies, moved into the Northeast by American planes at the close of the war with Japan, were routed in late 1948, and again effective communication beween the Synod and the General Assembly was cut off.

Synods in areas divided by the war with Japan and the civil war that followed, such as Shantung, Shansi and Honan, were unable to function or even to meet for many years.

In some other areas, the redrawing of synodical lines and the entry of new cooperating churches, as in Hunan and Hupei, came so late that it was not possible to develop a strong organization or program before the drastic limitation of church activities that came with Communist control. Hupei and Hunan had been a single synod from 1927 to 1948 (Lianghu Synod). Then entry of the Tsun Tao Hui (Evangelical United Brethren related) in Hunan and the Hsing Tao Hui (Swedish Missionary Society related) in Hupei led to the organization of separate synods for each of the two provinces.

One of the most important enterprises of the Church of Christ in China was its mission program. It constituted one of the strongest claims of the CCC to be a national church, for though modest programs of mission in nearby areas and among aboriginal people were carried on by some of the synods, particularly in the south, the considerable work of the CCC missions could have been conceived and administered only by the central agencies of a national church, particularly during the disruptions of the war years. It was a unifying factor in the life of the Church, and the concept of the responsibility of the whole Church for mission was accepted throughout all sectors of the Church. It was an effort of the whole Church, even though some congregations could take little part in it and in some cases were hardly aware of its work. The entire program gave evidence of the sense of mission on the part of the national Church and its leadership, an essential and distinguishing mark of a true church. It was almost unique in China, for though there were some modest efforts by other churches, notably the Sheng Kung Hui, the CCC mission program was on a scale not undertaken by others, and it drew support in contributions and personnel from all over the nation.

A strong measure of acceptance of the Church of Christ in China as a national church was indicated by its steady growth. Every General Assembly saw new churches coming into membership. The denominational range was quite wide, for though in the early years denominations in the Presbyterian tradition predominated, the union also drew Baptists, Congregationalists, and Methodists, as well as churches related to such American groups as the Evangelical United Brethren, the Evangelical and Reformed Church, and the Swedish Missionary Society of Lutheran background, to say nothing of many independent Chinese congregations. As has been indicated, the churches related to the Church of the Brethren and the Christian

Church (Disciples of Christ) were interested and might have become affiliated with the CCC in time.

The existence of a strong, though small, central administrative secretariat throughout the life of the Church and the high quality of staff leadership were unifying and cohesive factors. This was almost unique among Chinese churches, for though the larger denominational churches had coordinating and consultative agencies, staff was minimal, national programs and staff activity were very limited, and administration and program were largely at the regional level, usually related to ties with a particular overseas mission. The General Assemblies, even though they could not meet during most of the Sino-Japanese War, were an instrument of integration and helped to build up a sense of oneness in worship, faith, and service.

Was the CCC Too Strongly Presbyterian?

Was the Church of Christ in China too Presbyterian? This charge was often levelled at it by its critics. Certainly the Presbyterian influence was strong, particularly during the Church's formation—and quite naturally, since the nucleus of the union was Presbyterian. But those of other denominational backgrounds who came into the Church did not find its strong Presbyterian elements a great difficulty and, as has been pointed out, these included a fairly wide variety—Baptists, Congregationalists, Methodists, and others. It is true that major Baptist and Methodist groups remained outside the CCC, as did the Anglican-Episcopalians, though union was at least discussed. The Lutherans also remained entirely separate. But there was a strong admixture of several major traditions besides the Presbyterian, and a significant proportion of Protestantism in China joined its forces in the Church of Christ in China.

The national leadership of the Church was always aware of the divergent heritages of its member bodies. While missionary associates in the work of the General Assembly office came chiefly from Presbyterian missions, other denominational backgrounds were well represented in the Chinese leadership: C. Y. Cheng a Congregationalist, H. H. Tsui a Methodist, W. B. Djang a Baptist, to mention only a few. Early agreement that local churches should have full freedom of belief and practice—e.g., the statement in Article 4 of the Constitution that "Any constituent church, in addition to the acceptance of the bond of union, may retain its original standards of faith"—provided safeguards to those of other than Reformed background.

Doctrinal Issues

If there had been progress in the proposal to formulate a more specific doctrinal statement, this no doubt would have posed difficulties between those of the Presbyterian or Reformed tradition, accustomed to specific credal statements, and those of noncredal or anti-credal traditions, such as Baptists, Congregationalists, and Methodists. That happened in the postwar development of a comparable union, the United Church of Christ in Japan (Kyodan) and led to much debate and heart-searching. A position generally acceptable to the diverse elements in that church was finally achieved, though the most conservative elements of the Reformed group had already withdrawn from the union.

In China the national crisis with all its ramifications prevented the development of a church that might have wrestled with such issues. In those synods where varied denominational elements had been merged, preoccupation with practical problems of program and of mere survival were so pressing that there is little evidence of doctrinal debate or disagreement.

On the other hand, doctrinal considerations were important in the decision of at least two groups to stay out of the union. The North China Kung Li Hui (Congregationalist) made its decision not to come in primarily on the issue of the autonomy of the local congregation, but was also wary of Presbyterian conservatism. On the other hand, the Presbyterians of Shantung and Anhwei who stayed out, though both groups eventually came into the union, did so chiefly because they were uneasy about union with churches of other than Presbyterian background and Baptist and Congregational liberalism.

Self-support

One of the goals of the Church of Christ in China was self-support. No other theme was emphasized so persistently in the pronouncements of the Church's councils and the exhortations of its leaders. A large measure of self-support would seem essential to true autonomy and indigenousness. To what degree was self-support attained in the Church of Christ in China?

We would have to say in all honesty that it was attained only to a limited degree—chiefly at the local level, hardly at all at the national level. The difficulties, as with any young and struggling church, were formidable. The economy was not prosperous; the concept of church support of a professional ministry was alien to the Chinese culture; church buildings and especially church institutions were beyond the capability of the church to maintain. These difficulties were compounded by the destruction and disruption brought by civil strife and a major war. All Asian churches lost ground in self-support during the years of the Pacific War, including those in Burma and Korea, among the most advanced in this respect.

Within the CCC, self-support was most advanced and leadership was strongest where church members were numerous and there were prosperous communities. This was notably true in Kwangtung (including the Swatow area) and South Fukien, areas where the church was strongest in membership and leadership and, significantly, where self-government and self-propagation were also well developed. These were areas where there had been substantial emigration, and the flow of funds from overseas Chinese was an important factor in the general prosperity and in the strength of the churches. These were also the areas where Christian missions found entry into China, had their longest history, and (along with Manchuria and Shantung) had their greatest success.

There was general agreement that the Chinese churches were too dependent on mission support. The system of subsidization almost universally used in the early days created dependence. But in many areas where the church was strong, it surmounted that handicap.

The Chinese sects such as those mentioned in Chapter III certainly achieved self-support. Almost exclusively without connections with foreign missions, they had no alternative. They did so by employing a lay and largely untrained ministry, by vigorously emphasizing tithing, by using simple structures for worship, and by maintaining no institutional programs. Such sects had little concern for the wider community and were to a considerable degree dependent on the work of the traditional churches in Christian education, Christian literature, and medical services. Indigenous churches elsewhere in Asia, some of which had broken away from mission groups with which there had been earlier affiliation, had also achieved self-support, but almost always at the cost of adequately trained leadership, the absence of competent theological education, and a low and often superstitious level of church consciousness and religious life.

Complete self-support for every congregation is an unattainable goal in any country. In the United States, for example, most churches in new residential areas are supported by general denominational funds in their early development, and increasingly long-established and one-time self-supporting churches in areas of urban change are forced to seek aid from without or survive only by merger or by sharing ministries with a minimum of professional leadership and church activity. Self-support in China would probably not have been possible to a large degree without a much more prosperous economy. In comparable Asian churches with freedom to develop and much more prosperous economies, considerable progress has been made.

Progress in Self-support in Other Asian Churches

The United Church of Christ in Japan (the Kyodan), a united church including many of the same elements as the CCC, and in the most prosperous economy in Asia, has achieved a high degree of self-support. By 1971 local congregations were completely self-supporting with the exception of a few mission churches. In many instances, however, this was at a very low level, with pastors' salaries comparable to the salaries of unskilled labor, forcing many to seek supplemental work to support their families. The central administration of the Kyodan is completely supported by Japanese church contributions. In 1970 the total giving of the Church for all Church causes was approximately four and a half million in American dollars for a total membership just over 200,000, with about 2,000 ordained ministers. Support from the cooperating North American missions has for the most part been in the form of missionary service and in projects undertaken jointly.

In early 1972, in a remarkable development, this church and its related agencies in a sense went beyond self-support. The cooperating mission boards were forced to reconsider their commitments because of decreasing income and in many instances faced a reduction in missionary staff. The Kyodan's Council on Cooperation (church, schools, and Social Work League) pledged itself to work out a maintenance schedule for the more than three hundred missionaries

working within the Church and related institutions, so that no
missionary would have to leave cooperative work in Japan for
financial reasons.

The Hong Kong Council of the Church of Christ in China, with
about 20,000 members, has made a serious effort to attain self-
support. A plan mutually approved by the Church and its cooperating missions in 1953 called for an annual decrease of 10% in
mission subsidies (c. US$42,000 in 1963) with complete self-support
by 1973: a schedule which has been maintained and seems well on
the way to successful culmination. Mission aid continues in the form
of the services of a decreasing number of missionaries, some of them
in church institutions, and in assistance to interdenominational theological education at Chung Chi College. The substantial educational
program of the Church is maintained by fees and government subsidization, available to all private schools meeting government standards.

The Presbyterian Church in Taiwan reported a communicant membership in 1971 of approximately 70,000 (of which almost 30,000
were aboriginal tribespeople), with 50,000 baptized children and
46,000 inquirers under instruction. Of its nine hundred nineteen
congregations, four hundred seventy-five are listed as self-supporting.
The total contributions of the congregations amounted to approximately US$900,000. No mission funds go to the support of local
congregations, church buildings or presbytery programs, though
some presbyteries have endowment funds resulting from the sale of
former mission property. Aid to local congregations, where needed,
comes from the presbyteries.

The General Assembly office, including office expense, travel, etc.,
has a budget of c.US$20,000, of which about 31% comes from
related missions. Substantial aid from the missions goes to the
institutions for theological training, averaging well under 50% except
for the training of aboriginal church leaders, which receives about
70% subsidy from the missions. Institutional programs receive virtually no mission aid, but support goes to special programs such as
urban-industrial evangelism, mountain work, and student work. Total
grants from the supporting missions, not including the services of
missionaries, come to about one-tenth of local support.

So we see that in other churches in the area, a large measure of
self-support has been reached in the years since the end of the Pacific
War. Would a comparable measure of self-support have been possible
for the Church of Christ in China if it had been able to continue its
life and program? If a less restrictive society had been maintained in

China and there had been the kind of growth in prosperity that has come to other Asian nations, it is likely that the pressure for self-support would have had a similar measure of success. There was the will to achieve it on the part of the leadership of the Church, supported by many of its members, and there is no reason to believe it would not have taken place with the growth of self-reliance.

Under a Communist regime, the Church had to adapt to a different way of life. Christian schools, hospitals, orphanages, and rural and social work, important in Christian program in the past, soon disappeared or were taken over in a socialist state which saw responsibility for such programs as its own. More critically, it is difficult to see how a meaningful program of theological education could be maintained in a subsistence economy in which the commune and its units are the chief elements. If the Church had been permitted to continue its activity, pastoral leadership would have had to be, like that of the early church, dependent on tent-making ministries. Theological education would probably have had to be developed by individual tutorship rather than institutionally. Whether the kind of theological scholarship and corporate life needed by any true church could have come out of such a program or can come out of it in the future is a serious question.

As there presently seems to be some disposition toward permitting a limited amount of church life, evidenced by the renewal of some worship services in Peking, we may see what is possible for the Christian church in China under Communism. It has been possible for the Christian churches under European Communist regimes to maintain some activity, though usually not with more than worship services and in some cases with some degree of state subsidization. It is interesting that some of the members of the group of Japanese church leaders who paid an extensive visit to China in 1957 told the author that they felt the Chinese church was still a dependent church and that only the source of dependency had changed. The church was no longer dependent on the missions but on the state, which through the use of rentals from former mission property was at that time providing subsidization for congregations which were useful as showplaces and whose leadership was cooperative.

Pensions

One element in the concept of self-support that would seem essential is that of providing for the workers of a church in old age or deprivation. Very few Asian churches have been able to make any provision for such needs, a notable exception being the United Church of Christ in Japan, which has been able to establish and maintain a modest pension plan for its clergy.

The need for a system of pensions was frequently referred to in General Assembly reports and discussions and Church leadership was keenly aware of the need to make provision for the old age of church workers who had given years of service at subsistence levels and for the widows and children of men who died relatively early, especially for the education of their children. In spite of such concern and frequent discussions, however, no practical scheme was ever developed at the national level. At the Fifth General Assembly in 1948, the synods were urged to do something about this need and the plans developed by the Kwangtung and Szechuan Synods were mentioned as models.

Here again, the economic and physical disruption of the years of the Japanese occupation and the civil war after 1945 made it impossible to implement this genuine concern. Here, as in the general problem of self-support, success would certainly have depended to a considerable extent on the generosity of well-to-do Chinese Christian businessmen at home and abroad, who had contributed generously to the CCC mission program and other needs. It is worth noting that one such Christian had provided funds for a denominational missionary retirement center in the United States and reportedly had offered the Church of Christ in China a large sum for a similar retirement center for Chinese church workers. Changing circumstances made it impossible, however, for any such scheme to be carried out.

Church-Mission Relationships

Throughout its life, as we have seen, the Church of Christ in China, in its effort to become an indigenous Chinese church, had to wrestle with the thorny problems of church-mission relationships. From the first its leadership asserted the primacy and centrality of the church in Christian work and the necessity of recognizing the church as the body responsible for continuing Christian mission. As reported in Chapter VI, the General Council and the Second General Assembly endorsed a set of basic principles on church-mission relationships worked out with representatives of the cooperating missions in 1929. These clearly stated the "church-centric" principle of church responsibility for the administration of program and missionary personnel, church control of every aspect of Christian work, and "the right of direct relationship with the mission boards and church bodies"—i.e., recognition of the Church of Christ in China as an independent, sovereign, national church. The acceptance of that position implied the disappearance of the traditional mission organization of foregin missionaries standing between the Chinese Church and Christian bodies abroad. There was also quiet insistence that the work assignment of missionaries be the responsibility of the church courts and, especially in the latter years, the finances and personnel be channeled through the national church.

In this history, we have dwelt on the rise of a Chinese church and the growth of Chinese responsibility and leadership. But while the missionary role has not been emphasized, it was of course a very important one. The missionary was essential to the beginning of Christian work in China. As Chinese leadership and Chinese church forms began to evolve, the missionaries, some of whom have been mentioned briefly, were in full sympathy with the desires for a Chinese church and worked loyally within its structures and for its establishment. Through the years much of the ongoing evangelistic work was essentially that of the missionary. He played a major role in pioneer evangelism, penetrated areas where the Gospel had not reached, and made a substantial contribution to the work of Christian institutions. For the most part, the missionary's relationship with Chinese colleagues was warm and friendly—he worked under difficult circumstances, self-effacedly, frequently in danger.

As relationships between Chinese churchmen and individual missionaries were usually harmonious, so were those between the Church of Christ in China and its cooperating missions. Pronouncements on the Church's claims to churchhood and its right to control over programs were always worded in a conciliatory tone and were never recriminatory. There was frequent expression of appreciation for the help of the missions and the missionaries. These were not mere expressions of Chinese politeness, but genuinely felt sentiments. But from its earliest history there was no mistaking the insistence of the CCC on its sovereignty and autonomy. Unfortunately, while most of the cooperating missions recognized their validity, the implementation of these claims was all too slow.

While unquestionably there would have been an element of risk in moving too rapidly in this direction, especially where mature and capable Chinese leadership was in short supply, in areas where responsibility for policy and funds was early transferred to church bodies, the results were on the whole satisfactory. Indeed, it might be argued that the very shift of responsibility helped bring about the growth of capable leadership and the Church of Christ in China might have been much stronger if all the mission societies had moved in this direction sooner.

Fisher points out that while the mission boards and societies of the Western churches rendered "magnificent service" to the Christian cause with their work and had the aim of establishing indigenous churches, in fact the result of their work was often a case of "transplanting the church of the sending church to the mission field." He quotes C. Y. Cheng on church-mission relationships:

> We may regard the mission as a nurse engaged in looking after children. The nurse is big, capable, kind, wise, (sometimes not wise) in performing her task, but it is clear that it is not to be expected that a nurse will remain in the household forever. We believe that the relationship between the Christian church of the East and the Christian church of the West will, in the future, be a more direct one, requiring no such intermediary organization as the "mission".

One of the greatest obstacles to the development of a strong Chinese Church was a lack of trust on the part of some missionaries and mission organizations—trust in Chinese leadership, trust in a Chinese church, trust in God's power to work through a Chinese church and build it up. It is true that there were a few Chinese Christians unworthy of trust, motivated by selfishness and the desire for power—just as there were some missionaries who were reluctant to relinquish power, who were misled by the myth of racial superiority and were unable to understand and accept Chinese cultural patterns, and who were unable to assess accurately Chinese desires for autonomy and a Chinese church. True, the Chinese church might have fallen into heresies, as some missionaries feared. Chinese leadership was often divided. But some missionaries seemed unable to grasp the fact that the Chinese church had to find its own way and think through its own theology to be a true church, just as the churches of the West had done, not without deviation and error. So long as the missionary remained the arbiter of doctrine, the source of power, the paymaster—so long was it impossible to draw and hold strong and able Chinese leadership.

R. Pierce Beaver, in a paper prepared about 1943 for his own board (the Board of International Missions of the Evangelical and Reformed Church), said:

> We have been talking about devolution, transfer of administrative responsi-

bility and the assumption of the "colleague" relationship for the last quarter of a century. . . . It is now time to stop talking about these things and proceed along these lines that the majority of missionaries and national leaders have long since decided to be the only right procedures. . . . The autonomy which this Church [CCC] claims is in reality denied, not in theory, but in action, by many of the missions associated with it.

The process of devolution, the transfer of control over program, personnel, and funds to the Chinese church, while early recognized as the proper procedure to follow (it was a major theme at the 1927 Jerusalem Conference), was implemented very slowly. In the Synods of Mid-Fukien and North Fukien, the mission organization was dissolved in 1927 and full power given to the Synods. This had happened even earlier in Kwangtung and the principle was accepted and carried out in relation to church work, but synodical authority over institutions did not come until the mid-thirties. Even so, it appears that most of the missions continued to maintain direct links to the districts with which they had been historically related to channel their aid through them. This was generally true even in such advanced synods as South Fukien.

Progress was more rapid after 1945. Many of the boards recognized that the churches to which they had been related had been completely self-governing and in occupied areas self-supporting during the war years and did not claim the kind of authority which many mission organizations had exercised before the war. Thus the Board of Foreign Missions of the Presbyterian Church in the USA, on the recommendation of their postwar study deputation, which had conferred with church leaders, permitted reorganization of mission structures only along limited lines to care for missionary maintenance. The Missions Council of the Scottish Presbyterians in Manchuria was not reestablished. Instead an Advisory Council of Chinese and missionaries was formed to work with the Northeast Synod.

Missionaries were generally assigned to areas where the sending boards had traditionally worked, rather than through the General Assembly office to areas where the need was greatest and where particular skills were most suited. The one place where this pattern was broken was in the missions of the CCC. For the most part the missionaries assigned to these programs were those unable to work in the traditional areas of their mission's work. It was the beginning of a procedure which if more fully implemented would have helped to break down old denominational loyalties and strengthen the sense of national unity of the Church of Christ in China. Even here problems arose. Margaret Brown in her *History of the Honan Mission* reports that the United Church of Canada boards in 1940, when some of their displaced missionaries were reassigned by the CCC Provisional Assembly, accepted the procedure but wanted them assigned to their own mission's field of work in West China (Szechuan Synod). They challenged the authority of the CCC "to negotiate with Board of Foreign Missions in North America in matters affecting the work of missionaries from the Western churches."

Among the few steps taken by the mission boards that confirmed acceptance of the "church-centric" principle was direct support by a number of boards through the General Assembly of the missions of the Church. Another evidence was the postwar handling of relief and rehabilitation funds for Church workers by grants directly from several boards to the General Assembly office, giving it full freedom in distribution. Such action demonstrated a growing confidence by the boards in the national church and the recognition and strengthening of church-to-church relations.

At its meeting on May 25, 1950, in New York, the North American Advisory Committee, representing North American boards cooperating with the CCC, recognized the full authority of the Church of Christ in China over missionary personnel, property, and finances, but the hour was already late and the changing situation did not really permit testing such a position, so long sought by the Church and so belatedly acquiesced in by a group of mission boards.

In some ways, the Church of Christ in China was further along than most other churches in China in its claim to be a national and autonomous church with the right of control over supporting boards and societies. Certainly this was true in the leadership of the Church, with Chinese in every top position except one from the very beginning, and in its establishment and maintenance of a program of national missions. In contrast, Bishop Y. Y. Tsu of the Sheng Kung Hui reports in his autobiography that in May 1945 the five bishops in Free China drew up a "Memorandum to Cooperating Churches Overseas" entitled "The Crisis of the Chung Hua Sheng Kung Hui." This urged a central administrative office for the Church with central planning and funds and implementation of a 1941 recommendation of the House of Bishops that the Chinese church be free to elect its own bishops. "The recommendations involved a radical change in missionary policy, in the assigning of missionaries and funds, not to the individual dioceses but to the Chinese Church as a whole."

Although the established central office was maintained, the other recommendations were not implemented. According to Bishop Tsu, the three American bishops were opposed to giving up historical relations with their dioceses. As the critical situation in 1949-50 made it wise for Western missionaries to evacuate China, nine of the ten dioceses related to Western mission societies were still headed by missionary bishops, though in short order able Chinese bishops, most of whom had been serving as suffragan bishops, took their places. (The two dioceses established by the Sheng Kung Hui—Yun-Kwei and Shensi—were led by Chinese bishops.)

Summary—the Direction Was Right

Fisher begins his account of the Church of Christ in China by saying:

> As an organic union, the history of the Church of Christ in China does not cover a long period of time. It is not its length in time but what it is and stands for that makes it significant. It has been recognized as an event of sufficient importance to have received the notice of nearly every large gathering of Christians in and out of China for the last twenty years. It has been both commended and criticized. It has been an inspiration to many as the fulfillment of an ardent hope for church union. It has given impetus to other bodies of Christians to unite.

Fisher also expresses the intense commitment of most of the leaders of the CCC, missionaries as well as Chinese, to a Chinese church uniting various traditions: "We have a conviction that the formation of the Church of Christ in China is a part of God's plan for His Church here upon earth."

While it did not completely achieve its self-proclaimed goals (what church does?), it was a brave effort which would quite certainly have succeeded to an even greater extent if it had been permitted to continue. Its measure of success in hardly more than a generation as a functioning identity was not inconsiderable.

It was in process of becoming a truly Chinese church. Its leadership from the beginning had set the goals of autonomy, indigeneity, and witness—self-government, self-support, and self-propagation—and had held firmly to them. All sections of the nation were represented in its membership, probably the most far-reaching of any Protestant church in China. It was sufficiently meaningful as a nationwide Chinese church to attract leadership of high character, as able as any which came out of the life of the Christian church in China.

The stigma of "foreign religion" was understandably difficult to eradicate, but the experience of the war years, the growth of Chinese leadership, the sense of identity with the nation during the years of the Japanese threat, the commitment to mission during those years— all of these strengthened the position of the CCC as a truly Chinese church, a reality increasingly recognized by Chinese outside the Church as well as within. While throughout its brief history the Church continued to receive substantial aid from the cooperating missions, the top leadership throughout its life was Chinese. With the growth of Chinese nationalism, this was extremely important to the Church's survival.

It was an ecumenical church. As long as it was possible, it maintained its ties with the churches which historically had been related to its constituent units through missions, with ecumenical and confessional world bodies, and with other Chinese churches. Throughout its history, the CCC was in full cooperation with and gave full support to the National Christian Council of China and other agencies of Christian cooperation. It held the door open for wider union in China in a generous and undemanding spirit.

It was a church in mission. While its efforts and accomplishments in mission were modest, hardly more than a beginning, they were undertaken in the spirit of obedience to the Lord's call to mission and out of deep concern for the physical and spiritual well-being of neglected people of their own land, with strong and growing support from all segments of the Church. It was a church that exercised an important influence on Chinese society, perhaps more so than any other Christian body, through its program and its effort to be truly the Church of Christ in China—self-governing, self-supporting, and self-propagating.

It was a church with an increasing sense of selfhood and increasing self-reliance, clearly expressed in the words of an editorial in *The Church* for February 1949, probably written by one of its ablest leaders, H. H. Tsui:

> After more than twenty years, the Church of Christ is small in numbers, but not discouraged; it is dependent upon help from abroad, yet determined to undertake great tasks; it is a Chinese church, yet it is conscious of its ecumenical relationships; in a sense, it is *one* of the churches in China, yet it strives to be a united and uniting church, constantly praying for the time when there will be one Church of Christ in China.

The Constitution
of the Church of Christ in China

PART I. Name, Purpose, Bond of Union

Article 1: This Church shall be called "The Church of Christ in China," "Chung-hua Chi-tu Chiao-hui."

Article 2: The Church shall have as its object to unite Christian believers in China, to plan and promote with united strength the spirit of self-support, self-governance and self-propagation, in order to extend Christ's Gospel, practice His Way of Life and spread His Kingdom throughout the world.

Article 3: Based on the principle of the freedom of formulating her own faith, the bond of union shall consist:
(a) In our faith in Jesus Christ as our Redeemer and Lord on whom the Christian Church is founded; and in an earnest desire for the establishment of His Kingdom throughout the whole earth.
(b) In our acceptance of the Holy Scriptures of the Old and New Testaments as the divinely inspired word of God, and the supreme authority in matters of faith and duty.
(c) In our acknowledgement of the Apostles' Creed as expressing the fundamental doctrines of our common evangelical faith.

Article 4: All Churches who accept this Constitution are qualified to become constituent parts of this united body.
  Any constituent Church, in addition to the acceptance of the bond of union, may retain its original standards of faith.

PART II. Grades of Church Councils

Article 5: The Church shall administer its affairs through the following councils:
(a) Local Church—A local church is a company of believers regularly organized and assembling statedly for public worship in one or more places, and

recognized by the district association in whose bounds it is located. The method of its organization shall be decided by such district association.

(b) District Associations—A district association is a body composed of the lay representatives of the churches within a defined district and their ministers and their evangelists or licentiates who are recognized by such district church officers within its bounds.

(c) To promote evangelistic, educational, medical and social work within its bounds.

(d) The General Assembly—The General Assembly, the highest council of the Church, is a body composed of commissioners elected by all the respective synods.

PART III. Duties and Powers of Respective Church Councils

Article 6: The local church is the basic organization of the Church. Its duties and powers shall be determined by its district association.

Article 7: The duties and powers of the district association shall be as follows:

(a) To organize, supervise, assist, or disband churches within its bounds.

(b) By consent of the synod, to train, examine, ordain, install, or discipline all church officers within its bounds.

(c) To promote evangelistic, educational, medical and social work within its bounds.

(d) To decide references and appeals regularly presented by the churches within its bounds.

(e) To review the minutes of the churches within its bounds.

(f) To appoint representatives to the synod within whose bounds it is located.

Article 8: The duties and powers of synods shall be as follows:

(a) To organize and determine the boundaries of the district associations within its bounds.

(b) To decide all appeals and other matters referred to it by the district associations within its bounds.

(c) To decide all questions respecting doctrine and church government which may arise in the district associations within its bounds.

(d) To train, examine, ordain, install or discipline officers of the district associations or local churches within its bounds.

(e) To inaugurate, promote and supervise evangelistic, theological, educational, medical and social work within its bounds.

(f) To review minutes of the district associations within its bounds.

(g) To appoint representatives to serve as commissioners of the General Assembly.

Article 9: The duties and powers of the General Assembly shall be as follows:

(a) To be the representative of the whole Church and to constitute a bond of union among all grades of church councils.

(b) To consider and settle questions that may arise concerning church government or doctrine among the synods.
(c) To determine the standards for the ministry and regulate the reception of ministers from other denominations.
(d) To plan and administer all matters in connection with the interest of the whole Church.

PART IV. Amendments

Article 10: This Constitution shall not be altered, increased or diminished, unless there are two-thirds of the votes from all district associations of the Church affirming such alteration, increase or diminution. District associations in voting on any amendment to the Constitution shall have their number of votes determined by the number of communicants, namely, one vote for every five hundred (500) communicants or fraction thereof.

Article 11: Votes by district associations on proposed amendments shall be categorically "yes" or "no". The district associations may in separate overtures propose amendments or change, but such must in no wise limit or affect that "yes" or "no" vote on the proposed amendments transmitted to them for approval.

By-laws of the Church of Christ in China

PART I. Doctrinal Basis of Union

Article 1: The Church of Christ in China has the prerogative of formulating her own doctrinal statement.

Article 2: Every office bearer in the local churches and district associations of the Church shall declare his acceptance and observance of the bond of union as stated in the Constitution.

PART II. Missionaries

Article 3: Each synod shall have liberty to define for itself the place of the missionary in its organization.

PART III. Local Churches

Article 4: Each local church shall appoint delegates to the district association within whose bounds it is located.

Article 5: Each local church may adopt its own by-laws which must be in harmony with the Constitution of the Church.

PART IV. District Associations

Article 6: The representatives appointed by the local church to its district association shall be chosen from among the church officers in proportion to the number of communicants. Churches with two hundred (200) or more communicant members shall appoint two (2) representatives; churches with five hundred (500) or more shall appoint three (3) representatives. But each local church shall appoint at least one (1) representative.

Article 7: A district association may permit the local churches within its bounds to increase their number of representatives to attend the district association meeting.

Article 8: A district association may, whenever necessary, appoint special committees for all branches of work within its bounds and give them instructions and suitable authority and receive their reports.

Article 9: Each district association may adopt its own by-laws which must be in harmony with the Constitution of the Church.

PART V. Synod

Article 10: Each district association shall appoint representatives to the synod according to the number of communicant members in the district association. For each five hundred (500) in active membership, it shall appoint two (2) representatives, one of whom shall be a layman. With the permission of the synod, the representation of the district associations may be increased.

Article 11: A synod may, whenever necessary, appoint special committees for all branches of work under its jurisdiction and give them instructions and suitable authority and receive their reports.

Article 12: Each synod may adopt its own by-laws and rules of order, which should be in harmony with the Constitution of the Church.

PART VI. The General Assembly

Article 13: The number of commissioners from each synod to the General Assembly shall be according to its communicant membership. For the first three thousand (3,000) communicants or fraction thereof, there shall be two (2) commissioners. For more than three thousand (3,000) up to six thousand (6,000) communicants, there shall be four (4) commissioners. For more than six thousand (6,000) up to ten thousand (10,000) communicants, there shall be six (6) commissioners. For more than ten thousand (10,000) up to fifteen thousand (15,000) communicants, there shall be eight (8) commissioners. For more than fifteen thousand (15,000) communicants, there shall be ten (10) commissioners. In each case half of the commissioners shall be ministers and one-half laymen.

Article 14: Alternates shall be elected for each one of the commissioners appointed.

Article 15: In the election of commissioners to the General Assembly, care should be taken that there is a proper proportion of men and women, Chinese and missionaries, laymen and ordained pastors.

Article 16: The officers of the General Assembly shall be:
(a) A Moderator—The Moderator shall be chosen from among the commissioners present and shall be elected at the close of the General Assembly preceding the one of which he is to be the Moderator.
(b) Vice-Moderators—The two Vice-Moderators shall be elected at the first session of the General Assembly and shall be chosen from among the commissioners present. They shall serve only during the meeting of the General Assembly.
(c) Temporary Clerks—Two Temporary Clerks shall be elected at the first session of the General Assembly and shall be chosen from among the commissioners present. They shall serve only during the meeting of the General Assembly.
(d) A Stated Clerk—The office of the Stated Clerk shall be held concurrently by the General Secretary of the General Council.
(e) An Honorary Treasurer—The Honorary Treasurer shall be elected for a term of four years at the close of each Assembly.

Article 17: The General Assembly shall meet once every four years. The time and place for such a meeting shall be determined by the General Council of the General Assembly one year previous to the meeting.

Article 18: Twenty commissioners assembled at the time and place appointed shall constitute a quorum for the transaction of business. But these twenty delegates must represent at least two-thirds of the synods and at least one-half of them must be ministers.

Article 19: Except in special circumstances, the General Assembly should not receive appeals directly from local churches, or district associations.

Article 20: The General Assembly may, whenever necessary, appoint special committees, commissioners or boards to conduct or study the business of the Church.

Article 21: The General Assembly may, subject to the approval of district associations, prepare, revise, or amend the Directory of Worship, Form of Government, Book of Discipline.

Article 22: The General Assembly may appoint the Church's representatives on all interdenominational or union agencies which deal with "extra" or "inter" synodical matters.

Article 23: The functions of the General Assembly, necessary between assemblies, shall be exercised by its General Council.

Article 24: The General Assembly may adopt its own by-laws which should be in harmony with the Constitution of the Church.

PART VII. The General Council

Article 25: The General Council shall consist of the following members:
(a) The Moderator of the General Assembly.
(b) A representative from each synod who is elected to this office by the respective synods at the time they elect the commissioners to the General Assembly and from among the commissioners, and the election confirmed by the General Assembly. Each synod shall also elect an alternate, the election to be confirmed by the General Assembly.
(c) Members-at-large.
(d) The Honorary Treasurer.

Article 26: The General Assembly shall elect from the Church-at-large as members of the General Council, one (1) from each four (4) synods or fraction thereof.

Article 27: The officers of the General Council shall be a Chairman, a Vice-Chairman, a Recording Secretary, a General Secretary, and two Executive Secretaries. The Moderator of the General Assembly shall serve as the Chairman of the General Council.

Article 28: The General Secretary and the Executive Secretaries shall be nominated by the General Council and elected by the General Assembly for a term of years covered by two (2) General Assemblies, subject to re-election at the pleasure of the General Assembly.

Article 29: The General Council shall meet at least once every two years. The time and place shall be determined by its Executive Committee.

Article 30: Actions of the General Council at its Biennial Meeting shall be operative where power has been conferred, but the same may be reviewed or reversed by the General Assembly or by a vote of a majority of the synods.

Article 31: The actions of the General Council shall be transmitted to the synods immediately after each meeting. If a synod takes no action on the minutes of the General Council within one year, such synod will be considered as having approved the said minutes.

Article 32: The General Council shall pass on the budget of the General Council Office and all boards and commissions authorized by the General Assembly.

Article 33: The General Council shall prepare a digest of its actions to be submitted to the subsequent meeting of the General Assembly.

Article 34: The General Council shall serve as the Nominating and Business Committee of the General Assembly and shall be ex-officio members of said General Assembly.

Article 35: The term of a General Council shall begin on the adjournment of the General Assembly and continue until the adjournment of the succeeding General Assembly. Any vacancies within the General Council among the members-at-large shall be filled by appointment by the Council. Vacancies from among the synod representatives shall be temporarily filled by the General Council until a successor is elected by the synod concerned.

Article 36: The General Council may adopt its own by-laws which should be in harmony with the Constitution of the Church.

Article 37: The functions of the General Council, necessary between regular meetings, shall be exercised by its Executive Committee. The method of organization of such Executive Committee shall be decided by the General Council.

PART VIII. Amendments

Article 38: These By-Laws shall not be altered, increased or diminished, unless there are two-thirds of the votes from all district associations of the Church affirming such alteration, increase or diminution. District associations in voting on any amendment to these By-Laws shall have their number of votes determined by the number of communicants, namely one (1) vote for every five hundred (500) communicants or fraction thereof.

Article 39: Votes by district associations on proposed amendments shall be categorically "yes" or "no". The district associations may in separate overtures propose amendments or changes, but such must in no wise limit or affect that "yes" or "no" vote on the proposed amendments transmitted to them for approval.

(From *An Adventure in Church Union,* 1944, pp. 23-30)

Appendix B

Statistics of the Church of Christ in China

(from the *Revised Directory of the*
Protestant Christian Movement in China, 1950)

Synods of the Church of Christ in China

Name	Area	District Associations	Organization as CCC Synod	Cooperating Missions
Kiangnan	Kiangsu, Anhwei (South of Yangtze)	3 ⎫ East China Synod 1927	1948	PCUSA/PCUS
Kiangan	Kiangsu, Anhwei (North of Yangtze)	3 ⎬	1948	PCUSA/PCUS
Chekiang	Chekiang	4 ⎭	1948	PCUSA/PCUS/LMS
Kianghuai	Anhwei, Shantung	6	1948	PCUS
Hupeh	Hupeh	11 ⎫ Lianghu Synod 1927	1948	LMS/CS/SMS
Hunan	Hunan	5 ⎬	1948	PCUSA/E&R/EUB
Szechuen	Szechuan	10	1934	UCC
*Hopei**	Hopei (West)	3	1933	PCUSA
Honan	Honan	2	1933	UCC
*Shantung***	Shantung	6	1929	PCUSA/BMS
Shansi	Shansi	3	1933	BMS
Shensi	Shensi	3	1933	BMS
South Fukien (Minnan)	Southern Fukien	9	1919	LMS/PCE/RCA
North Fukien (Minpei)	Northern Fukien	3	1927	ABCFM
Mid-Fukien (Minchung)	Central Fukien	3	1927	ABCFM
East Kwangtung (Lingtung)	Eastern Kwangtung	3	1927	PCE
Kwangtung	Kwangtung (West)	10	1925	EUB/LMS/PNZ PCUSA/UCC

Hainan	Hainan Island	3		1932	PCUSA
North China* (Hwapei)	Hopei (East)	4		1931	LMS
Northeast (Tungpei)	Manchuria	14		1927	CS/PCI
Malaya***	Singapore/Malaya			1948	PCE

*United 1950 as Hopei (Union) Synod
**3 additional presbyteries joined 1950
***Withdrew 1950

Cooperating Missions

ABCFM	American Board of Commissioners for Foreign Missions
BMS	Baptist Missionary Society
CS	Church of Scotland
E&R	Evangelical and Reformed Church
EUB	Evangelical United Brethren
LMS	London Missionary Society
PCE	Presbyterian Church of England
PCI	Presbyterian Church in Ireland
PCUS	Presbyterian Church in the US
PCUSA	Presbyterian Church in the USA
PCNZ	Presbyterian Church in New Zealand
RCA	Reformed Church in America
SMS	Swedish Missionary Society
UCC	United Church of Canada

The Presbyterian Church of Australia and the Presbyterian Church in Canada were also cooperating with the CCC, especially in its missions.

Other Statistics of the Church of Christ in China

Communicant members	176,983*
Ordained ministers	496
Evangelists (Men and women)	1448
Organized churches	1053
Preaching places	1714
Universities**	10
Middle schools	78
Hospitals	82
Theological schools	14

*Not including c. 25,000 in three Shantung presbyteries which affiliated later.
**Much institutional work was interdenominational.

Appendix C

Church of Christ in China
General Assembly Chinese Staff

(Arranged in chronological order of service)

Name	Synod (or Denomination)	Title(s)	Period of Service
T. C. Fan (Fan Ting-chiu)	Hunan	Associate General Secretary Executive Secretary	1930-34 1934-35
Ch'en Wen-hsien	Mid-Fukien	Student Work Christianizing the Home	1931-36
H. Y. Chang (Chang Hsueh-yen)	Shantung	Assistant Secretary	1933
C. Y. Cheng (Ch'eng Ching-yi)	North China	General Secretary	1934-39
H. H. Tsui (Ts'ui Hsien-hsiang)	Methodist	Executive Secretary General Secretary	1935-43 1943-59(?)
George Y. H. Geng (Keng Yuan-hsueh)	Kiangan	Student Work	1936-37
C. K. Lee (Li Ch'iung-chieh)	Hsing Tao Hui (Swedish Missy. Soc.)	Secretary Church Missions	1937-42
C. T. Tsai (Ts'ai Chi-ch'eng)	So. Fukien	Young People's Work Secretary for Missions	1938-43 1943-?
Ch'i Yu-chen	Northeast	Christianizing the Home	1939-?
W. B. Djang (Chang Po-huai)	Shantung	Director Border Mission West China representative Exec. Sec'y. Provisional Comm.	1939-48 1940 1942
S. L. Hsieh (Hsieh Shou-ling)	Lutheran	Literature Work	1941-?

S. S. Chu (Chu Hsin-sun)	East China	Acting Secretary	1943-46
Ch'en Heng	Hunan	Field Director Kweichow Mission	1944-?
S. S. Sun (Sun Shou-hsin)	Shantung	Field Director Yunnan Mission	1944-?
C. S. Chu (Chu Chen-sheng)	Shensi	Rehabilitation Secretary Editor *Kung Pao*	1946-50 (?)
Wu Yik-wan	Kwangtung	Executive Secretary (c. 3 months)	1948
Henry D. Tsui (Ts'ui Te-jun)	Shantung	Field Director Border Mission	1949-?
Liu Ling-chiu	Shantung	Ass't. Director Border Mission	1949-?

Bibliography

Books

Baker, Richard Terrill. *Ten Thousand Years* (The Story of Methodism's First Century in China). Methodist Joint Division of Education and Cultivation, New York, 1947.

Bates, M. S. (ed.). *China in Change*. Friendship Press, New York, 1969.

Boorman, Howard and Richard C. Howard (eds.). *Biographical Dictionary of Republican China*. Columbia University Press, New York and London, 1967 (3 vols.).

Bush, Richard C., Jr. *Religion in Communist China*. Abingdon Press, Nashville and New York, 1970.

China Christian Yearbook, 1927-1939. Christian Literature Society, Shanghai.

Clark, William H. *The Church in China*. Council Press, New York, 1970.

Crouch, A. R. *Rising Through the Dust*. Friendship Press, New York, 1948.

Fulton, Austin. *Through Earthquake, Wind and Fire*. St. Andrews Press, Edinburgh, 1967.

Jolliffe, R. C. *The Chinese Church Rides the Storm*. Friendship Press, New York, 1946.

Jones, F. P. (ed.). *Documents of the Three-Self Movement*. Far Eastern Office, National Council of Churches, New York, 1963.

————. *The Church in Communist China*. Friendship Press, New York, 1962.

Lacy, Walter N. *A Hundred Years of Chinese Methodism*. Abingdon Press, New York, 1948.

Latourette, Kenneth S. *A History of Christian Missions in China*. Macmillan, New York, 1942.

Miao, Chester S. (ed.). *Christian Voices in China*. Friendship Press, New York, 1948.

Rattenbury, H. H. *The Seven Churches of China*. The Cargate Press, London, 1935.

Rattenbury, H. B. and Hilda M. Porter. *Let My People Know*. Methodist Missionary Society, London, 1947.

Smith, C. Stanley. *The Development of Protestant Theological Education in China.* Kelly and Walsh, Ltd., Shanghai, 1941.

The Revised Directory of the Protestant Movement in China. National Christian Council of China, Shanghai, 1950, mimeo.

Tsu, Andrew Y. Y. *Friend of Fishermen.* Trinity Press, Ambler, Pa., n. d. (c. 1966).

White Unto Harvest, a Survey of the Lutherans, the China Mission of the Norwegian Lutheran Church of America, written by the Missionaries. The Board of Foreign Missions, Minneapolis, Minn., 1934.

Williamson, H. R. *British Baptists in China.* The Carey-Kingsgate Press, London, 1957.

Young, George A. *The Living Christ in Modern China.* Carey Press, London, 1947.

Pamphlets, etc.

An Adventure in Church Unity in China. North American Advisory Committee, Church of Christ in China, New York, 1944.

Annual Reports. Hong Kong Council, Church of Christ in China, 1968, 1971.

Beaver, R. P. *The Church and the Mission in China.* N. d. (c. 1943-44), mimeo.

Brown, Margaret H. *History of the Honan Mission,* typescript.

Church Unity in China and Church and Mission Cooperation. Church of Christ in China General Assembly, Shanghai, 1938.

Clark, William H. "Are You the Man?" N. d. (c. 1949), typescript.

Digest of the Important Actions of the 1st, 2nd, 3rd, 4th, 5th General Assemblies of the Church of Christ in China.

Djang, W. B. An Address to the Provisional Council of the General Assembly of the Church of Christ in China, February 10, 1943, typescript.

Fisher, A. J. *Building a Christian Church in China.* Shanghai, 1947, typescript.

Let Us Unite (Hoh er wei ih). Church of Christ in China General Assembly, Peiping, 1935 (revised and re-issued 1938).

MacGown, David J. *Presbyterians in the Church of Christ in China.* Yale University B. A. thesis, n. d., typescript.

Minutes of the Federal Council of the Presbyterian Church in China, 5th Meeting.

Minutes of the North American Advisory Committee of the Church of Christ in China.

The Missionary Enterprise of the Church of Christ in China, n. d. (c. 1948), typescript.

The Missions of the Church of Christ in China, n. d. (c. 1950), mimeo.

Together, Information on the Cooperative Effort of Canadian Presbyterians with the Chinese Christians. Board of Missions, Presbyterian Church in Canada. Toronto, 1947.

The Church of Christ in China, n. d. (c. 1948), mimeo.

What is the CCC? General Assembly of the Church of Christ in China, Nanking, 1927.

Periodicals

China Notes, 1962 ff. East Asia Department, National Council of Churches, New York.

Information Service of the Kwangtung Synod, Church of Christ in China. 1925 ff.

Newsletter. The General Assembly of the Church of Christ in China. Occasional issues, 1943 ff.

The China Bulletin, 1948-1962. Far Eastern Office, National Council of Churches, New York.

The Chinese Recorder. Shanghai, 1920 ff.

The Church (English-language bulletin of the Church of Christ in China). Chungking, 1945-46; Shanghai and Hong-kong, 1948-50.

Index

American Board of Commissioners for Foreign Missions 21, 64, 70
Anti-Christian Movement 40ff.

Baptist Missionary Society 40ff., 60, 144
Bates, M. Searle 10
Bau, T. C. 105
Bell, Gerald 123
Bible Societies 31, 103
Bible Union, The 23
Book of Common Worship 102, 116-17
Border Mission 121, 124, 133, 136ff., 149ff., 159, 161, 167, 170
Boxer Uprising 18-19, 41, 46, 47, 52, 79

Canadian Methodists 61
Canton Medical Hospital 103
Chang Hsueh-liang 85, 86ff.
Chang, H. Y. 103, 114, 123
Chang Tso-lin 83, 85
Chao, T. C. 29, 47
Chekiang Synod 74
Chen, C. C. 116, 121, 159
Chen Heng 135
Chen Wen-hsien 92, 100
Chen, W. Y. 38, 106, 113, 156, 185
Cheng, C. Y. 27, 29, 34, 45, 46, 51, 55, 92, 93, 96, 97, 101, 104, 105, 106, 119, 137, 159, 168, 197, 201, 209
Cheng Ching-yi Memorial Church 134
Cheng Ching-yi Memorial School 124
Chi, Y. C. (Ch'i Yu-chen) 119, 120, 123, 124, 131, 134
Chia Yu-ming 46
Chiang Kai-shek 47, 85, 156
China Christian Educational Association 30, 106, 158
China Continuation Committee 25, 26ff., 43, 55
China Inland Mission 15, 22, 24, 29, 60, 104, 134, 149
China Sunday School Union 24
Chinese Home Missionary Society 32, 44, 132, 133, 143, 147, 148, 149
Chinese Independent Presbyterian Church 70
Chiu, T. K. 143, 146
Chou En-lai 175, 177
Christian Farmer 103, 113-14, 123
Christian Literature Society 15, 23, 31, 113, 160
Christian Manifesto 174ff.
Christian Medical Council (China Medical Missionary Association) 16, 23, 106, 142, 154
Christian Student Movement 89, 100
Chu, C. S. 159, 165, 189
Chung Hwa Hsing Tao Hui 98, 169

Chung Hwa Sheng Kung Hui 34ff., 45, 67, 116, 149, 157, 211
Chung Hwa Tsun Tao Hui 169, 170
Church Committee for China Relief 112
Church-Mission Relations 60ff., 92ff., 163ff., 207ff.
Church of Christ in China 9, 10, 27, 33, 37, 38, 43, 54ff., 59ff., 63, 64ff., 68ff., 89ff., 103ff., 107ff., 119ff., 124, 130, 132ff., 150ff., 155, 158ff., 167ff., 170ff., 176ff., 188ff., 194, 195ff.
  Bond of Union 66, 195
  General Assemblies 65, 94
    First 54ff.
    Second 95ff.
    Third 99ff.
    Fourth 115ff., 133
    Fifth 167ff.
Church Union 34-35, 37ff., 56-57, 116
Clark, W. H. 10, 124, 142, 145, 146, 147, 148, 159, 170
Coonradt, Ralph G. 145, 147
Copland, E. Bruce 10, 123, 124, 141, 159, 162, 170, 176, 185, 198
Crouch, Archie R. 141

Directory of the Protestant Christian Movement 63, 70
Directory of Worship 59
Djang, W. B. (Chang Po-huai) 119, 121, 123, 125, 131, 133, 135, 137, 139, 140, 151, 159, 161, 170, 201

East China Synod 74
East China Union University 157
East Kwangtung Synod (see Lingtung Synod)
Edinburgh Missionary Conference 27, 55, 66
Evangelical and Reformed Church 76, 124, 164

Fan, T. C. 37, 56, 60, 118, 159
Feng Yu-hsiang 47, 71

Fisher, A. J. 9, 83, 107, 121, 122, 159
Five Year Forward Movement 97, 104
Forward Movement 113, 156, 168

General Assemblies (see Church of Christ in China)
General Council (CCC) 89, 90ff., 102ff., 115, 159ff.
Geng, George Y. H. (Keng Yuan-hsueh) 119, 159
Gih, Andrew 50
Goforth, Jonathan 47, 77, 81
Gotch-Robinson Theological College 62

Hainan Synod 72
Hayes, John D. 120, 134, 136
Hayward, Victor E. W. 120, 134
Honan Synod 46, 77, 125
Hong Kong Council (CCC) 10, 33, 128, 192-93, 205
Hopei Synod 78-79, 182ff., 187
Hunan Synod 77, 182, 200
Hupei Synod 77, 200
Hwapei Synod (see North China Synod)
Hymns of Universal Praise 102, 116

International Missionary Conference 51, 104, 113

Jesus Family, The 49, 186
Joint Conference Representatives of Mission Boards 163

Kaung, Z. T. (Chiang Ch'ang-ch'uan) 47
Kepler, A. Raymond 9, 22, 23, 53-54, 56, 60, 62, 73, 89, 98, 103, 118, 119, 121, 123, 137, 143, 159-60, 168
Kiangan Synod 74
Kianghwai Synod 63, 81, 169, 182
Kiangnan Synod 74, 188
Kiangsu Synod 189
Koo, T. Z. 48

Kwangtung Synod 68, 70ff., 99, 126, 128, 166, 181, 182, 199
Kwantung Synod (see Northeast Synod)
Kweichow Mission 133ff., 149ff., 159
Kung Pao 123, 159, 176, 189

Law, Lau Sam Tsz (Mrs.) 166
Lee, C. K. 117, 123, 125, 133, 134, 135
Leger, Samuel H. 96, 107
Leung, S. C. 96, 158, 161, 185
Lew, T. T. 29, 47
Li Yung-wu 77
Lianghu Synod 76-77, 126, 165
Ling En Hui 48-49
Lingtung Synod 72
Little Flock, The 49
Liu Ling-chiu 170, 190
Lobenstine, E. C. 29, 105, 106
London Missionary Society 21, 55, 70, 73, 192
Lutheran Church in China 29, 35ff.

Malaya Synod 82, 169, 198
Mao Tse-tung 177, 186, 190
May 4th Incident 39
Mei Dao Hui 36, 77, 98, 107
Methodist Church, Chinese 37, 143ff.
Methodist Church in China (Methodist Episcopal, Methodist Episcopal South) 36ff., 45, 89, 102
Miao, Chester C. S. 105
Mid-Fukien Synod 72ff., 165, 178, 182, 210
Missionary Conferences 21, 25, 43
Missions Cooperating Council 120, 121-22, 160
Mott, John R. 26, 55

Nanking Incident 42
Nanking Theological Seminary 25, 161, 181, 187
National Christian Conference (1922) 27, 37, 43, 53
National Christian Council of China 28ff., 31, 58, 97, 104ff., 108, 112, 156ff., 168, 178, 213
National Christian Service Council for Wounded Soldiers 117ff., 130, 133, 159
National Committee on Christian Religious Education 31, 105
New Zealand Presbyterian Mission 44
Ni To-sheng 49
North American Advisory Committee 63, 124, 144, 211
North China Christian Rural Service Union 101, 103, 114
North China Kung Li Hui 67, 98, 103
North China Synod 58, 64, 69, 78, 101, 182
North China Theological College 25
North China Theological Seminary 62, 66
Northeast Synod 63, 80, 91, 104, 115, 164, 199
North Fukien Synod 74, 210

Presbyterian Church in Canada 61ff., 199
Presbyterian Church in China 33ff., 70, 144
Presbyterian Church in Ireland 144
Presbyterian Church in the U.S. 122, 164
Presbyterian Church in the USA 45, 144, 155, 160, 210
Presbyterian Church of Australia 144
Presbyterian Church of England 73, 144
Presbyterian Church of Formosa 63, 169, 205
Presbyterian Church of Korea 76
Presbyterian Church of Scotland 76, 80
Price, Frank W. 123, 185
Provisional Council (CCC) 122-23, 124, 125

Rawlinson, Frank 51, 59, 105
Reformed Church in America 21, 72, 144

Richard, Timothy 31
Rural Life Improvement 100, 103

Self-support 99ff., 180, 184ff., 202ff.
Shansi Synod 79, 101
Shantung Christian College 62, 119
Shantung Synod 63, 75-76, 182
Sheng Kung Hui (*see* Chung Hwa
  Sheng Kung Hui)
Shensi Synod 79, 101, 182
Smith, C. Stanley 105
Sommerville, Jean 134, 136
South Fukien Religious Tract Society
  113
South Fukien Synod 21, 37, 58, 72ff.,
  100, 126-27, 165-66, 199
Statistics
  CCC 103ff., 188
  Hospitals 31, 111, 154
  Missionaries 15, 20, 42
  Protestant 14-15, 35, 36ff., 71, 111
  Roman Catholic 13, 14, 15
  Schools 14, 97, 111
Sun, S. S. 146-47, 170, 183, 189
Sun, T. H. 68, 114, 168
Sun Yat-sen 17, 39ff., 47, 97
Sung, John 50
Swedish Missionary Society 60
Szechuan Synod 77, 101, 125, 183,
  184

Three-Self Movement 174, 186, 188,
  189-90, 191
T'ien Feng 114, 186
Ting Li-mei 46
Tom, Y. S. 71, 96, 101, 107, 187
True Jesus Church 49
Tsai, C. T. 119, 121, 125, 131, 168,
  182, 189
Tseng, Lindel 34

Tsou, Ping-yi 167
Tsu, Y. Y. 185, 211
Tsui, H. H. 60, 62, 104, 106-7, 119,
  121, 124, 125, 131, 137, 156, 159,
  162, 164, 165, 174, 179, 182, 185,
  186, 187, 201
Tsui, Henry D. 140, 170

Union Theological Seminary (Canton)
  51, 95, 127
United Brethren 59, 71, 76, 144
United Christian Publishers 113, 187
United Church of Canada 70, 81, 211
United Church of Christ in Japan
  (Kyodan) 66, 203, 204

Wang Chung-hui 48
Wang, C. T. 47
Wang Ming-tao 50, 186
West China Union University 26, 77
Williamson, Alexander 22, 31
Women in the Church 57ff.
Wong, K. C. 31
Wong, Peter 128, 192
World Council of Churches 66
Wu, George K. T. 156, 157
Wu Yi-fang 58, 105, 113, 157, 178
Wu Yik-wan 134, 162
Wu, Y. T. 114, 188

Yen, F. C. 42
Yen Hsi-shan 83
Yen, W. W. 42
Yen, Y. C. James 48
Yenching University School of Reli-
  gion 25
Yuan Shih-kai 39, 40
Yui, David Z. T. 29, 47
Yunnan Mission 142ff., 150ff., 159,
  167